Center for International Trade Development
C I T D
A Los Rios Community College/ED>Net Initiative
A Gift for Glob
SACRAM
CENTER FOR INTERNATI
CALIFORNIA MEXIC
916
D0340442
LIBRARY

One Billion Shoppers

Accessing Asia's Consuming Passions and Fast-Moving Markets – After the Meltdown

Paul French & Matthew Crabbe

NICHOLAS BREALEY PUBLISHING
LONDON

This book is dedicated to:

artist and grandmother Myfanwy Kathleen Croley (1907–98)

Margaret Ann French (1927–94)

First published by
Nicholas Brealey Publishing Limited in 1998

36 John Street
London
WC1A 2AT, UK
Tel: +44 (0)171 430 0224
Fax: +44 (0)171 404 8311

671 Clover Drive
Santa Rosa
CA 95401, USA
Tel: (707) 566 8006
Fax: (707) 566 8005

http://www.nbrealey-books.com

ISBN 1-85788-210-5

British Library Cataloguing in Publication Data
A catalogue record for this book is available from the British Library.

Printed in Finland by Werner Söderström Oy.

Contents

Acknowledgements

This book was the product of conversations and research conducted over a number of years of studying, analyzing and visiting Asia. Those conversations were many and varied and were with sources and contacts too numerous to list here.

Special thanks go to those people and organizations that paid us to work in the field of Asia and allowed us time and permission to write this book. They include Robert Senior, Sarah Holmes and Heather Greig of Euromonitor, Dr Derek Smith, managing director of the DIALOG Corporation, and Nigel Taylor, managing director of Fourth Communications Network in Europe, as well as the staff of Virtual Business Information in London.

Special thanks must go to Nicholas Brealey who saw this project through the boom times, the meltdown and the bounce back. Thanks must also go to our editor Sally Lansdell. By far the greatest thanks go to Nicola Everitt and Phoebe Harkins for their sterling support above and beyond the call of duty.

After the Meltdown

Something epoch shattering occurred in Asia in 1997. Almost overnight the surety many had felt at the 'economic miracle' ended. The Japanese economy had already been giving cause for concern, but when the so-called tigers started to slip – Thailand, Malaysia, Indonesia, Hong Kong – the world sat up and worried. The region suffered an economic crisis that required drastic financial restructuring and International Monetary Fund (IMF) loans of unprecedented size to keep countries such as Thailand from sliding into bankruptcy.

Fifteen years of solid economic growth at astoundingly rapid rates had excited manufacturers and financiers alike. The opening up of China and latterly Vietnam coincided with the advance of consumer societies throughout east Asia. Even India appeared to be pulling out of the abyss of absolute poverty. The prospect of over two billion new consumers led to a rush of inward investment and talk of tiger economies and waking dragons. Western multinationals promised their shareholders great profits from the Asian region and a goldrush mentality appeared in boardrooms and the business press.

However, all too often this exaggerated view of Asia's prospects was based on a model of the region as a monolithic entity: one large mass of expanding economy from Mumbai to Tokyo with a thousand cities of conspicuous consumers in between.

Many of the same pundits who were so quick to laud the rapid expansion of the region were also the first to start using terms such as the 'Asian contagion' and 'Asian flu'. People talked about total meltdown and continued to speak as if the economic blip would be a pan-Asian phenomenon rather than looking country by country. In doing so they missed the intricacies of the region.

Surely if Hong Kong was suffering, what could stop collapse in China? If Malaysia and Indonesia were hurting, how could Singapore escape? And wouldn't trouble in Japan affect Korea and Taiwan? Also, it was generally believed that if all these economies crumbled the emergent economies of India, Vietnam and the Philippines wouldn't stand a chance. It was the domino theory all over again but applied to economics and not communism – fall one, fall all.

Without doubt, events in Asia had ramifications for the whole world, although the fallout has not been as great as initially predicted. Each country in the region has been affected in different ways. Some have had temporary blips, such as Hong Kong and Singapore. Others have been forced to undergo a period of belt tightening, witness South Korea and Thailand; while others have entered unstable phases, for example Indonesia. By and large China, Taiwan and India have been left unaffected while Vietnam and the Philippines have taken one step back before two forward. Just as the pace of economic development had not been constant across the region over the previous 15 years, different countries grew at different paces for different reasons.

This book examines the differences between Asia's nations from the viewpoint of their consumer economies. All were at a different stage of development and sophistication prior to the crisis – all have responded to the effects of the crisis in different ways. The need to understand the diversity of Asia's economies, consumers and cultures has never been greater.

This book is not about Asians as cheap labor or demon exporters, protectionists or potential enemies, but simply about their role as consumers. Before the end of the twentieth century Asians will constitute in excess of half the world's total population. There will be over one billion people in China and southeast Asia with significant purchasing power. Five hundred million east Asians will have spending power equivalent to their middle-class counterparts in North America and western Europe. They cannot be ignored.

One Billion Shoppers does not give you an in-depth guide to every market segment in every country, though we provide an appendix of further reading and relevant Web sites. It is intended to provide an alternative way of thinking about Asia, of considering the region's diversity and differing levels of economic and consumer sophistication. It is about Asian consumers and their motivations, aspirations and intentions.

We have chosen our countries carefully. The richer nations of the region – Hong Kong, Singapore, South Korea and Taiwan – have developed consumer markets that reflect international trends but refuse to jettison all trace of their domestic cultures. Malaysia, the Philippines, Thailand and Vietnam are burgeoning tigers with consumer markets in perpetual flux.

India and China are Asia's two dragons. India is called a subcontinent but is very much a part of Asia. It is moving closer to its Asian neighbors and further from its British colonial past, and is on the cusp of full-blown consumerism. China stands alone, infinite possibilities juxtaposed with myriad difficulties to be overcome. But few doubt that time spent deciphering the world's most populous nation is wasted, given its enormous potential.

The all new Asian consumer

First in this book we look at the new consumers in Asia. They have reacted to the economic turmoil in a number of ways. Many have simply stopped buying the luxury goods and expensive imports that were the status symbols of the newly rich across the region. Those who considered themselves rich are scaling back their spending, becoming more selective, perhaps even buying the T-shirts one sharp Bangkok street merchant had printed up announcing that the owner was a member of the 'Former Rich' club. Others have reined in their spending to take account of the new economic situation. Most consumers continue to spend but have become wiser, making choices based as much on value and quality as on need and desire.

This new wisdom among Asian consumers makes an understanding of the region and its consumers even more of an imperative. Much more attention must be paid to advertising and marketing: to how efficiently goods are distributed, just who the target audience is and how to reach them. These factors, along with competitive pricing, are now fundamental to success in Asia. Previously a marketing campaign could afford to make a few mistakes; the market was big enough and forgiving enough. This is no longer true. Asian consumers have become as unforgiving as their counterparts in the boom-and-bust economies of the US and Europe. Consequently, it is now essential for producers, advertisers, retailers and marketers to have as deep an understanding of their chosen Asian markets and target audiences as they would seek to gain in the west.

Families and children have become increasingly important as they become wealthier and open to new influences. Teenagers are a defining group, setting trends and acting as the vanguard for new products. Women have become a major focus of numerous marketing campaigns as they increasingly leave the home to work, study or travel. They are having profound effects on consumption patterns as they change their lifestyles and demand convenience and choice.

A good example is karaoke, a very Asian phenomenon. Rather than daytime television or local coffee mornings, Asian housewives spend their afternoons practicing their repertoire while finishing off the ironing or preparing dinner. They will even compete in amateur karaoke competitions. And this love of karaoke is helping to push sales of digital videodisc technology on Asia's high streets while similar technology is still hard to find in the west. What does this say about Asian women, their place in the family, their role as consumers, manufacturers' approaches to the markets? These are the kind of topics that this book addresses.

Asia's new middle class is slightly more difficult to pin down, as definitions vary from country to country. What is certain is that this emergent middle class is the backbone of consumer change in the region, reinforcing it and making it permanent. The middle class is also the group of consumers most affected by the economic turmoil and their reaction to the crisis will be crucial to the future direction of consumer markets across the continent. They are beginning to relocate in new out-of-town suburbs. This is propelling sales of cars and telecommunications along with household goods and fostering the development of out-of-town malls. The middle class is altering the consumption patterns of women and nuclear families and each change in lifestyle affects other areas. The themes in this book therefore cut across each other, just as a successful marketing campaign blurs the distinctions between different groups of consumers.

Asian consumers have one main benefit: they don't have to relearn the ways things are done. Asia is jumping straight to digital and fiberoptic, often bypassing older technologies. Teenagers assume computers rather than opting for them. Mobile telecommunications become the first phone people own, dispensing with land lines completely. If your first computer is a color laptop running Windows 98 and linked to the Internet, you have an advantage over those who have to upgrade and renew their equipment. You see the world differently.

The consumer environment

In Part Two, we look at the environments that Asian consumers inhabit; environments which are changing every bit as rapidly as the consumers themselves.

Increasingly Asia is an urban continent with some of the largest cities on earth. These are the home of the new middle class, the places where trends start and where the widest array of goods and services are available. Megacities are rising up alongside wholly new cities such as Subic Bay in the Philippines or the newly created industrial cities of southern China. These become engines of consumption with networks of retail outlets, the old neighborhood stores and street vendors giving way to air-conditioned malls and plazas combining retailing, food courts, bowling alleys, multiplex cinemas and leisure centers. The largest mall in the world is located in Manila.

Improvements in infrastructure are paving the way for further increases in consumption. Again, needs vary from country to country. China is embarking on a massive road and airport building program, Malaysia is laying fiberoptic cable, South Korea is constructing power plants and Vietnam is connecting eager subscribers to the telephone network at a furious pace. India appears finally to be tackling the water-distribution problem that has bedeviled the country.

Asia's media has undergone a profound revolution in the last 20 years. In the process, it has become a significant consumer product, as well as an effective means of communicating with consumers. Consumers' purchasing choices are being guided through advertising and their outlook through programming.

The introduction of modern technology has had wide-ranging effects on the region's consumers and we consider what the arrival of mobile phones, the Internet and satellites means for people.

Naturally, retailing is crucial to this book and is the main way in which Asians access consumer goods as well as being one of the region's main leisure activities. We show the differing stages of retailing across the region, its successes and failures, as well as the likely consequences of the economic crisis.

Lastly, we look at leisure itself. If Asian nations are to follow Japan's lead in turning themselves into 'lifestyle superpowers', then how much leisure time Asians have – and what they choose to do with it – will be a crucial issue for the future. Asia therefore continues to be a growing market for providers of entertainment and leisure goods and services.

Future trends

In the last chapter we attempt to draw together the interwoven themes of the book and examine ways in which Asia is bouncing back. The post-meltdown period offers opportunities for a wider variety of businesses and, while some sectors have suffered, others have risen. Finally, we attempt a portrait of the Asian consumer and look ahead to try to divine what the combined effects of the new consumers and their changing environment will mean for the region.

Throughout the book we have tried to let Asian experiences speak for themselves as far as possible. Where useful we have included concrete examples of business strategies, both successes and failures, as well as everyday examples of the impact of the new consumer economy in Asia.

Aspirations

Annually, several million southeast Asians become first-generation consumers of washing machines, microwave ovens and mobile phones while millions more aspire to travel abroad, eat in fast-food restaurants and purchase their own homes. It is this increase in desires that is behind the region's shift from being a group of exporting nations to increasingly a group of nations manufacturing to fulfill their own home-generated demands. The economic crisis may result in the region becoming an aggressive exporter again, but the home markets, though weakened, will remain.

As with everything in Asia, there are disparities. In Singapore young homeowners are remodeling their kitchens from the traditional Chinese style to a more western, range-style design, while in Vietnam consumer aspirations run to drinking a Heineken and smoking a Winston. In China, people are getting into computers, interior design and soccer; in Malaysia it is cars and scooters. Each to their own, depending on the state of development in the economy.

How do consumers choose what to buy? What makes people buy karaoke machines before hi-fi systems, why are Asians buying laser discs rather than videotape players, where do they want to go on their holidays and, when they get there, what exactly do they want to do?

This book illustrates the main forces propelling the consumer market, not so much in terms of inflationary expectations or GDP analysis but more in terms of the average shopper. Ultimately it is the average shopper, be they walking down the high street in Kuala Lumpur, Shanghai or Taipei, who makes the choice. This product or that, this service provider or the competitor, this financial outlay or that dream buy.

Controlling the wider economies of southeast Asia is beyond the powers of marketers. However, through careful and fully researched positioning, advertising and location, manufacturers can ensure that they reach their target audience in those parts of the region most receptive to their product.

1

Accessing Asia

The days have passed when salesgirls in Chinese department stores would move through the crowds with racks of clothing and return to their station minutes later with an empty rack. It is no longer sufficient to build a mall in Malaysia, Bangkok or the Philippines and simply assume that the shoppers will come. Asian consumers have become more sophisticated and with money now tighter for many they are looking for better quality and value for money.

In Hong Kong and Singapore, being a world-class brand is no longer enough to guarantee sales. You have to suit the consumer, match their needs. And the meltdown has made every consumer increasingly aware that every purchase has to be justified, afforded and accounted for. Not all retailers and brands will survive in the post-meltdown consumer economy. But for those that do persevere, the rewards of the bounce back will be significant.

The retail sector is closely linked to the wider economy. A strong economy means that the shops are full, the car showrooms busy and consumers out on the prowl. In the very good times the market boomed – in less than a decade Hong Kong built itself 1.75 million square meters of retail space across 65 separate shopping centers. Despite a slowdown, in 1998 there were still plans for a further 20 plazas in this Special Administrative Region (SAR). At the same time consumers have begun to make additional demands on retailers. They want convenience and choice and plush surroundings: additional costs that must be borne by retailers and developers at a time when both are looking to cut costs to remain competitive.

The new, sleek malls may well survive; the older-style malls across Asia may not. Those that marked the first phase of organized plaza retailing, typically located on the second and third floors of commercial buildings, are finding the going toughest. Their maze of shops with little organization, large clusters of no-brand independents and sparse catering and entertainment facilities are now ill matched to the gleaming retail centers with their brand-name stores, competitive discounts, food courts, multiplex cinemas and parking facilities.

Likewise, retail centers located away from residential areas are also suffering. In Singapore, Hong Kong and other countries, tourism sales are dwindling, so plazas located for convenience to residents are doing best. Those located around public transport stations, such as next to MTR stations in Hong Kong, or suburban malls like Tampines in Singapore are currently in a stronger position than either Causeway Bay or Orchard Road which are aimed more at tourists. This reflects the importance of the volume of throughput. Right now increasing prices is a recipe for bankruptcy, but boosting customer volume (in terms of shopper numbers) is a recipe for survival.

Another result of the economic turmoil will undoubtedly be a levelling off of retail rent levels. Any corrections to rental prices, particularly in the high-priced countries of Hong Kong, Taiwan and Singapore, will ease pressures on retailers. One thing is for sure: in Hong Kong's Pacific Plaza and Singapore's Orchard Road, charging rents in excess of New York's Fifth Avenue or London's Oxford Street will soon be a thing of the past.

However, while some retail businesses have closed in Asia, others have opened. Retailers such as Japanese-owned department store chain Yaohan that were struggling before the meltdown have found recent events too much for them. In contrast, niche retailers have been gaining ground, showing that when the demand is perceived correctly a business can succeed. These businesses are typically not international but are being built by people who have researched their markets and have strong contacts and roots in their local economies. For niche retailers the financial commitment of setting up shop is often far less than for an international retail giant, the stakes are lower and the breakeven point significantly different. This book offers many examples of such success stories across the continent.

The larger retailers have also had to change their strategies in order to remain viable. British retail giant Marks & Spencer announced in late 1997 – mid-crisis – that it was increasing its presence in Asia, not reducing it. But rather than attempt blanket coverage, being sucked into opening in every mall across the region, companies like M&S are choosing their locations very carefully. Again, they are looking at malls situated near where people actually live, where they catch the train and arrive home at night, where they do their essential weekend food shopping – not necessarily those locations they visit for special shopping trips. Additionally, retailers like M&S are stressing their value for money and quality reputations, and their lower-cost, high-value, own-brand products are proving winners in the new retail climate.

The genesis of the Asian consumer

The modern Asian consumer was born in the 1960s when countries such as South Korea, Taiwan, Hong Kong and Singapore began to follow the path initially charted by Japan. Many people forget the distance these economies have traveled in the last 50 years. During this time the region suffered periods of poor economic development, the Second World War, other wars both civil and otherwise in Indochina, India, Korea and Malaysia, revolutionary upheaval in China, bloody coups in Cambodia and Indonesia. The Federation of Malaysia was formed as recently as 1963.

The economic progress achieved in South Korea and Taiwan on the back of heavy industry and manufacturing production, as well as the successes of the service and financial industries in Hong Kong and Singapore, sent ripples of enterprise and industry across Asia. By the 1970s Malaysia, Thailand and Indonesia had charted courses set to emulate their neighbors' successes. By the early 1980s, the reform process was underway in China and Vietnam followed. India, with a sixth of the world's population, began to throw off the shackles of bureaucracy and its war with Pakistan, while simultaneously moving away from the socialist-leaning policies that had created its giant, slow-moving industries. Across the region entrepreneurs emerged to produce a plethora of services and operations to complement, support and thrive off the growing industrial base.

By the mid-1980s Asia had earned a reputation as a demon exporter and began to invest in Europe and the US as well as across east Asia. Regional giants such as Mitsubishi, Acer, Kia and a host of others invested throughout Asia and became internationally recognized brand names – Lucky Goldstar (LG), Hyundai and Lexus. This investment was boosted by the arrival of multinationals. Companies such as Colgate-Palmolive, Unilever and Ford stepped up their Asian operations as much to tap local market potential as to secure low-cost manufacturing sites.

While much of the Asian miracle was built on perspiration, a growing number of people began to lift themselves out of absolute poverty into a new middle class. Instead of simply exporting toasters, microwaves, PCs and TVs, Asian companies found they had a home market to sell to. Increasingly, international manufacturers targeted this market. The growth of business and higher per capita incomes fueled the development of a host of service industries, from the massive expansion in hotel space and airline schedules to amusement arcades and the film industries of Bollywood and Cantowood.

And all the while subtle changes were occurring at ground level. Across the region people began taking responsibility for their own housing, health and education. This was a seismic change in countries such as China after decades of rigid state control. Home ownership rocketed, education levels soared and private healthcare became standard in many countries. The wealth generated in government bank accounts also paved the way for consumerism. Massive infrastructure projects hooked people up to electricity, gas and treated water as well as public transport systems and roads.

By 1990 Asia was assuredly a world economic power, still a major exporter but also now an innovator, pioneer and a domestic market to be reckoned with. The tantalizing prospect of China opening up to capitalism continued to attract massive doses of inward investment (one third of all inward investment worldwide in one year). India, still awakening slowly, also offered a major new market and a growing middle class and was more consciously bringing itself within the Asian sphere of influence.

In the 1990s Asian consumers also became infinitely more accessible through the growth of the media and the proliferation of advertising media – cable TV, radio, newspapers. And Asian consumers became easier to find as urbanization increased – 20 of the world's 25 largest cities were located in Asia, suburbs were spreading and farm land becoming new airport runways, golf courses or condominium sites.

Asian consumers became just the sort of consumers marketers like. On the whole, many of the new middle class had retained high levels of savings, enabling the purchase of big-ticket items. But many Asians also took to credit surprisingly well and they showed themselves keen to devour the latest fashions, technology and fads. Perhaps best of all, over 50 percent of Asians are under 25 and an increasingly high percentage are literate, educated, urban based and entering the middle class.

The turmoil brings opportunities

However, although consumers had emerged and prospered, it became very clear that not all sectors of the economy had made the transition and a series of bad debts and loans culminated in the economic crisis. This turmoil forced both local and foreign companies to reassess their business strategies, sometimes dismissing them completely and refocusing their activities.

A major focus is now China and it may well be that Asia's crisis will be that country's next boost. While Asian and other retailers were moving cautiously into the Chinese mainland, the crisis at home and the relative stability in China have now instigated a surge of new investment. Chinese consumers are not as accustomed to the range and wide availability of clothing, food and other consumer goods as are consumers in Hong Kong or Singapore. Wealth has led to greater demand for these products in China and more retailers and manufacturers are now answering that call.

There are numerous examples of the booming Chinese market in this book, but for an initial flavor, consider the example of clothes retailing. Not so very long ago, China's new rich left the brand label attached to the sleeve of their new suit to show its prestigious origins and their newly acquired Rolexes meant that the fashion was to have your sleeves permanently rolled up whatever the weather. These people were the first wave of new consumers.

As the economy has continued to accelerate, the number of new consumers has grown. Conghua Li in *China: The Consumer Revolution* (1998) calls China's single kids the S generation, and claims that 'the closest parallel that can be drawn would be the baby boomers in North America in the early 1950s, a time of similar prosperity and rising expectations'. They must fulfill their parents' expectations and they are also the mass consumers of the next few years.

Consumers have begun to buy international, Asian and now also Chinese brands in greater number and with Chinese characteristics. The maxim of 'same but different' applies – everyone wants the latest 'in' brands but few people want to be startlingly different. This follows years of conformity.

A similar pattern is seen in Chinese-influenced countries such as Singapore, where often anything out of the ordinary is viewed with suspicion. The counter-culture kids depicted in Singapore author Claire Tham's short stories are viewed as outsiders because they are punks. In China, wearing Gucci is no longer out of the ordinary but conveys success – being a punk is extraordinary and may lead to rejection and other problems.

Similarly, just being foreign doesn't always work any more. South Korean and Taiwanese brands are increasingly sophisticated and value for money. Even Chinese brands are now much better quality than they used to be. Local brands can be successful and are major rivals not to be ignored by foreign companies, even at the upper end of the market. Examples include Panda brand cigarettes and Tsingtao beer.

The larger clothing retailers cannot afford to be complacent. Clothes retailers such as Hong Kong's Giordano chain and international retailers such as Esprit are building their presence in China to ride this wave. Retail franchising is growing in the clothing industry. Bossini (part of the Giordano chain) has over 100 franchised stores and is planning more to compensate for the slowdown in its core Hong Kong market. Goldlion, an upmarket menswear chain, is also offering franchises to build a China-wide network as quickly as possible.

The recovery begins here...

Following the economic crisis many analysts abandoned the region, predicting that the crash would be total. But it wasn't.

First, the countries of Asia – with the exception of Indonesia – have remained stable through both political and economic turmoil. China did not plummet into civil war after the death of Deng Xiaoping; Hong Kong did not see riots on the streets following reunification with mainland China. Taiwan still acts independently and has held democratic elections; Japan rode out the worldwide recession despite property prices crashing; South Korea has survived all the political scandals, riots and armed sparring with its northern sister nation and managed a successful democratic election in the midst of severe economic downturn. Thailand came through its coups and the Philippines has survived political upheaval.

Secondly, the currency crash did not stop the vast majority of people going out to shop in department stores, buy their groceries and cans of Coke and iced tea. There has been belt tightening, and at the premium end of the market a decline in sales of luxury goods, but life goes on.

Thirdly, consumers have become increasingly cautious and conscious of value for money. With the rise in credit and debit cards across the region a credit-based spending binge was a possible reaction to the meltdown, with consumers using credit facilities to maintain their pre-meltdown lifestyles. All the evidence so far points to the fact that this has not happened. Rather, consumers have become more cautious, more considering in their purchasing, and have forced retailers to look to their pricing structures and margins to win business. The market shift has been from premium brands at high prices to mass-market volume sales, from the new rich to the mass of emerging consumers. These one billion shoppers are the future of the Asian market.

People still need food and clothing as necessities, but over the past 15 years branded and packaged quality goods have become semi-essential consumer items. The key to Asia now is the ability to get both essential and semi-essential products to consumers with greater attention to distribution and distribution costs as well as to maintaining competitive pricing to boost volume sales. This need to reach the mass market is leading to higher levels of investment in retailing and distribution, growing markets in the post-meltdown environment that we look at more closely in the final chapter.

Bouncing back

All countries and regions go through periods of economic crisis, not least the US and Europe in the late 1980s. They often bounce back stronger and more prepared for future problems. In hindsight, the devaluation of the Mexican peso, while severe, forced structural change on that country and surrounding Latin American nations. Mexico's crash highlighted government debt while in Asia private company debt exacerbated the crisis, but the Asian currency crisis also brought some much-needed structural change to financial institutions. As the region recovers so the new systems will be stronger and less susceptible to a rerun of 1997.

Thailand and South Korea have begun to implement IMF restructuring plans for their financial systems and are demonstrating conscientious approaches to recovery. China has begun to restructure its financial and government systems to root out corruption and prepare its institutions for a consumer economy. The ascendancy of Zhu Rongji as Prime Minister in March 1998 is the most overt symbol of this change. Ordinary people are prepared for short-term economic hardship in the form of layoffs and withdrawal of subsidies to ailing enterprises in order to allow the country to move forward.

In Thailand manufacturers and exporters are already taking advantage of the low value of the baht to increase exports; a similar process is occurring in Malaysia. In South Korea newly elected President Kim Dae Jung pushed through a new accord allowing troubled companies to lay off employees and struck a deal with the country's powerful unions to allow this process to occur. He has also persuaded some *chaebol* heads to inject their own capital into companies. In another sign of the historically ultraprotectionist South Korea's new approach, Procter & Gamble was allowed to purchase the Ssangyong Paper Group and German industrial company Robert Bosch bought control of its joint venture with the Kia motor group.

Asia still has numerous underlying strengths. Most of the the column inches devoted to the crisis were concerned with stock-market performance. However, stock markets are only one indicator of wealth. It is essential to consider all the underlying indicators of wealth and economic performance, indicators in which Asia is abundant.

On the economic side, Asian nations generally have extremely high levels of savings and investment and low inflation, and trade budgets are invariably in surplus as are national current accounts.

On the social side, Asia retains its strong work ethic. In the face of crisis a strong national spirit emerged – not least in South Korea where the public donated gold jewelry to repay debts created by the economic crash. There is still a strong emphasis on training and education and, according to the 1998 *Index of Economic Freedom*, Hong Kong and Singapore are the two most open economies in the world.

While some of the much vaunted infrastructure projects such as Malaysia's longest building in the world have been put on hold, inward investment remains high. It is even possible that it will accelerate with cheap currencies propelling multinational spending sprees as well as boosting Asia as a holiday destination for westerners. Multinationals operate globally and for most their exposure in Asia is a small component of their total investment spread. Domestic companies are likely to avoid additional overseas investment to protect their home base – bad news for Welsh and French workers assembling Lucky Goldstar microwaves, but perhaps a boost for the domestic Korean economy.

Writing in the *International Herald Tribune* in December 1997, Tommy Koh, former Singapore Ambassador to the US and executive director of the Asia-Europe Foundation in Singapore, stated: 'I have no doubt that after a period of adjustment, which may take two to three years, East Asia will bounce back, stronger, more disciplined, more transparent and more competitive. The rise of East Asia in the world economy has suffered a temporary setback, but is unstoppable.'

The fact that so many Asian countries have survived blips in their histories and come through the other side fairly unscathed points to its underpinning strength as a region of rapid economic and social development. The experiences of the first two-thirds of the twentieth century will not be ones Asians wish to repeat, and so predictions of economic collapse followed by social turmoil are scare-mongering, just as overexuberance about the growth of the tiger economies was foolhardy.

The fact is that Asia has always been rich – rich in culture, history, natural resources, manpower, educated people, inventors, financiers, entrepreneurs and so on. But this potential was held back by the interference of western colonial powers over the last 200 or so years, bringing to Asia commercial exploitation, war and drug abuse. Now that Asians have reclaimed control of their region, they are eager to pick up their old skills in inventive manufacturing, rich agricultural output and ambitious financing, coupled with new skills learnt from their former conquerors.

Asians feel that it is their turn to show the world what they can do and show no signs of being afraid of rising to the challenge. Despite the recent turmoil in Hong Kong, the currency crisis, the downturn in tourism and the retail slump, a December 1997 survey by the American Chamber of Commerce (AmCham) reported that 96 percent of the nearly 600 Hong Kong-based companies polled had a 'favorable' outlook for the future. It also saw the ongoing turmoil as a necessary price to pay for long-term stability.

This environment continues to create the kind of entrepreneurial ambition not really seen since nineteenth-century Britain or the US in the 1950s. The difference is that Asia is much, much bigger, comprises many more countries and cultures, a huge slice of the world's population, and has so far only achieved a fraction of its potential. Within this environment, new types of consumers are emerging, particular to Asia in terms of what they buy and why, and with the kind of purchasing power that allows them to experiment with new interests, ambitions, pastimes and lifestyles.

The Asian consumer takes center stage

The first lesson is to remember that the very term 'Asian consumer' is shorthand. Asia is a network of countries with both a great deal and very little in common. The countries of China and southeast Asia share only a broad geographic positioning in common. They are neither all the same race, religion, ethnicity or temperament.

The region varies from the giant landmass of China to small city states such as Singapore. Understanding the nature and dynamics of any one country is easier with the others in view – in particular, the Chinese-dominated communities of southeast Asia have strong similarities whether in Taiwan, Singapore or Thailand – but these are only comparisons. And in those comparisons lie other contradictions, the main one being that size is really no indicator of consumer power in Asia. It is the diversity that is crucial to understand.

Population

China has over one billion people, India is nearing the billion mark while Singapore has just under three million and Hong Kong just over six million.

Religion

Thailand is 95 percent Buddhist, the Philippines 99 percent Roman Catholic while Indonesia and Malaysia remain dominantly Muslim. Increasingly China is a 'divine supermarket' of religions both ancient and modern, though there remains a majority of atheist socialists.

Urbanization

Vietnam is over 70 percent rural. China is just under 30 percent urban but has cities such as Shanghai with populations in excess of 15 million. Singapore, Hong Kong and Taiwan are largely urban societies. Rural countries are often poorer, such as Thailand (81 percent rural) and the Philippines (69 percent rural), but others can be relatively wealthy, such as Malaysia which has a 51 percent rural population.

Politics

Both Taiwan and Singapore have made significant steps towards fully fledged democracy in recent years. However, China and Vietnam remain ruled by their respective Communist Parties. The demonstration in Tian'anmen Square caught wider public attention than did riots in Bangkok and Jakarta. Indonesia is undergoing a fresh wave of pro-democracy upheavals and President Soeharto has been forced to resign. South Korea has seen scandal after scandal rock the political establishment and with the economic crisis in full swing elected a liberal candidate. Hong Kong reverted to Chinese rule in 1997 and Macao will do so by the end of the century, marking the end of European colonialism in Asia.

Economic disparity

The annual incomes of Hong Kong or Singapore residents are already equal to those in many western countries; they are 100 times higher than the incomes of peasants in the Mekong Delta or the Chinese hinterland. According to the World Bank, in 1995 Singapore's average citizen earned US$23,360; the average American brought home US$25,860. Gross mean income per head in South Korea is US$11,000, approximately half the western European average. However, the average Chinese earned just US$530. In China, Indonesia, Thailand, the Philippines and Vietnam, eight out of ten of the combined two billion population survive on just US$2 a day. Even if we calculated these sums in purchasing parity terms, the disparity would still be enormous.

Same yet different

Same yet different is a pattern throughout the region. Every country has a middle class which is growing in size and importance. However, the definition of middle class varies dramatically from nation to nation. And the middle class may not always be instantly recognizable. The notion of a global middle class, a class with common values across both sides of the Atlantic, has not yet stretched to the Pacific. Asians may be middle class in income terms but they remain very traditional and still have a plethora of national peculiarities and values.

All the countries of the region have dynamic economies but they are built on different bases. They range from the financial and service-based economies of Hong Kong and Singapore to those with large raw material deposits such as Indonesia. Manufacturing industry has necessarily been a motor of growth in many countries but rarely in similar industries. The shipbuilding and steel production that have developed South Korea are in contrast to the high-tech computer chip and fiberoptic technologies that are powering Malaysia's development.

Inward investment

Despite the hiccup in 1997, inward investment into Asia has been spectacular. In 1995, China sucked in fully one third of total inward investment to the developing world and continues to swallow massive gulps of investment on a daily basis. Many conclude that Asia, and China in particular, is the playground of the multinational corporation. Certainly they have been able to make major inroads. Recently Colgate-Palmolive bought up China's largest toothpaste factory (the biggest manufacturer of toothpaste in the world) and the auto companies have entered the region with a vengeance, as have the tobacco firms.

But the benefits of the Asian consumer market are also being felt by smaller companies and niche industrial sectors. The Scottish whisky industry offers up prayers to Taiwan, the world's largest per capita consumer of the spirit. British retailers such as Marks & Spencer and the Body Shop have found lucrative markets in Asia and the tiny Redruth Brewery of Cornwall has become a major supplier of real ale to the burgeoning Hong Kong dark beer market.

Deconstructing Asia

Asia is far from being an undiscovered Shangri-la but it is underdeveloped and underexploited territory. The region is certainly overwhelming at first glance and the primary requirement is to break it down into its components. If you do this then you can build the parts back up into a regionally sound picture with which to work on marketing, advertising and distribution plans.

Hot spots

China is a multibordered nominally communist country, which absorbed Hong Kong in July 1997. It continues a semi-hot dispute with Taiwan and is grappling with an internal pro-democracy movement and the rebellious provinces of Tibet. Essentially, China has followed a policy of plenty of *perestroika* with no *glasnost*: keep the lid on the society while freeing the economy. The shift has been dramatic. In the Cultural Revolution Mao exhorted the Red Guards 'to change heaven and earth' – barely 20 years later Deng declared: 'To be rich is glorious.' However, if not properly addressed soon, the widening gap between the rich cities and the poor hinterland could recreate the kind of social divisions which brought down the nationalists and put the Communists in power in 1949.

China is not the only potential hot spot. Indonesia's occupation of East Timor continues. Protesters take to the streets regularly in Jakarta, Bangkok and Seoul. Burma remains a dictatorship. Singapore is as well known for its social rigidity as its low crime rate. North and South Korea remain sticking points. There are border disputes throughout Indo-China and the drug trade and piracy hamper trade agreements.

The reality is that business does go on and consumer markets continue to emerge. More importantly for the international business community, we have passed through two kinds of war in Asia that have profoundly affected the climate for consumers in the region:

- ✦ The investment wars were not violent but left plenty of regional politicians with bloody noses. The fight to open up investment, particularly in isolationist countries such as South Korea and Taiwan, was hard fought and won an inch at a time.
- ✦ It was the same with the trade wars that were fought on the battlefields of the GATT negotiations and the formation of the World Trade Organization (WTO).

With the region now open for investment and trade we are entering the consumer wars.

Consumer wars

Many of the consumer battles seen first in the US and later in western Europe have been or are being replayed in Asia. The cola and tobacco wars are in full swing. Just as the major music retailers are battling for market share along Oxford Street in London or around Times Square in New York, so too in Asia. In June 1996 HMV announced that it was entering the southeast Asian market and taking its rivals Tower and Virgin head on in a battle for supremacy of the CD retailing sector. But although the names may be familiar, Asian consumers have invariably modified and adapted western brands, products and services to their own uses.

As previously in Europe and the US the growth of credit has radically altered the consumer market. Despite many regional governments' attempts to curb spending and restrain inflationary pressure, both consumer spending and retail sales have continued to rise. Across the region consumers' aspirations have undergone great leaps, made possible by greater access to goods, services and credit. Since 1991 the number of credit cards in use has expanded by 80 percent, with over 95 million payment cards now being swiped in Asia-Pacific, excluding Japan.

Sheer size alone will not mean instant success for the uninitiated. Asians demand to be respected, and only the foolish now enter the region without first trying to understand the kind of beast they will have to deal with, be it dragon or tiger.

Part One

Consumers

2

The Asian Family

In assessing any market one must consider the consumption patterns of individuals and families. In the west, where the cult of the individual has tended to take precedence, the family as a consumer unit often takes secondary place. In Asia, the family is the central consumer unit and understanding why that is so is crucial to getting to grips with consumption in Asia.

The family plays a central role in Asian countries' history, culture and society. The family is considered to be the basic unit of society and of consumption, and is therefore the natural place to start a discussion about Asian consumers. It is, after all, the family that provides the next generation of consumers and imparts a values set from one generation to the next. Within it are Asia's children, teens, middle class, women and new homeowners.

The family unit is especially crucial to a basic understanding of the Asian consumer market right now because the nature of families and family life are changing. The following are some of the key trends:

- Increasingly the typical middle-class Asian family is a nuclear one, with middle-aged parents and children. Previously the extended family unit was the norm.

- The growth of the nuclear family is leading to higher spending levels per child as parents and grandparents dote on their one or two children or grandchildren. The pressures of large populations are encouraging people to have fewer children.
- The children of middle-class parents are growing up in high-consuming, smaller families and gaining whole new expectations of consumption patterns. This means more money to spend per person than in the past.
- Spending on all things baby and child is rocketing, from maternity wear and soft toys to educational books and fast food. Children are a focus of family attention in Asia, perhaps even more than elsewhere.
- Services such as private kindergartens, tutoring colleges and summer camps are appearing all over the region to cater to the needs of Asia's pampered children. The new generation is growing up in very different ways to their predecessors.

Asian families have traditionally been the backbone of society, supplementing the myriad roles assumed by governments in the west and the arena where the concepts of self-reliance and responsibility are first learnt. The family provides support and security. Asian parents don't assume that the state will pay for education and healthcare because few of the region's countries have anything like a European-style welfare state. This means that parents take it on themselves to provide more for their children. It also means that in the post-meltdown period, spending on children's education and welfare will be one of the last things affected.

The nuclear family

Increasing urbanization and social pressures have led to growing levels of extended-family breakdown, particularly in urban areas. One prime example of this process is the rapid rise in divorces, such as in China where the number grew by 23 percent between 1990 and 1994, according to official statistics. However, despite the prophets of doom for the family in Asia – and there have been many – the main trend is away from the extended family and

AVERAGE HOUSEHOLD SIZE

Across Asia the average size of households is shrinking due to several factors. Not least among these are the reduction in family size, falling birthrate and the breakdown of the extended family as grandad and grandma stay put and the children and grandchildren visit by car.

Country	Number of people per household		
	1990	1994	1998*
China	4.4	4.1	3.7
Hong Kong	3.7	3.5	3.3
India	5.6	5.4	5.3
Indonesia	4.5	4.4	4.3
Malaysia	5.0	4.8	4.6
Philippines	5.1	5.3	5.2
Singapore	3.9	3.7	3.7
South Korea	4.0	3.8	3.4
Taiwan	4.0	3.8	3.6
Thailand	4.6	4.6	4.6

Source: National statistics
Note: *Authors' estimates based on historical trends

towards the nuclear family. In China, for example, family size is shrinking rapidly to 3.7 people per household and going as low as 3.4 people in urban areas. Nuclear families now comprise 30 percent of all households in the country.

This change doesn't necessarily lead to breakdown but more often a reconcentration of the family on a smaller, more compact scale. Some commentators have argued that the emergence of smaller family units represents a shift towards a more western ethos. Others have counter-argued that the change is simply the result of the impact of more freely available birth-control measures and family economics. In reality it is a mixture of factors: women choosing careers over childbirth at a young age, men choosing careers and late marriage, growing personal incomes along with financial commitments and different lifestyles. Another consideration is that couples who can afford to (of which there are increasing numbers) will buy their own home, away from the in-laws, so that they can set up their own family environment in a way they feel is more in tune with their generation's values.

On a Malaysian daytime TV talk show one morning a panel of parents who had built their own nuclear families were arguing vociferously for the benefits of smaller households. The claim that nuclear families improve communication between parents and children and allow them more time together was acknowledged as a good thing. Most of the parents came from families of six or seven children and they had consciously opted for the nuclear version in reaction to their own upbringing. Essentially, the emergence of the smaller, nuclear family should be taken as a sign of a maturing society, wealthier and better able to sustain itself than previously.

Birth rates

Birth rates are of concern across the region, but for differing reasons. Vietnam and China have sought actively to reduce the birth rate and foster smaller families. The Chinese one-child policy is the most overtly coercive example of this form of social engineering. Strict rules on family size have lowered the birth rate from an average of six babies per woman in 1970 to about two today. This still means there are an additional 14 million Chinese born annually.

In Vietnam the Communist Party's current five-year plan has enshrined the aim of reducing the nation's population growth rate of 2.1 percent a year to a projected 1.8 percent by 2000. The United Nations Family Planning Association (UNFPA) provided Vietnam with US$87 million between 1978 and 1996, which included the cost of building a condom manufacturing plant.

India has a birth rate of 28 per 1000 population, growing at 2 percent a year, and will have a population in excess of 1 billion by 2000. Birth control is a sensitive area politically and forced birth-control measures attempted in the past have left a bitter taste.

ASIAN BIRTH RATES

Overall birth rates are falling across the region. South Korea has had a successful birth control campaign reducing population growth from 3 percent in 1960 to 1 percent in 1997 – a demographic transition achieved in one generation. In the Philippines birth rates have remained high (the Philippines is also Asia's only majority Catholic country), although they have begun to decline as the economy has picked up. China's particularly low population growth is due almost entirely to the enforcement of the one-child policy. The Chinese have described the introduction of effective family planning as the 'No. 1 difficulty under heaven'.

%	Population growth rate		Population aged 0–14	
	1997	2000	1997	2000
China	1.1	1.0	26.0	25.3
Hong Kong	1.0	1.0	18.1	16.5
Indonesia	1.8	1.5	32.1	30.8
India	1.0	1.0	34.5	33.5
Malaysia	1.0	1.0	36.9	35.2
Philippines	2.3	1.8	37.5	36.4
Singapore	1.0	1.0	22.3	21.6
South Korea	1.0	0.8	23.0	22.2
Taiwan	1.0	1.0	25.6	25.6
Thailand	1.8	1.4	27.6	26.5
Vietnam	2.0	1.8	36.7	35.7
World average	1.4	1.2	26.9	26.1

Source: National statistics

Given India's multicultural and multireligious nature, a broad policy to tackle population growth is virtually guaranteed to be unworkable.

Indonesia, with over 100 million people, is the largest Muslim country in the world in population terms. Like India, its birth rate remains relatively high at about 25 per 1000 inhabitants each year.

And in Malaysia the annual birth rate is 26 per 1000. In both these majority Muslim countries, family structure has been less dramatically altered by economic development than in other east Asian cultures.

In contrast, several of the more developed nations in the region are showing concern at their falling birth rates. South Korea's population will start to fall dramatically by 2020 if the current decline in population growth continues. The Seoul government has become concerned that a shrinking labor force may not be able to sustain the expanding number of elderly citizens, and also that North Korea's population, while only half that of the south presently, is growing twice as fast. Across the East China Sea, Taiwan's shrinking birth rate has forced the government to revise its somewhat dry slogan 'Two Children is Just Right' to the more upbeat 'Go For Two'.

In wealthy Singapore, the lack of pregnancies and the increase in the number of DINKYs (Dual Income, No Kids) is partly the result of growing national wealth, job opportunities, improved healthcare and an effective birth control policy during Lee Kuan Yew's premiership. Now, however, the government is keen to increase the birth rate backed up by television adverts exhorting educated and newly affluent singles to marry. A dating agency for university graduates has been set up to encourage like to marry educationally qualified like in an attempt at social engineering. Those tying the knot and producing offspring are rewarded with personal income tax breaks, a true incentive for the middle class.

In Japan, which in many ways is the role model for development in Asia, the average family size is almost exactly 3. Birth rates fell during the 1990s, from 10 births per 1000 population in 1990 to 9.6 in 1994. This reflects the country's highly developed state, both economically and socially, where many more women are pursuing careers and having children later in life, or not at all. Japan has one of Asia's highest percentages of the female population economically active, with 41 percent of its women in work. An inescapable conclusion is that growing national wealth and personal incomes tend to presage falling birth rates.

On the whole, the decline in birth rates and family size is an urban phenomenon. Thailand's rural growth rate is perhaps as high as 3 percent but the rate in Bangkok is much lower. Countries alarmed at falling birth rates such as South Korea and Singapore are heavily urbanized. Even the Chinese one-child policy is more abused in the rural rather than the urban areas where transgressions cannot be so easily hidden from the eyes of the authorities.

Rural families in China have been targeted with particularly inventive campaigns to encourage family planning, attempting to appeal to the new entrepreneur in the countryside. One sign that appeared in villages read: 'If you want to get rich, have fewer kids and raise more pigs.' You can't argue with that.

Demographic shifts

The age composition of Asian society is also changing. The more developed Asian nations (such as Hong Kong and Singapore) now have over 50 percent of their population aged over 30 and often less than a third aged under 15. In India male life expectancy has accelerated rapidly from 56 in 1995 to 59 in 1997, and is projected to reach 61 by 2002; and in China, male life expectancy is now 67 years.

By the year 2000, there will be 130 million retired people in China alone. Indonesia will have 15 million elderly people by the year 2000 and they will not all have golden old ages. Even in countries as advanced as Singapore, surveys have shown that seven out of ten old people rely on their children for money, an especially surprising result given that the country has one of the world's highest personal savings rates. The pattern is similar in other Asian countries, nearly 50 percent in Thailand and nearly 40 percent in the Philippines.

But in some of the more populous nations, the younger sections of the populations are much larger than in the rest of the region. The country with the largest 0–14-year-old population is the Philippines at 37.5 percent, closely followed by Indonesia at 36.7 percent, Vietnam at 25 percent and India at 24 percent. This reflects the less developed state of their economies, where parents tend to have more children to ensure they can be cared for when they are too old to continue working.

In Thailand alone there are 4.9 million people aged over 60 and 10.9 million aged under 10 – that's two kids to every senior.

Children under the age of 12 make up about 16 percent of Asia's total population.

In Beijing, the average family spends around US$375 per annum on their children. Since the average per capita household income in Beijing is about US$1500, this means that spending on parents' one child is worth approximately a quarter of total household income.

Such large amounts of investment by parents in their children are illustrative of trends right across Asia. Children are therefore, without spending much themselves, one of the most important consumer groups. The current generation of kids in Asia have earned themselves the title 'the golden children'.

All companies in Asia are interested in these consumers of the future – the children who are changing Asian people's attitudes to their place in the world and what they expect the world to provide them with. It is crucial to understand how they interpret their world.

Asia is moving at a rapid pace and, while social trends may be embedded through family and tradition, there is little chance that today's kids will see the region as their parents did. Their education now includes surfing the Web, watching foreign documentaries on TV, listening to foreign music etc. The influence of education on any child's perception of the world is huge, and education plays perhaps an even more significant part in children's lives in Asia than elsewhere.

An Asian education

It is virtually impossible to overstate the importance of education in Asian society. Even in countries where economics determine that children should enter the world of work at the earliest possible moment in order to contribute to the family kitty, every effort is made to maintain some sort of ongoing educational program.

Education starts young, with parents eager to get their children off to a good start. Governments are investing heavily in pre-school education. Private kindergartens are appearing throughout the region, not just in solidly middle-class enclaves but also in remote rural communities. Even those countries whose fiscal resources are scarce, such as Vietnam, have managed seeming miracles in education. The Vietnamese have managed to ensure that over 90 percent of school leavers are literate, both rural and urban. Enrollment in primary and secondary schools is in the high 90 percent bracket. Government spending on education has risen to 14 percent of the national budget in 1997 from under 5 percent in 1989.

At primary and secondary schools, truancy rates are low by western standards and schools are becoming better equipped year by year. Curricula are being extended and teacher training improved.

And the importance of education doesn't stop after primary or secondary school. For many families across Asia, sons and daughters come home just in time to see their parents leave for school as they attend the region's numerous evening classes in the hope of attaining that additional degree, professional qualification or second-language proficiency that will enhance their career prospects. For an Asian middle-class child, education is a part of life, not something to be endured till they reach fifteen or sixteen.

In Taiwan and Japan, cram schools are filled with children outside normal school hours, all of whom know that if they want to get to the right university, they have to get exceptional grades. The competition for places at the 'rated' universities has put massive pressure on students. It is often the case that good jobs are assured to those who get to the best universities, without much regard to their actual performance in higher education. So school results really matter to these children, and just as much to their similarly ambitious parents.

The Asian Chinese living outside mainland China have been sending their kids to the world's best colleges and universities for decades. There is hardly a leading business school in the world that does not have an active alumni association in Hong Kong or Singapore. It seems to work. Taiwan has a population one-third the size of the UK, but produces more engineering graduates annually.

SMART SCHOOL, SMART KIDS

One of the flagship programs in Malaysia's Multimedia Super Corridor (see Chapter 9) is the creation of Smart Schools throughout the country.

According to the *New Straits Times* (March 31, 1997): 'The core element of the Smart School concept is the use of information technology as a key means of educating students who will form the generation of a technology-oriented society.'

Meanwhile in Singapore, the Education Ministry is planning to incorporate Smart Labs, a computer-based education delivery system using network computing and Web-based technologies, as a component in the country's Smart Schools concept nationwide. Through the system, students will also gain easier access to a wider range of resources including productivity tools, information on the Internet and e-mail.

Undoubtedly, the pupils at Smart Schools will want the same sort of technology in their homes as they have in their classrooms.

Western universities actively target Asian students. Leading institutes such as London's prestigious Imperial College of Science, Technology and Medicine actively employ staff to visit the region and sell their college and courses to an increasingly discerning Asian undergraduate market. Nearly every North American and European university of any worth is doing the same.

Malaysia's Kolej Unitek advertises several advantages of enroling in the institution, the first and second being: 'choose to complete your degree in a reputable university in the UK or New Zealand' and 'choose to spend your final year abroad to make it easier on your pocket'.

And the mainland Chinese are increasingly sending their children overseas to study, with the government's blessing, and in a reversal of fortune that goes against the last 50 years of enmity, Taiwanese and Singaporean parents are becoming keen for their children to attend mainland Chinese universities.

In 1998 European and US universities and colleges found that many of their Asian students were suddenly departing for home.

The economic crisis had meant that their national currencies had depreciated to a level where western education was too expensive. This is hitting the western colleges hard, as some depended on Asian students for as much as a third of their income. However, there has also been a rush to establish branches in Asia. Britain's University of Leeds has established a business studies department in Singapore. Pennsylvania University's Wharton School of Business has signed an agreement with the Singapore Institute of Management to create an undergraduate studies program in that country, while UCLA's Anderson School is establishing business management departments in Beijing and Shanghai.

Educational book buying is increasing. In Thailand, where book buying has not traditionally been widespread due to limited access and income, the Bangkok government has heavily encouraged reading by increasing the budget for the national literacy program, stocking libraries and encouraging local publishers through tax breaks for textbooks. The result has been a significant growth in reading as a hobby. The market for textbooks exceeded US$47 million in 1997, 44 percent of total book sales.

In Singapore, the fastest-growing sector of the book industry is children's books and encyclopedias. A recent report on the industry noted that parents' concern for their children's academic well-being was boosting the market for assessment, supplementary and educational books. Two leading Singapore bookstores, MPH and Times – The Bookshop, both stock in excess of 5000 titles aimed at children. Both stores report growing sales of computer books, educational and reference books to parents for their children.

In Indonesia the 7–24 age group controls an estimated 80 percent of the retail book market, with 10 percent of total book sales being for children. Parents are actively encouraging their children to read, even though it may not be a pastime they enjoy. One problem in Indonesia is that books are expensive, with quality often low, while many foreign titles are never translated into the national language.

In the Philippines, a new development has been the Goodwill bookstore, which caters solely for children. This not only stocks children's books, toys and educational material, but also offers its young shoppers their own shopping baskets and trolleys, reading and play areas – firmly, and consciously, putting the child in charge of their book shopping.

With fewer children to spread the family money around there is extra cash for piano lessons, sports activities, computer clubs and school trips. Children with computers in school want computers in their bedrooms, those with a leaning towards music want their own instruments, more sports means more sports gear and everyone wants the books, bags and packed lunches that go with school life.

The head of the family

The basic unit of most Asian societies is the family, and obedience to the family is a strong influence and value. The head of the family is therefore a potent force in deciding how it spends its cash. Asian society is outwardly patriarchal, so the head of the family is invariably the father. However, it is often the mother who wields real practical power and is usually the dominant force behind much of a family's spending.

Mothers undertake most of the family's day-to-day shopping and make everyday purchasing decisions. Fathers are usually more involved in the purchase of large and/or expensive goods, and also deciding about the allowances given to the children.

Mothers still spend more time with their children than do fathers, and so women are more attuned to the change in their children's aspirations, shaped by the new media and technology.

Children are therefore a strong influence on the purchasing decisions made by their parents, often being better informed about new products than their parents are. This has changed the relationship between the child and the parent, and between the parents themselves.

Increasingly affluent families

The growth of the nuclear family and the rise in affluence across the region are crucial to the growth of consumer markets and the region's long-term success. Parents are going shopping with money in their pockets and looking for ways not just to ensure that their children grow up successful and educated but also that they grow up healthy. Many of these new parents grew up in very different circumstances, in environments of poverty, hard manual work and insecurity. The parents of a 10-year-old Vietnamese child were born into a country at war, in China they may have been a Red Guard, in Hong Kong an immigrant from southern China. This is not what they want for their children and they are doing, and buying, just about anything that will ensure that the pattern changes for the next generation.

This investment is largely being made in children's education, so they will have better career prospects than their parents did. But this investment also includes better food, better clothing, more stimulating toys, involvement in sports and other social activities. This is not only creating a new generation with a different outlook to their parents, but is also changing the way parents view the world and act as consumers.

And across Asia the children's market is developing in sometimes surprising ways. The market for artificial insemination is booming. Infertility clinics have opened across India with six in Hyderabad alone. One Indian clinic, The Infertility Institute and Research Center, has dealt with over 11,000 cases since opening in 1990. In Malaysia, the national Fertility Society has brought what was once a sensitive and taboo subject out into the open and managed to persuade an increasing number of men to attend for a sperm count. Ten years ago this would have been impossible. Even if couples could have brought themselves to attend, the high cost of many infertility treatments would have been beyond them.

Thai babies

The increasing affluence of many Thais is filtering down to the next generation. Thai parents have become massive consumers of baby powder, formula milk, pacifiers and specially marketed baby foods, not to mention the ever-necessary diapers. The country now imports over US$80 million worth of powdered milk and every year Thais spend US$40 million on diapers and US$60 million on baby powder.

Birth rates are falling annually and incomes have grown. The simple equation is more money to be spent on fewer children. Actual spending has boomed (around US$242 million a year in total in Thailand and rising every year). The economic crisis will not affect spending on children until absolutely necessary, as it is no longer considered to be a luxury.

And the new mums are doing better too. A Thai Farmers Research Center study found recently that the average mum-to-be was spending US$1400 on maternity wear, clothes and shoes: all before they buy the first rattle or change the first diaper. This is a new phenomenon in Thailand and is due to the rapidly growing number of working women, obviously some of whom are pregnant. At the higher end they are spending on pre- and ante-natal classes.

Thai retailers have been quick to recognize the trend. Bangkok department stores now devote large segments of floor space to all things baby. Angel Baby, a new all-baby chain store, is spreading rapidly across Bangkok and also establishing a direct marketing division to target pregnant mums stuck indoors.

And Beijing's big babies

The desire by Asian parents to provide well for their children is natural enough, although sometimes the attention can be lavished a little too thickly. Chinese city kids are increasingly overweight. Obesity rates among urban children have grown by 10 percent every year since 1986 for under-7s – that is, every year there is a threefold increase in the number of kids weighing in excess of 15 percent more than they should. The problem is a uniquely urban one, the rural areas being largely still too poor to produce fat children.

Chinese researchers believe that parents, many of whom have themselves endured famine, are regularly overfeeding their children, both to express love and to flaunt their new wealth. The researchers have drawn parallels to 1940s America (a country that still has the most obese children internationally) and also admit that the one-child policy has led to spoiling by parents and grandparents, who outnumber the kids six to one. The research also found that many urban children were eating four, or even five, meals a day plus numerous snacks and drinks.

The new Chinese urban fatties are showing signs of depression as well as, not surprisingly, performing poorly at sports. All this has meant added profits for the growing number of fast-food chains in China, but also for one enterprising Beijing businessman who has opened a 'fat farm' designed specifically to help under-15s shed the pounds.

The new Asian family model

An increasing number of Asian children are being brought up in families with disposable income, ready access to consumer goods and aspirations to further ownership. Despite the recent economic difficulties, consumer aspirations have already been fostered; perhaps more significantly, this aspiration is focused on providing a better standard of living for the next generation, which will ensure that spending on providing for the children will tend not to be sacrificed.

The new Asian family increasingly has a car and a mortgage, goes on holiday, often abroad and maybe twice a year, and has cable TV. There are more families where both parents are working in professional occupations; they are finding good schools for their offspring and looking forward to them going to college. More than ever before children are being raised in the new middle class, with parents who are active consumers, already far removed from their grandparents' and great grandparents' lifestyles. These are the children who will become mass consuming teens and the professional middle class of the twenty-first century – and they have a passion for consuming.

How to market to Asian families

- *Stress the educational value* – Dorling Kindersley's books and CD-Roms, with their overt educational values, have proved popular with parents and children alike, despite their relatively high cost.

- *Stress the health benefits* – Savory snack manufacturers are increasingly cutting the salt content of their products, pandering to health-conscious parents who are increasingly concerned about their children's diets.

- *Target new ideas and products at the younger generations* – Newly popular sports, such as soccer and basketball, have found great popularity among children and teenagers in particular. New flavors of soft drinks are more readily accepted by teenagers and young adults.

- *Increase product ranges to target different age groups separately* – Johnson & Johnson has been particularly successful with its children's personal care products, and over-the-counter medicine companies have also benefited from targeting the children's and women's markets separately.

- *Provide for families* – Ampang Point Shopping Centre in Kuala Lumpur, like many others in the region, specifically features a Toytown area for children and fast-food restaurants for teenagers to congregate in. The aim is to develop kids' and teens' loyalty so they keep coming back.

- *Advertise to children* – Kentucky Fried Chicken in Malaysia purposely targets all advertising at kids and teens, not adults, in the belief that it is children who take their parents to KFC, even though it's the parents who pay.

3

Teen Frenzy

Asia currently has just under 2 billion residents below the age of 30, of whom 640 million are teenagers. That's 21 percent of the total regional population – the largest teenage market in the world:

- Millions of teens increasingly indulged in nuclear families, increasingly in middle-class families, increasingly fighting the sociocultural battle between western and Asian values – defining their own tastes and increasingly demanding consumer goods of their own choosing.
- Millions of teens with greater access to the media, to TV, to advertising, to music, magazines, billboards and travel – much of it, such as MTV Asia, increasingly aimed specifically at them.
- Millions of teens increasingly well educated, fed and housed and now looking for consumer goods aimed at them, brands targeted to them.
- Millions of teens with a growing influence in the region, who are changing the social landscape.

Take just one example from the oil-rich sultanate of Brunei, where teens have been at the forefront of the drive to open up the country to outside influences. Bandar Seri Begawan, the capital city, now has a multiplex cinema catering to teen tastes as well as a real-time link bringing to Brunei London's Capital FM radio station, which

NUMBER OF TEENAGERS 1997

China	214,783,000
India	214,340,000
Indonesia	42,361,000
Vietnam	18,077,000
Thailand	11,517,000
Philippines	11,206,000
Korea	8,477,000
Taiwan	3,876,000
Malaysia	3,828,000
Hong Kong	839,000
Singapore	415,000

Source: National statistics

is now heard blaring out of cars throughout the city's streets.

With low unemployment in most Asian countries, teens don't have many of the same worries as their western cousins. Even in those countries with relatively high teenage unemployment, such as Vietnam with 20 percent teen joblessness, this is more a temporary situation resulting from population shifts to the cities and the restructuring of the economy than the long-term youth unemployment seen in Europe. They may be temporarily unemployed and hungry for work, at the start of their careers or studying, perhaps even just enjoying life before responsibility sets in, but they are eager to become consumers and not jaded in the way many European teens are, or crime and drug besieged like many disadvantaged American teens.

Teenagers in Asia may wear the clothes, follow the trends and walk the walk of Generation X (even in some cases copy the talk of their western counterparts) but they are not disillusioned, not the so-called slacker generation. Exactly the opposite. In fact, all the evidence indicates that Asian teens are carving a youth culture for themselves, on the one hand undeniably influenced by western trends and fashions, but on the other retaining and rediscovering many traditional Asian values from their own cultures.

Compared to their western counterparts, Asian teens emerge as an extremely well-balanced, moral and responsible bunch. Educational standards are improving annually. The statistics may be doubted, but anyone who has visited a McDonald's on a Sunday in Singapore will find themselves among tables of coke-swilling, burger-munching teenagers with their textbooks out looking deeply concerned about the next morning's test. And a survey by McCann Erickson India found that 72 percent of Indian teenagers still look up to their parents as role models compared to just 12 percent of US teens.

And these teens are an advertiser's and marketer's dream. Consider the results of a recent survey of teen life in Manila: teens spent an average of three hours a day watching TV, mostly between 6 pm and midnight, seven days a week. Those same teens listened to three hours of radio a day, preferring FM music stations, spent between two and five hours three times a week in a shopping mall and visited the cinema once a fortnight on average.

Lack of conflict

This balance between the new world that Asian teenagers inhabit – a world of opportunity, travel and access to foreign culture along with the traditions and values of Asian society – is not showing the signs of conflict that many pundits had predicted. Of course, there are examples of rises in juvenile crime, dropping out and drug taking. In April 1997 Singapore announced its first death from Ecstasy, the drug that has been labeled the narcotic of choice for Asia's affluent young professionals.

In many Asian countries, infractions of the law that would seem petty in the west are treated harshly. Another example from Singapore: Garrence Neo Yong Hao is a 16-year-old student at Pierce Secondary School. He was caught smoking four times and fined US$34. Garrence and seven other teen smokers also had their names printed in the *Straits Times* revealing their habit and punishment.

Overall the evidence points to the fact that the vast majority of Asian teens are remaining remarkably straight compared to their

THEIR WORLD ... AND THEY LIKE IT

Perhaps nothing better reveals the positive attitude of Asian teens than a survey conducted among students between 15 and 19. Asked if they believed that 'the world will improve in my lifetime', all Asian teens, except the Japanese, proved more optimistic than their European or US peers. Chinese were the most optimistic, with 69 percent believing good times to be ahead, followed by Koreans at 49 percent, Taiwanese at 44 percent and Vietnamese at 40 percent.

***New World Teen Study Wave II*, The Brain Waves Group**

western peer group. A survey by condom manufacturer Durex, reported in the *South China Morning Post* (22.5.96), found that teenagers in Hong Kong were postponing their first sexual encounters until they reached the age of 18, with only 2.3 percent of males and 1.1 percent of females having sex before they were 15.

Spending power

Hong Kong teens have an average monthly allowance of US$84 per month. The average pocket money for Singapore teens was US$30 a week, though 17 percent worked part-time and 49 percent full-time in the holidays. And 4 percent of Singapore teens admitted to having taken out a bank loan to support their lifestyle. Malaysian and other Asian teens are not far behind and those in countries such as the Philippines and Vietnam are catching up quickly. Teens have become discerning consumers in their own right and their loyalty must be sought and cultivated.

Although disillusionment may be very low, easy access to the newest gadgets, the latest popular culture, worldwide media and money have left Asia's teens with a need for challenge.

Spirituality

Asian teenagers are not growing up as carbon copies of their parents. As a new generation they are developing their own sets of values and ambitions. The increase in their media exposure, be it MTV Asia, targeted magazines or music, has brought them examples of lifestyle alternatives outside the get-rich and workaholic mindset of many of their parents.

In recent years, children have grown into young adults who question their parents and the parent–child relationship has therefore altered. For example, South Korean students demonstrating for reunification with the North are at direct odds with their parents and grandparents who may well have participated in the Korean War that divided the nation. Likewise, Taiwanese youth have begun openly to question the role of the KMT old guard, the political direction of the country and its relationship to mainland China. In Indonesia, the young have led the opposition to the ruling clique and in Singapore, they have enraged leading politicians by suggesting that life in the city state is bland and lacking in challenge and variety.

Having been born into surroundings where money has often not been an issue, technology is nothing new. Where just about anything is available to buy, many Asian teenagers are looking for new kicks and trying to fill the cultural void left by years of sheer capitalism. They are children of the 'tiger' years and don't know the more deprived Asia their parents grew up in.

In Taiwan, some teenagers are becoming Buddhist monks or nuns, in an attempt to add some value to their existence. This is not the same as the growth of New Age cults in the west, where the turn from capitalism has been a search for new ideologies based on mixtures of ancient beliefs, science fiction, the Judeo-Christian tradition and popular culture. There is evidence Asia-wide of a growing interest in new philosophies and religions that invariably harp back to real or imagined Asian belief systems. Thai authorities have become increasingly concerned at the number of young people joining religious cults. However, the attraction of religion tends to be more about rediscovering the theoretical roots of their values set. It is not so much a rejection, or a reaction, as a process of reclaiming.

Even Asia's 'pulp fiction', the Manga comic, which is read just as much by young adults as by children, tends to have quasi-religious moral storylines, many of which quote classical Buddhist and Taoist teachings, in a format that has remained fairly constant over the centuries. In many respects, this is just an extension of the kind of moral tone taken on by the classic *kung fu* movie genre. Classical themes and even morality are still very potent with contemporary youth in Asia, and although these may be repackaged, usually with a lot more sex and violence, the old ways still hold true.

India has been the Asian nation most profoundly influenced by the west. English is one of its official languages and it has remained a democracy (the world's largest), coupled with a western-style legal system. However, India's politics remain strongly influenced, almost ruled, by religion and the spiritual divisions within the population. Even its political parties tend to be split on religious lines. However, despite religious sectarianism often reaching violent conflict, India has survived for 50 years as a nation, and as a democracy, with an increasingly strong identity of its own, away from the albatross of its colonial past.

Taiwan's economy has grown so rapidly that the latest generations often do not sense the nascent nature of their country's wealth, having never witnessed poverty or economic decline. In some ways it can be said that the youth in Taiwan has been spoilt, and that like spoilt children this new generation is rebelling against its parents and is not interested in overthrowing their enemies on mainland China. One form of rebellion is to reclaim what your parents have rejected.

Many parents can offer little in the way of spiritual guidance, especially in China where official communist dogma dismisses religion as an 'opiate of the masses'. All they can offer are Asia's jumbled-together philosophies and quasi-religious traditions.

Teenagers' demands for more from their parents will in turn push many parents to look for some answers, and this whole process will (and already is in such places as Taiwan and Hong Kong) create new trends in consumer behavior. Awareness of separate age groups, with separate generational cultures, is creating new consumer markets where they did not exist before.

Asianization

The search for something new is rekindling an interest in Asian artistic forms, both visual and oral. This is creating new demand not only for Asian painting, music and calligraphy, but also for more concrete products, such as interior design, CD and book covers, Asian-style product logos and brand names, and even for more Asian-looking car designs. David Tang's Shanghai Tang clothes chain best exemplifies this use of traditional Chinese materials and design along with western influences – but always with the inner label reading 'Made by Chinese'.

Another good example are the cheap and widely available ready-to-drink tea drinks. Previously packaged in bland cardboard bricks, there are now new drinks with fresh flavors, packaged in increasingly interestingly shaped metal cans, with more imaginative designs, such as stark black bamboo on a white background. The aim was to move up market and appeal to the new rich consumer. But brands of such drinks are now also looking for an image, be it youthful, sporty or healthy. Youth, sport and health awareness all existed in Asia before – but what is new is that these things are now lifestyle statements.

The west is no longer the only benchmark of success and Asians are now much more aware of their own credibility as a civilization. Leading western consumer goods manufacturers are now giving their products Asian names (often Chinese). Take Coca-Cola's Fei Yang (Uplift) brand of fruit teas, introduced into Taiwan – a Chinese-language brand from a quintessentially western company. By providing flavors such as guava which are popular with the Taiwanese, Coca-Cola has produced a product which will probably never be seen in the US. This will be the key strategy in years to come – make a 'local' brand to local tastes rather than trying to sell a foreign brand which has to be heavily marketed to gain recognition and consumer favor.

Teens in transition

It is an interesting development that in Hong Kong, teenagers are no longer so impressed by the names Calvin Klein, Gianni Versace and Donna Karan. They now appear to want something different from the mainstream. This doesn't seem too revolutionary a request, especially to the manufacturer of less well-known branded goods, but in effect Hong Kong's youth, like others in the region, are in transition.

On the one hand the influence of the west is apparent, as in the example below.

> **Jakarta – Seven teenage girls in worn-out bell-bottoms or micro mini-skirts with cowboy boots are clustered around a cramped Revlon cosmetics counter trying on fire-engine red lipstick that promises not to 'kiss off'.**
>
> **Next to Revlon is the counter for Sari Ayu, one of Indonesia's traditional *jamu*, or herbal, cosmetics brands. It's deserted.**
>
> **'Those products are for the older women,' says Hexa Arum Purwanti, 19, as she stands in front of a poster of model Cindy Crawford, Revlon's spokeswoman, looking brash and confident. 'For me, I like the bright colors and the way Cindy looks.'**
>
> **Ms. Crawford's look is a very visible sign of a generation gap that has Indonesia's home-grown brands on the defensive against the likes of Revlon as they compete for the faces of the country's young women.**
>
> **On youth's side is Revlon Corp. – unapologetic about using American supermodels and global advertising campaigns. 'We're not going to be all things to all people. We're about glamor and fashion,' says Revlon adviser Sherry Abbott in Jakarta. Revlon doesn't plan to use Indonesian models or to 'localise' its cosmetics, she adds.**
>
> ***Asian Wall Street Journal*, February 1996**

On the other hand, the power of regional brands and marketing approaches is also affecting the consumer market. In August 1997 Japanese cosmetics giant Shiseido began running TV commercials promoting the Za brand of cosmetics. The company used regional satellite channels such as Star TV and MTV Asia as well as women's magazines and also employed a Hong Kong movie star to endorse the range. The campaign was aimed at young, middle-income Asian women, using Asian branding, Asian stars and Asian media.

Increasingly the trend is for western companies to use local celebrities and models in their advertising. L'Oréal's Color Endure range is promoted by Deanna Yusoff, who has made personal appearances throughout the region at plazas and department stores. The company's Malaysian managing director Paul-Henri Duillet says: 'She [Deanna] is not only a beautiful, competent singer and actress, but she is also a self-confident warm individual and an inspiration to all Malaysian women.'

Asian teens are adapting, molding, taking from western culture what they like and largely leaving behind what they don't. But they aren't doing this consistently. The examples of Revlon, L'Oréal and Za show that in some markets young consumers are targeted in a local manner and in others they face western-derived campaigns. The daily reality is that they are exposed to both approaches and they make choices. They like McDonald's and rap and Revlon. But they also like Hindi and martial arts movies from the studios of Bollywood and Cantowood, noodle bars and Cantopop.

Teenage influence

Asian teenagers have power in sheer numbers and this is affecting the development of the consumer culture across the whole region. Their influence is twofold. First, they increasingly have personal disposable incomes approaching western levels, making them fully fledged consumers in their own right who have to be sought out, understood and targeted by manufacturers. Secondly, they have a crucial influence over their parents' purchasing decisions and therefore direct, to a degree, the way the family's disposable income is utilized.

Parents may pay for Nintendo but the teenagers choose the games, parents usually pay in Benetton, or more likely Asian equivalent Giordano, but it's the teenagers who choose to shop there. Parents hand out the pocket money but the teens choose what to spend it on. Many have part-time jobs giving them independent incomes.

And this phenomenon isn't limited to richer countries like Singapore or Hong Kong. China and the Philippines are also reporting the trend. Just ask yourself:

- Who is ensuring that McDonald's is able to expand rapidly throughout Asia?
- Who is the target of the Asian cola wars?
- Who are the tobacco companies trying to get puffing away?
- Who is supposed to wear merchandise from Reebok, Giordano, The Gap and Benetton?
- Who is propelling CD sales, the growth of local pop music and the spread of Star TV's V music stations across the region?

Not fortysomething Vietnamese rice farmers, that's for sure – teens, in their millions, with their universal teenage problems of fashion, sex appeal, brand consciousness, acne and street style.

Don't think Asian marketers aren't aware of them. Take these responses:

- Takashimaya department store in Singapore has introduced Nex.is, a department for teens complete with a fashion 'lab' and easily changeable decor to reflect rapidly changing styles.
- Across the region the sounds of Cantopop – and in India, Indopop – fill the air. Stars attract massive followings of teenagers who then demand cable TV to watch their favorite stars' videos and have also driven the expansion of retail music stores.

But regional governments are alert to the teen fads and are not always encouraging them. In 1995 rap music was banned in Indonesia and Thailand. Michael Jackson was prevented from performing in South Korea despite sellout crowds and the city

REBELLION

Music symbolizes teens staking their own ground, reflecting their own lifestyle choices. Try a typical night in Ho Chi Minh City as described by Jason Folkmanis in the London-based *Sunday Business* newspaper:

'Fashionable youth gun their motorcycles past the red and yellow neon of the Rex Hotel, once the home of war correspondents. In a side street just down Hguyen Hue Boulevard is the notorious Apocalypse Now disco, raided in June [1996] by the police looking for prostitutes.'

authorities in Kuala Lumpur recently forced all nightclubs to close at 1 am in an attempt to stop the spread of alcohol. In Brunei no further permits for video game arcades have been granted, as the government believes that this is where teens get into trouble.

At the high end, teens in Singapore are a significant component of the regional telecommunications revolution, buying up pagers and mobile phones in order to keep in touch. At the low end, girls in Jakarta were making their first tentative purchases at the cosmetics counter. To most teens, branded is still best.

Listening teens

Music artists like Jacky Cheung and Faye Wong are not household names in the west, but in the Chinese-speaking world (including communities as far flung as London and San Francisco) they are big acts – Asian role models for the region's youth. Undoubtedly these singers and others like them are influenced by western music as well as Chinese tradition. Pop music throughout Asia is largely the domain of solo acts, and many happen also to be movie stars.

The base for the Cantopop phenomenon is Hong Kong and, by extension, the southern Chinese coast. The big four acts currently are Jacky Cheung, Leon Lai, Aaron Kwok and Andy Lau. Female stars have their own hierarchy and there is also an underground scene.

MTV Asia broadcasts both Mandarin and English-language programming across the region from several cities. It competes directly with local music cable station Channel V. The main advertisers on MTV Asia are the likes of Coca-Cola, Levi's and Tower Records – in other words, pretty much the same advertisers as on MTV in North America or Europe. In 1996 MTV Asia signed a deal with the Hong Kong terrestrial network ATV to air four hours a week of programming. This has allowed it to circumvent its problems with the main cable provider, Wharf Cable, which had argued that it didn't have sufficient channel capacity to carry the station. Since then MTV Asia has spread from country to country, adapting to national tastes with local output. And Rupert Murdoch's V channel has also been spreading from country to country and influencing chart sales since its launch.

Star TV's Channel V has launched a 24-hour international music service in the Philippines, reaching one million viewers via 50 leading cable operators. It already had a strong presence in the Philippines, where it was aired on terrestrial broadcaster Citynet 27, along with its own 24-hour Mandarin service. A highlight of the channel in the Philippines is the Pepsi Sigaw Manila, presented by local VJs and shot on location in the Philippines. Channel V Thailand has advertising sponsorship with German beer Kloster worth a reported US$250,000. Its target audience is 15–34-year-olds.

In 1996, southeast Asians spent in excess of US$10 billion on music – almost a quarter of total worldwide music sales. And that ten billion doesn't include pirated CDs (in Singapore alone in 1996 it was estimated that S$11.8 million worth of pirated CDs were sold). It's a safe bet that a large percentage of the spend was teenage cash. As ever the region breaks down by market. Hong Kong and Singapore are sophisticated markets with major retailers such as Tower Records and HMV, while China is an emerging market. The international music business is excited. Record sales are slacking in Europe and the US and the business needs new impetus. Industry experts in the region are talking about a 75 percent increase in sales by the end of the century, something like US$33 billion in total.

Music sales seem somewhat immune to the retail recession. Tower Records has opened two stores in Singapore, at Pacific Plaza and Suntec City Plaza. The stores stock a range of over 140,000 CDs along with books, magazines, multimedia and catering facilities from speciality coffee store The Coffee Bean. Meanwhile along Orchard Road is HMV, with 25,000 square feet of music and multimedia.

The big western acts are doing OK in Asia and will continue to do so. Novelty western acts have found themselves millionaires thanks to Asian sales – just ask UK girl groups the Spice Girls and Shampoo. One British act, Kavana (actually a 21-year-old from Manchester called Anthony Kavanaugh) has attracted a massive following in Asia, particularly Malaysia, where he is known as Kavvy Baby to his numerous fans. In the UK his first album was released with a small picture of the singer dressed all in white. Following his success in Malaysia his label, EMI Malaysia, released the album with a different cover – Kavana all across the front in a black leather jacket and with additional tracks.

Music industry professionals are finding that terms such as Mandopop and Cantopop are as important in their speech as grunge and punk were in the past. The knock-ons are massive. CDs are the dominant market sector. Walkmans, Discmans and DAT are all selling in volume. And there is an influence on fashion too. Despite the ban on rap in Thailand and Indonesia, across Asia an LA Raiders jacket or a pair of Nike Air Jordans says it all.

Watching teens

So far domestic terrestrial TV's attempts to target teens have been pretty lame. Asian teens are not getting anything as risqué as British teens got from Channel Four's *The Word* where drugs, sex and swearing were part of the weekly fare, or America's *Saturday Night Live* where young comedians lampoon authority figures and celebrities on a weekly basis. At the moment Asian TV's teen programming consists of shows similar to *Teen Talk* on Malaysia's TV3. This features a teenage, or until just recently teenage, host who poses questions along the lines of 'Why don't our parents understand us?' In a move probably unacceptable to western teenage audiences, the question is answered by parents with just a few comments from teens and all summed up by an 'expert' who invariably manages to be simultaneously cringingly condescending and dismally uncool. This is programming *at* teens rather than *for* teens at the moment. It's enough to make anyone subscribe to cable.

Then there's the movies. Hollywood product from the likes of Sylvester Stallone and Arnold Schwarzenegger translates virtually instantly – the all-action blockbuster that relies on effects and action rather than script and nuance is finding a rapidly expanding movie and video audience in Asia and often it has little trouble with the local censors. The popularity of these particular films and stars is partly due to the region's traditional penchant for action movies and also the lack of any requirement to speak perfect English. Sly and Arnie's Planet Hollywood restaurants aren't doing badly either; most Asian capitals now have one.

Reading teens

A bunch of new magazines have been launched aimed directly at teens, mostly glossy and full color. Attracting advertising has not been a problem. Examples include *Ya*, a pan-regional magazine launched in 1995, and *Amoeba*, published out of Hong Kong. More general magazines in Hong Kong have increasingly sought to capture a share of the youth market. Typical of this has been Oriental Press Group's title *East Touch* which has 19 percent of its readership between the ages of 9 and 14. In Malaysia, Star Publications launched *Galaxie* back in 1974, a light reading bimonthly entertainment magazine aimed at teenagers and young working adults.

In Singapore the 15–19 age group comprises 7 percent of the population and a survey found that 74 percent of them regularly read the *Straits Times*, the leading national newspaper (though this may reflect lack of choice rather than preference). Approximately 50 percent of teenage girls read *Her World* magazine and 67 percent of teenage boys read the magazine *8 Days*, giving advertisers in

BOOK FAIR 'CENTRE FOR LURID MAGAZINES'

'More than 1500 teenagers camped outside the Convention & Exhibition Centre all night to get the pick of publications on sale at the eighth Hong Kong Book Fair. The main draws were Japanese and local comics portraying sex and violence ... former legislator Andrew Cheng Kar Foo said "The book fair should be a healthy activity that promotes reading ... but these magazines are eroding our youths' impressionable minds." ... About ten Television & Entertainment Licensing Authority officers were monitoring the stalls to ensure that such comics were not sold to anyone under 18.'

***Singapore Straits Times*, 25.7.97**

those publications unprecedented coverage of the affluent teen market.

As the teen market has developed in Singapore so new titles have sprung up. The Eastern Publishing group launched *Teens* magazine in 1995 and organized a nationwide modeling competition for teenage girls. Magnum Publishing's *Teenage* title is pretty much what you would expect from teenage magazines anywhere in the world. Typical articles include 'How Charming Are You?', horoscopes, 'Four Signs He Likes You', endless interviews with Jennifer Aniston and revelatory true confessions such as 'I Was Hooked on Ecstasy!'

In China, home interiors magazines, women's magazines and music magazines are now competing with the old prescribed political magazines. Books with content ranging from explicit sex to fierce, quasi-Maoist political philosophies are all in vogue, as are translations of novels such as Michael Crichton's *Jurassic Park* and the works of Jane Austen. *Young Generation*, a youth-targeted magazine, has proved popular.

With high literacy rates among urban teens, India is a major market for niche publishers aiming for the youth market. Publisher Living Media launched *Teens Today* in 1996 and eight months later had 50,000 readers, 20,000 of whom took out subscriptions. The magazine manages an ad-to-edit ratio of 1:3. Living Media has spent a great deal of time pinpointing its readership and found that its targets are 13–17-year-old school-attending upper-middle-class kids in families with one car who speak English.

While *Teens Today* is broad based in its editorial focus, other Indian magazines have targeted niches within the teen market. Young music lovers have the *Rock Street Journal* which comes with a lyrics booklet sponsored by Suzuki Shogun, the college kids have *JAM* (Just Another Magazine) and there are others including *Jetset*, *Upbeat* and *Sun*. Several teen mags have developed pullouts to reflect the different tastes in India's various regions where parents also have varying ideas about what their sons and daughters should be reading. New Delhi parents worry about westernization, southern parents ponder the apparent liberalism of the content, but publishers are willing to adapt and listen to parents and teenagers in a market as potentially vast and lucrative as India.

Wired teens

Despite all that is said about how comfortable western teens are supposed to be with technology, how a kid can set the video but grandfather can't and all that, Asian teens are truly technology comfortable. With the young the bulk of the population, this means that Asia is a generally pro-technology market.

If the first phone in your house is a GSM mobile, you tend to see telecommunications differently. If your first computer is a laptop with Intel inside, a Netscape Communicator Web browser and a fax/modem, you tend to see the power of personal computers differently too. If your first piece of software is Windows 98, how do you see software?

Asian youth are not upgrading, catching up or retooling. They are entering the market at the top level. Technology ownership is extremely high among teens and they start state of the art.

Hong Kong has one of the highest level of mobile phone ownership in the world at 12.7 phones per 100 people and this is

PAGERS BANNED IN AT LEAST FIVE SCHOOLS

'Miss Teo arched an eyebrow. Her sensitive face had detected the distinct sound of a vibrating pager, slightly muffled. Experience told her that it was probably buried in a school bag ... In a sweet voice, which all the students immediately recognized as being lethally dangerous, she enquired, "Whose pager just went off?" ... she began to walk around the class. Each student's bag underwent an inspection to which all customs officers should aspire. Eventually she arrived at Beng Huat's desk ... before the trembling Beng Huat she triumphantly fished out the pager and held it aloft. "Perhaps you would care to explain, Beng Huat?"'

***Straits Times*, 20.10.95**

exceptionally high among teenagers desperate to keep in touch with each other.

Telecoms growth is not confined to the wealthier countries. Vietnam's teens, newly unleashed in an open telecoms market, have helped propel the country's pager system subscribers to in excess of 200,000.

HMV, Tower Records and Virgin, along with local chains such as Hong Kong's KPS, are competing to open retail outlets throughout Asia selling CDs, videos, software, games and CD-Roms to teenagers with money to spend and the technology to use the products. Big players in the educational CD-Rom market such as Microsoft and Dorling Kindersley are increasingly looking to the region for sales growth.

Asian teens are Internet crazy. Web pages are springing up by the thousand and connection rates are rocketing, pushing up telecoms, computer and software spending from notoriously wired Singapore to Vietnam which introduced a national Internet provider in 1995.

Singapore is in another league compared to most Asian countries. A recent survey found that 12 percent of teen girls were saving up to buy a car, as were 6 percent of boys.

The ownership level of pagers among teens in Singapore is extremely high at 90 percent – the highest in the world. Motorola developed several of its bestselling pager models in the country using local talent.

The burger wars, Asian style

It seems that no one has profited more from the teenage revolution than the burger companies. They love kids, all kids, any kids. Their products are increasingly coming within the reach of a growing number of teens, certainly of their parents, and Asian teens have adopted the burger and fries habit with a vengeance. Not just burgers either but all fast food.

Religious restrictions have not stood in the way – Muslims have helped build up Kentucky Fried Chicken's market share in the region, vegetarians have chowed down on rice burgers and Dunkin' Donuts. American fast food has become a way of life. The Europeans have a share too. There is pizza at Pizza Hut (or one of its many imitators such as Shakey's – the People Pleasing Pizza Place in Malaysia and Singapore). The Hong Kong branch of Harry Ramsden's, the noted north of England fish-and-chip shop, is a major draw. And French-inspired Delifrance chain is expanding with croissants, baguettes and pastries. The company now has 14 outlets in Hong Kong alone. Oliver's sandwich shops are expanding throughout the region too.

Shakey's is a brand undergoing a major revamp in Asia. Throughout the 1980s and early 1990s this chain of franchised pizza parlors stayed in business but couldn't compete with the flasher, brasher chains. The company almost exited Asia altogether. But it responded to the changing food market by introducing freestanding takeaway units – quick service and high branding. Originally a California-based chain, the company has adapted to the Asian market by emphasizing chicken and family-oriented rotisserie meals. Fast food is still the order of the day and it has introduced the Shakey's Turbo oven which cooks pizzas in 60 seconds, your whole meal ready in three minutes. Now Shakey's, the brand that never quite went away, is back in Singapore, India, Malaysia and the Philippines and attracting teens and families.

Burger giant McDonald's operates in excess of 400 restaurants in southeast Asia. Twenty-five of the company's most profitable establishments are in Hong Kong where there are over 80 golden arches restaurants alone. The company has made concessions to Asian tastes, introducing teriyaki and pork burgers.

Burger King, owned by British conglomerate Diageo (formerly Grand Metropolitan), has also spread rapidly throughout the region. But perhaps most impressive has been the growth of KFC. In Asia it has found a ready market among hungry teenagers for its chicken products. The company has established outlets on university campuses and introduced home delivery in some countries. In Indonesia and Malaysia, KFC has found a natural home among the Muslim population and in India with the Hindus. In Malaysia the company has over 150 outlets and has spread into neighboring Brunei too.

But the international brands have not had it all their own way. Asian teens have shown their usual ability to adapt western tastes and find something new, something hybrid. A host of local chains have become the places to hang out.

In the Philippines the market leader in fast food is Jollibee, part of the wider food conglomerate of the same name. The company operates 180 branches, outstripping McDonald's sales, with establishments selling burgers and pizzas. Admittedly the outlets look very similar to a McDonald's but the burgers have been 'Filipinized' with softer patties as well as eggs and spices added to make them sweeter.

In Hong Kong, the Café de Coral chain attracts teens with an eclectic menu featuring Spring Chicken Set, Super European Croissant and red bean ice cream.

In Taiwan, the Japanese-based MOS Burger chain has been successful and become a major teen hangout with its MOS Burger and MOS Hot Dog outlets. The stores offers Japanese variations on American fast food, such as rice burgers, allowing Taiwanese teens to combine their fascination with both cultures. The chain is now spreading into Singapore and on throughout Asia and the US west coast.

Land of the Maharaja Burger

In 1992 India had one foreign fast-food company, UK's Wimpy, along with several US-style outlets such as Nirulas, Monginis and Fast Track. These were mostly clustered around Bombay and New Delhi. In total the market was worth about US$30.5 million a year. But in 1996 fast food arrived in India with a vengeance as McDonald's, Pizza Hut, KFC and Domino's Pizza joined the fray.

Most of the international chains are operating as franchises in India. Domino's plans 100 outlets. McDonald's has no beef on the menu and is serving mutton burgers along with the renamed Big Mac, now the grandly titled Maharaja Burger. Vegetarians can eat burgers with rice-based patties.

McDonald's has invested US$40 million as has rival KFC. Colonel Sanders, however, is under no illusions about the potential of India – it knows it will be doing well if it captures 5 percent of the total consumer catering market which is largely confined to middle-class urban dwellers. KFC has also adapted to the local market with spicier varieties than are available elsewhere. The company has run ads stating that 'Hands are your cutlery', tapping into the traditional Indian practice of eating with the hands and thereby making KFC appear culturally acceptable.

However, not everyone in India has rushed out for a Chicken Zinger or a Maharaja Burger and fries. In 1995 KFC outlets in Bangalore found themselves besieged by farmers' groups and environmentalists and McDonald's outlets have found themselves the subject of protesters warning of cultural colonialism.

Cultural influences

Without doubt the new Asian teenager is picking and choosing from western culture. They want western fashions and designer labels but they can live without the general teenage rebellion that seems to occur in every generation of western teens. The new Asian teen is amalgamating what they like from the west with what they like about their own culture. Often this leads to some odd hybrids.

As Asia becomes more unified through travel and pan-regional media, so Asian teens are learning from each other. Taiwanese students adapt styles pioneered by the Japanese, who themselves have blended Japanese and US culture to create their look. Malaysian teens adapt styles they pick up in neighboring Singapore and Chinese teens in remote cities eagerly await the arrival of the latest styles from Hong Kong via Beijing.

For teenagers, more so than any other group, Asia is a cultural melting pot with a complex network of styles, reference points, interests and subcultures. From this pot is emerging the genesis of an Asian style symbolized in the rise of domestically based clothing designers, musicians, novelists and trendsetters. And perhaps even more importantly, along with all of this comes a new, brasher confidence among those who will increasingly come to determine Asia's future in the twenty-first century.

Teens need special treatment

Of course, not all Asia's teenagers are wealthy and can afford pagers, cars and magazine subscriptions aplenty. Many are still living on the cusp, avoiding absolute poverty but not quite able to enjoy the full fruits of consumerism. However, the majority are in a better position than their parents were at their age, and the vast majority are aware of themselves as teens, as a group with needs and interests. Manufacturers and retailers need to remember this. It's not just the 'big ticket' items that offer potential profits.

Bicycles are items that vastly improve the life of many Indians; they are effectively their form of mass rapid transit. The US has Detroit, the motor city – India has Ludhiana, the cycle city. The US has GM, the largest auto company in the world – India has Hero Cycles, the largest bicycle manufacturer in the world. A foreign eye might not notice the change afoot in Ludhiana but the locals do. India's 50 million or so bicycles are invariably black, functional, inexpensive and boring.

Right now, however, everything in India has the whiff of change about it. Flash cars are appearing in provincial cities, new office blocks are going up, the major cities are creating a new rich – and the so-called fancy cycles market is booming, with models like the BSA Street Cat, the Atlas Rebel and Hero's own challenge, the Ranger range. But in this fast-changing market Hero is perceived as the sort of cycle your dad would ride if he lived in northern India and rode a bike. So the company decided to target the teen market and repackage itself as the fanciest of fancy cycle manufacturers.

All Hero's fancy cycles now come grouped into a series called 'Generation X', 20 models all with slight differences important only to people keen to stand out from the crowd. The range will introduce three or four new models a year to keep up interest. Different bikes for different teens – the Hawk for the urban cyclist, the Impact for those preferring a lighter frame, the Ranger BMX for the tricksters, the Allegro for those cycling for exercise and Miss India for the stylish woman cyclist in need of a particularly fancy cycle.

The Generation X series has been a success, especially in the richer and more fashion-conscious south of the country. Sometimes teenagers don't have much money, but they find a way to rebel. In India one way has been to reject the tradition of having a black bicycle and get yourself a dayglo orange Rebel to shock your parents and impress your friends.

China's teens emerge

In China, teens are facing many uncertainties, issues which their parents did not have to worry about. Employment is no longer prescribed by the local Party bureau, but it is also not secure and unemployment levels are increasing as economic necessity causes increasing numbers of workers to be laid off from ailing state-owned corporations. This is causing changes in society too. Workers now have to migrate to find work, the poverty gap between rich and poor, urban and rural is widening, money has replaced the Party as the ruling ethic and western influences are now widespread. All these factors are creating a whole new society, which teenagers' parents are not equipped to advise them how to approach. Competition for work begins at school, and the pressure on children, and especially teenagers, increases, especially where the child is the parents' sole offspring.

Where such a pioneering generation exists, the opportunity for social change is great and the current young generation in China will develop into the model for the following generations of capitalist Chinese. As a body of consumers, they will be highly influential in shaping the consumer market of China for years to come.

Teens to adults

On the whole it is clear that Asian teenagers are getting on with the job of being the next generation. If we've made them sound too squeaky clean it isn't because we are ignoring the strains and stresses of the new generation – it's because the overall message is a positive one.

Of course, many teens in Asia are resisting the conformity their anxious parents would wish on them. The rapid development of many countries has led to some 'lost boys' and the strict nature of societies such as Singapore, Malaysia and China has also meant rebellion.

Malaysian authorities have instituted a movement for teens called Rakan Muda or 'young friends' which organizes sports and activities. And juvenile delinquency still shocks Singapore. Teens taking Ecstasy are decried, taxi cabs carry ad hoardings proclaiming 'no casual sex, no Aids'. An 11-year-old schoolboy who was beaten up by six teenage attackers for no apparent reason made front-page news – people were shocked by the fact that when the boy asked his attackers why he was being beaten they replied 'for fun' and walked away smoking cigarettes.

Perhaps some Asian countries just didn't want to admit that their youth would learn some bad habits. It's hard to believe that those politicians who bemoan teenage sex believe that it is a new phenomenon and purely caused by western influence. An older, more straitlaced generation of Malaysians was shocked by a government survey that found that 71 percent of teens had smoked, 40 percent had seen a porno film, 28 percent had gambled and 14 percent experimented with drugs. Obviously there are pockets of society that have not benefited from Asia's economic growth. However, it is important to focus on the bigger picture, the general flow of the tide, not the hidden undercurrent that most never see or feel. Western experience perhaps also tells us that today's teenager who experiments with drugs or listens to rock music just may be tomorrow's corporate executive or even, who knows, president.

Teenage girls have emerged as particularly important to the Asian consumer boom. They are looking for personal growth, with increasing numbers opting for college and travel as well as their own power as consumers, saving for cars, buying phones and cosmetics. But, as every father knows, girls become women, and in Asia the new generation of female consumers has truly become a force to be reckoned with.

The boys are looking to the future too and, despite changes, it is more than likely that they will remain the gender that will benefit most from the region's continued economic emergence. Today's teenage boys, starting work, college or even families, are tomorrow's managers, politicians and middle-class fathers.

Advertisers have noticed the predictable phenomenon that teenagers tend to become adults rather quickly. San Miguel, the region's largest brewing concern based in the Philippines, has shifted its advertising to target the 18–25 age group, just at the point where smart teens become young professionals. Its ad campaigns feature MTV-style images highlighting supposed teen concerns such as the environment, racism, politics, Aids and personal appearance. They play on teenage angst, that unsettling period between adolescence and adulthood. San Miguel is hoping for consumer loyalty – that a teen who sips a beer to ponder why his spots won't go will still be sipping when his main concern becomes why his hair won't stay.

How to market to teenagers

- *Think small* – Small companies usually perform better than large ones in the teen market. This isn't surprising, since teenagers change their minds in a nanosecond and companies have to respond, especially those in the fashion and trend sectors. For makers of acne cream it's easy – all teens get it, all teens want rid of it. Sports shoe makers and soft drink producers may have to be a little more proactive. Also there's one extremely fortunate thing that retailers and manufacturers should remember – teens don't tend to cut down their spending during an economic slowdown.

- *Celebrity promotions* – These work well in most Asian countries. In South Korea Samsung used a little-known 19-year-old singer called Kim Won-june to promote its Count Down teen clothing range. Kim is now a national star and Count Down is turning over US$150 million in less than six years. The US influence has been strong here too. Everybody knows about Hollywood film stars sneaking off to sell beer and cigarettes in Japan on the quiet, but it's happening all over the region. Across Asia, basketball has become a major sport with NBA stars becoming spokespersons for a wide range of products marketed to teens. With the rise of the half-Thai American golfer Tiger Woods another level in pan-regional celebrity endorsement has been reached, one that ethnically bridges the gap between east and west. But remember that as with teens globally today's idol is tomorrow's sad case.

- *Stretching brands* – The Revlon example earlier fits this strategy, as does Ribena with its regular drink targeted at mothers, its fizzy version at teens. The holy grail of branding is to get a cradle-to-grave brand. Cover every base – Marlboro, Marlboro Light, Marlboro Menthol, all ages, all tastes.

- *If the name fits* – Whereas western teens are still hankering after the post-punk trauma, first reviling anything that is alleged to be establishment fashion then worshipping the badges of so-called underground or alternative fashion companies, in most of Asia it is the opulent, establishment names which excite teen allegiance. Calvin Klein now markets most of its products to teens in Korea, for example, even going to the extent of adapting its products to suit its teenage followers. However, this may change as western brands become too common and the market shifts.

- *Watching the locals* – Western manufacturers need to watch local markets, as many successful product launches have been built on domestically derived trends. One development, coming out of Japan as so many do, is for the creation of virtual stars, star personalities who exist only in cyberspace. This includes the creation of virtual pop stars, who can have their own singles and TV shows and even personal lives created by marketing gurus. Such plastic pop stars can be used as advertising images and of course they are far less temperamental than the real thing.

- *Offer choice* – Asian teens invariably grow up with less personal freedom and different notions of democracy to those in the west. Yet with cable TV, liberalized airwaves and a deregulated retail sector, freedom has been epitomized in choice at a consumer level if not always a political one. Retailers able to offer wide ranges will find teens in their stores more and for longer.

- *Ride the wave* – In markets with reduced access either due to limited expenditure or limited stock, such as Indonesia, Thailand and Vietnam, exaggerated trend cycles have been evident. Suddenly every teen has a pair of Nike shoes, or a pager, or a certain brand of shirt. Companies that have ridden the wave have found it immensely profitable. Those that haven't need to look out for the approaching surf – teen trends change very quickly. Essentially, Asian teens don't have fixed brand preferences. They have grown up in emerging consumer societies where every month new brands have become available, therefore the notion of trying something new is strong and they will switch brands as rapidly as style dictates.

4
Asia's New Women

To say that it's the men who earn the money and the women who spend it may be rather a sweeping statement, and perhaps not very politically correct, but there is an element of truth in it. We have already explored how the family unit is the key to understanding society and consumption in Asia and mentioned how it is often the woman within a family who makes most of the day-to-day spending decisions. She usually buys the weekly groceries, purchases the children's clothes and also looks after the grandparents. Women are not only a consuming group in themselves, but also represent a channel towards other consumer groups.

During the 1990s, women in Asia have emerged as powerful consumers and increasingly powerful citizens in their own right. It is a fallacy that Asia is a male-dominated society and that women do not have any power or say. In fact, women across the region are enjoying careers, establishing companies, pursuing education and exercising a range of choices that many of their mothers, and certainly their grandmothers, would never have considered possible. A failure to appreciate this changing role can cost countless sales, but there are tremendous rewards for companies that are clued up to the real situation.

ASIA'S WOMEN 1997 ('000S)

	Total	% working
China	609,641	36.3
Hong Kong	2,925	36.8
Indonesia	104,301	38.8
Malaysia	10,394	35.5
Philippines	35,613	37.2
Singapore	1,434	40.1
South Korea	22,710	40.1
Taiwan	10,853	36.8
Thailand	29,832	46.8
Vietnam	39,071	39.4
TOTAL	866,774	39.1

Source: National statistics

Traditionally, Asian husbands handed their earnings straight to their wives, who then decided how the money was spent, and this often continues to be the situation. However, as Asian women are now increasingly educated and entering the workforce at all levels – from basic production requiring extreme dexterity to management and politics – so their sophistication as consumers has increased.

For many women marriage is no longer their first priority but is something to be chosen rather than sought. Women are increasingly delaying childbirth, preferring to get an education, have a career and enjoy a successful marriage before becoming mothers. The emergence of such lifestyle choices, as opposed to more traditional expectations, is making women more aware of their rights both as individuals within society and as consumers. And choice as consumers means demanding better goods for a better price with better after-sales service.

These themes were borne out in a recent Philippines Department of Labor survey. This found that women accounted for 60 percent of the country's total labor force growth between 1982 and 1992 with a participation rate of 57.8 percent. By 2005 women will account for half the workforce, with growth in the number entering the managerial and professional sectors as well as providing the bulk of the workforce in services and administrative support. This is more than just a demographic indicator – it represents women's increasing influence in society, at work, in the home and as consumers.

To try to examine all the areas that women have influenced in Asia's consumer markets would take another book in itself. Suffice it to say that their influence and opinion extends from choice of house, holiday and credit cards to child rearing, services and consumer goods.

- Avon, the third largest company in the Indonesian cosmetics market, has established a door-to-door network of agents busy introducing competitively priced toiletries to rural women across the archipelago. Not only is its direct selling ideally suited to this fragmented market, but the increasing number of women using makeup for work has also skyrocketed. Confidence in the market was such that Avon's leading competitor, Amway, has also entered Indonesia. The two now compete in most countries in the region.
- In Hong Kong sales of spirits and mixer drinks have been revitalized by women adopting a fashion for cocktails. This is also representative of the increasing trend for women to get together socially separate from men.
- Across Asia sales of microwave ovens are growing as women increasingly go to work and seek out convenience and packaged foods. More and more they don't have time to earn a salary, build their careers and cook every night. Microwave ovens have also been a shortcut to upgrading many Asian kitchens that lack the room for European-style range units. In Hong Kong, sales of microwaves have grown by 40 percent in the last four years and in Singapore by nearly 70 percent. Even Indonesia and Malaysia have seen sales increase by 15 and 150 percent respectively.
- Chinese women have traditionally favored functional cotton-blend underclothes, if not by taste then by availability. Now,

with rising incomes and changing tastes, a market for luxury lingerie has emerged in the big cities. Major international lingerie companies are entering the Chinese market – for example, Japan's Wacoal Corporation is aiming for a 50 percent increase over its 1996 sales of US$4.4 million.

The woman's place in Confucian patriarchy

Confucius was basically a failed bureaucrat, who went around ancient China in search of government employment, making up time between jobs working as a teacher. His pupils became disciples and interpreters of his moral philosophies. These were principally focused on the moral duties of people within their society, based on everyone having a set place and a specific set of duties related to their position and in accordance with the other echelons of society.

Five guiding relationships ruled the basic teachings which were introduced by Confucius' antecedent Mencius:

- the ruler and his ministers or subjects
- father and son
- husband and wife
- elder brother and younger brother
- friend and friend.

This emphasizes that women only exist as wives in traditional Chinese society and that outside this position they have no social standing. The interpretation of this was always that the wife was subservient to her husband. In fact, Confucius saw more equality between a husband and wife, just as the first relationship was meant to indicate a two-way relationship – the ruler was responsible for his subjects, just as much as a citizen is expected to be loyal to the ruler.

Some assume that a patriarchy simply means a society ruled by men. However, many women have been reiterating the idea that it is in fact the strong woman behind the powerful man who is actually pulling the strings (including the purse strings). Asian women are not subservient – fighting your way on to a Beijing bus, against wizened old grannies with elbows as sharp as pickaxes, will only confirm this.

Challenging traditional roles

The traditional female role has been whittled away by both women and social-reforming men. One of the most significant aspects of socialist and liberal thinking in Asia has been the general trend towards the emancipation of women within society, giving them equal rights to men under law. As women became workers, they also began to become social shapers, educators and politicians, further challenging traditional views. This has been especially evident in relation to consumer behavior (both male and female). Women flex their consuming muscles, not only by buying goods and services but also by investing in the further improvement of themselves and their family. But the most important way in which women have empowered themselves has been by investing in education.

Women are increasingly educated throughout Asia. In Taiwan, women equal men in educational attainment. All across east Asia, daughters are being pushed into education as hard as sons are. They want education, they know that the well-paying posts, the careers, the jobs of the future require a good education. To be competitive in the post-turmoil job market requires a good education. They also know that lingering patriarchal traditions can often make it more difficult for them to do as well as their male counterparts, and are therefore usually even more determined and focused students than the boys.

An illustration of this thirst for knowledge is that throughout the region women are increasingly attending the growing number of evening classes. In Thailand, girls who have left their remote villages to join the ranks of factory workers in Bangkok are rushing from production line to evening school.

Exposure to new working environments is also giving women new training and expertise which is helping them to get ahead.

Increasingly, women are performing the most senior roles in the services sector, the cutting edge of the new consumer markets. They are very apparent in the catering industry, the travel business, the hotel sector and retailing. They are the people who welcome visitors to the region, who make their stay comfortable, who ultimately project the region's image abroad – remember Singapore Airlines' highly successful Singapore Girls advertising campaign. Women are therefore often becoming better equipped with the 'people skills' so crucial to the increasingly service-oriented consumer world than are their more often office-bound male counterparts.

The higher profile of women in Asian society is only the gloss on an undercurrent of their greater social involvement. Female administrative assistants and secretaries are often better equipped to face the challenges of rapidly changing technology than their usually older, male bosses. They therefore become indispensable specialists and earn more for their skills. More skills, more money, better lifestyles and more choices. The result is that Asian women are becoming a very potent consumer group, not only because they are wealthier and wiser than before, but also because women are becoming more diverse in the way they choose to live.

Smoking, drinking and having a good time

Young women are taking up smoking, drinking and other supposedly non-female pursuits. Women are going out together without the need for male company, deciding to live by themselves and choosing more unconventional lifestyles. Such behavior is radically changing the marketing dynamic of the region. Female sexuality is becoming a marketable commodity for advertisers, not just as images but as a positive lifestyle, going against tradition.

Women are doing all sorts of things that once they would not have thought about or had access to. Recreational drug use among women is increasing along with drinking. In 1996, the number of women in Singapore caught for drug offenses doubled to 532, with most users in their twenties. Women have their own cars, they travel the world alone or in groups, they ditch their boyfriends and they have premarital sex.

New marketing campaigns, such as in-bar drinks promotions, cosmetics demonstrations or door-to-door insurance sales, often led by direct-sales promotions, are usually fronted by young, attractive women. Female sexuality is no longer only mentioned through poetic innuendo, it is blatantly evident. This has clearly changed women's perceptions of themselves, but it has shaken the stubborn male identity too. Men have been just as influenced by the changing role of women as the women themselves have.

In 1996 the *Bangkok Post* surveyed Thai women with incomes between US$592 and 1185 a month. The survey found that while many women will use domestic brands in the home, outside they want international brands – 81 percent of the women surveyed wore jeans and favored Levi's, Lee and Mc. They also chose Seiko watches and Rayban sunglasses, Avon and St Michael (Marks & Spencer) talcs and Nivea cleansers with Clinique, Lancôme and Estée Lauder cosmetics ranges. The survey also found that they liked to put all their stuff in Guy Laroche baggage if possible. The economic crisis has adversely affected sales of luxury goods, but a growing number of women have become used to quality products and this is not a taste that they will lose quickly.

Such brand and image awareness as now exists among Asian women means that they are likely to expect a great deal more from their men. Arranged marriages are out and suitors need to be well dressed, clean shaven, courteous, generous and well educated. This is changing established patterns of marriage and relationships. In India, women are increasingly marrying outside of their caste. A growing number of Indian women living in cities and working in professional jobs are choosing partners who make them laugh, who dress well or have a good job. Wealth, happiness and personal taste are starting to replace superstition and convention.

Working women

In South Korea industrial expansion could not have happened without millions of women entering assembly jobs in the electronics, textiles and toy factories. By and large these jobs were low paid, mundane, unpleasant and unrewarded.

Women workers in Taiwan are the backbone of the thriving computer and electronics industries. In Malaysia, they have migrated in growing numbers from rural areas to the cities. They have learnt the business of electronics component assembly and provided the increasingly skilled labor force for the industry that has done more than any other to make Malaysia a world force in technology exports.

In Thailand and Indonesia it is women who are 'manning' the factories created by inward investment from Japan and the west. Nike, Gap and Timberland are just some of the western brands assembled by women in Indonesian factories for export. In India, women are the backbone of the textiles industry, now so important to the country's growth. In less developed nations such as Vietnam and the Philippines, women are entering the new industrial workforce at all levels.

In China the situation is even more dramatic. Its recent socialist past brought women into a role unique among Asian societies, because the Communist Party emancipated women and formally declared their equal status in society, at least in the eyes of the law.

This has often been more of a social policy than a social reality but, on the whole, women are 'holding up half the earth'. The revolution allowed women to become doctors, physicists, steel workers, train drivers, police officers and teachers, breaking the old Confucian traditions.

Since the opening up of China's economy, women have often been the main workers in the new industries which have mushroomed around the Special Economic Zones and beyond. These women are often the major income earners not only for their immediate but also their extended family.

And women are still prominent in agricultural life; they are still housewives, mothers, educators and shoppers. They do all the things they used to and more. They make decisions both in terms of their immediate lives – a dishwasher or a microwave? – and in terms of their long-term objectives – kids now or later, home ownership or renting, a holiday or a car?

Once a worker, always a worker

These changes have meant deep and lasting changes in consumption patterns too. Joint mortgages, car repayments, credit card debts, hire purchase. For most women these were all things at which their parents would have thrown up their hands in horror. But with regular and more substantial wages Asian women are becoming locked into a cycle of continuous consumption that is compounded by school fees, childcare costs, healthcare and holidays. With this comes the need to maintain a standard of living or to aspire to one that is even better, meaning that 'career' becomes more important than just 'work'.

And increasingly a woman's income is necessary to supplement the wider family income. Raised expectations mean a higher cost of living, aspiration means expenditure and women working is not a temporary phenomenon.

Of course, women's new position is essential for the Asian economy, especially in light of the economic crisis which struck the region in 1997. Authors such as John Naisbitt, Jim Rohwer and others have shown that without the large-scale participation of women in the national economies of east Asia, the tigers would not have roared so loud. Recovery will largely be down to building up exports, the more valuable the better, and it is very often the women who make the export goods.

More and better

The Asian recession has been a grave embarrassment for its male-dominated business world. There needs to be a radical rethink to salvage the region's economies. The industries being discarded in the recovery process are old style and ineffective. They are making way for new, better-conceived, better-managed and usually smaller, light industries. In these industries, so far, women have comprised the majority of the workforce. Examples include electronic components manufacturing, services, travel and tourism.

In some countries a service industry such as retailing can account for as much as 15–16 percent of employment, the majority of it female. As growing numbers of women move into better-paid, higher posts in management and the service industries, so they start to prioritize their careers. These working women enter the middle class economically, the new female urban professionals. They leave childbirth and family to later, if at all. They move around and, of course, they consume. They need, and can afford, holidays, business suits, makeup, cars to get them to the office, premium coffee to sip at their desks and gyms to ensure they remain stress free and productive.

It is not just in the higher echelons of the workforce that women are upwardly mobile. In Vietnam, China, Indonesia and the less developed nations, every day women are leaving the villages and farms and heading for the megacities and new jobs in factories. This shift is bringing new opportunities and greater access to goods to spend their wages on to a whole new group of female consumer.

Many retailers and manufacturers have successfully captured this market, from lingerie designers to car manufacturers. A prime example is the Episode chain selling upmarket fashions to professional women across Asia. The clothes not only reflect quality and modern design but are also made from fabrics most suitable to the Asian climate and therefore often preferable to less comfortable European designer womenswear. Malls across Asia have created floors dedicated to womenswear specifically targeting the professional working woman.

Broader horizons

Across the region the number of births is falling as women are going to work, going to college, postponing childbirth in order to build a career. The pressures of urban living, career demands and the desire for independence are all contributing to women consciously changing their lifestyle patterns. But even where women are still having children, they are not necessarily playing the traditional role.

Except at extremely micro levels, this emancipation is not organized. There is no mass women's movement to parallel those seen in Europe and the US. However, women are expanding their horizons.

Broadcasting and press regulations are being relaxed and there is a plethora of new women's magazines, both versions of western publications such as *Elle* and *Vogue* and domestic magazines such as *Her World* and *Go*. Top-selling magazines in China currently include *The Home*, *Best Friend* and *Woman's Companion*. Catching them up is *Family Doctor* with 1.7 million readers covering popular medicine, grooming advice and sexual information for women.

Also important is the growth of satellite and cable television which have brought western programming into Asia. Vietnamese cable watchers now enjoy *NYPD Blue* and *Seinfeld*. The effect of such a cultural invasion, especially the portrayal of women in these programs, is bound to be profound.

Asian women in the spotlight

As women become more prominent and take overtly public positions across Asia, they are also defining what women can be in modern Asia. These women are not confined to one country or one medium, be it politics, cinema, TV or literature. They are role models for young girls and increasingly they are speaking out about their position in their respective industries and societies.

Nadya Yuti Hutagalung

Nadya Yuti Hutagalung is 23, half Indonesian, half Australian, has been a model, become a mother, lived in several Asian countries, speaks her mind and is currently an MTV presenter. She also runs a sideline in product endorsement and has her own home page on the Internet on which she gets e-mails from viewers in the US, Malaysia, the Philippines and Australia. Nadya fits perfectly into the US flip TV format of MTV while remaining a promoter of Asian bands. In a recent interview with Malaysia's *Daylight Magazine* she denied that she was the Asian face of US culture, responding that MTV provides local programming country by country and is taking every market by storm.

Nadya may not be typical of Asian women, but she is an example of the new generation: women capable of taking the best from the west and the best from the east, of being independent and balancing career with family.

Gong Li

Gong Li is another Asian role model in the spotlight. Her face has become commonplace across the region in advertising, magazine profiles and television. She is China's best-known actress both at home and abroad and is the star of two of the country's most popular, controversial and internationally acclaimed films, *Farewell my Concubine* and *Red Sorghum*, as well as many others.

Gong Li is planning a record with Warner Brothers, will be the Asian face of L'Oréal until 2001 and has made a film with Jeremy Irons called *China Box*. She is married, had open affairs in fiercely puritanical China and won the Best Actress award at Cannes in 1992. She is the extreme face of women in China: financially independent, successful, outward looking and maintaining control of her own career.

Yui Phetkanha

Yui Phetkanha is proof that women can ascend from humble roots to the heights of fame. She originally comes from the rural northeast of Thailand, an area often thought of as more akin to Laos. After moving to Bangkok with hopes of making enough money to survive and send some back to her family, she was spotted eating noodles in a side street and invited to take part in a talent show which she promptly won.

Since then Yui has appeared in films with Bruce Willis, graced the cover of *Asiaweek*, appeared in a George Michael video and been picked by Chanel to front the campaign for Allure perfume. For the Chanel shoot she earned US$35,000.

Shahnaz Husain

India's most successful cosmetics company, Shahnaz Herbals, is run by its founder Shahnaz Husain who has built a US$100 million makeup empire from experiments in her kitchen. Her products now control over 80 percent of the Indian market as well as being favored by filmstars and models for their ayurvedic properties.

Women in politics

Women's public profile raising is also changing male attitudes. The women of the Hong Kong Legislative Council enlisted male support; hundreds of men have stood outside Aung San Suu Kyi's Yangon (Rangoon) home to listen to her speeches; thousands of men braved police repression to rally to the political cause of Megawatti in Indonesia in 1996. And who could forget Corazon Acquino leading the Philippines in its peaceful revolution, dubbed 'People Power', which toppled long-term dictator Ferdinand Marcos from power.

Sisters doing it for themselves

Women are doing all sorts of almost revolutionary things that affect their position as consumers:

- having children later
- expecting their men to take a role in the household
- getting divorced with increasing regularity
- staying unmarried for longer, preferring to concentrate on their careers
- still having children but choosing to remain single.

Increasingly women are having children later. In fact, many are deciding to reject motherhood altogether. Right now Hong Kong has one of the lowest birth rates in Asia. The richer countries have seen the most dramatic falls in birth rates, those where the consumer culture has been strongest, most rapid to develop and is now the most deep rooted.

Women are also expecting men to take a more active role in the household. This reflects the changing notions of what couples are: often unmarried, often both earning respectable salaries, in careers, united in postponing their families. Women are demanding more time to see friends, go out, socialize.

Though women's perception of themselves may be changing fast, the pace of change for men is slower. They are showing signs of getting more involved, looking after the kids, doing the shopping. Male shoppers have increased by 30 percent over the last decade according to recent research in the Philippines. South Korean men have increasingly been staying at home to look after the children. 'Househusbands' may not seem revolutionary in the west, or even in many parts of Asia, but in Korea, where society has remained strongly patriarchal and men take being men very seriously, this is radical.

Across the region many upper-income families are having to redistribute family tasks as the economic crisis means that the traditional home help or nanny is a luxury no longer justifiable. The thousands of Filipina housemaids in Hong Kong, Singapore and elsewhere are feeling very insecure in their jobs. Parents used to letting housemaids take care of the children are now having to take an increasing amount of day-to-day responsibility.

Women across Asia are discovering that divorce does not need necessarily have to lead to social isolation. In the past, divorce had been shameful and something to be avoided at all costs. But divorce rates in China have doubled since 1980 and look set to triple by 1998. Intellectual women and those with careers are the ones embracing divorce most keenly. And divorce rates are up throughout the region: Malaysia, Singapore, Korea, Taiwan all have more divorces annually.

According to the Thai Farmers Bank Research Center, the divorce rate in the country has been growing at 4.5 percent per year, compared to just 2.7 percent for marriage. The ratio between marriage and divorce is now 10:1 – not stupendous in western terms, but a seismic social shift by Thai standards. Divorce rates in large cities such as Bangkok and Chiang Mai are higher than in the rural areas, exceeding 5 percent. This is an important social development in a country which is on the whole devoutly Buddhist and has until fairly recently been politically unstable, populated mostly by rice farmers.

It seems that the increase in divorce rates is linked directly to the increase in wealth, living standards and the ability of women to survive economically outside of marriage. In Vietnam, the most recently emergent of the emerging countries tackled in this book, divorce is on the rise, with 114,123 cases passing through Hanoi's Supreme Court in the last three years. Women questioned on their reason for divorce replied that is was due to ill treatment (31 percent), adultery (15 percent) and conflicts with mothers-in-law (9 percent).

But why should divorce rates be interesting in consumer terms? Learning to avoid divorce has obviously become an issue, which leads directly to being choosier about men and what they offer. Couples across Asia increasingly meet outside the family network, in social institutions and not least the workplace. The new cafés, coffee bars, gyms and package holidays are the meeting places for professional couples. Lonely-hearts columns have sprung up and dating clubs and singles bars are also on the rise.

This in turn has meant that men have to behave differently if they are to get a wife. Entertainment is more important, especially if you are young, free and single. More variety in entertainment is being demanded, bringing with it a whole new bag of consumer tricks. Drinking with the lads, having a girls' night out, going bowling, watching a movie and traveling with friends are all new pastimes for many Asian people and they are changing the way people spend their money.

Asia's bachelor girls

Japan has been the model for Asia's new professional women. While Japanese women still have little effective institutional power (there are only a tiny number of women in parliament or senior positions at the powerful ministries), in society they have become increasingly important as living standards have improved. Japan's birth rate fell almost in line with the growth in women's employment to 1.46, one of the lowest in the industrialized world. The average age of marriage has climbed to over 26 and many Japanese women are staying single, with the number of single women in their thirties mirroring western European trends by the 1990s.

Japanese women have been starting businesses at a furious rate, often targeting their former selves, the phenomenon of Japan's office ladies (OLs). OLs were a marketer's dream when they first appeared: mass consumers of luxury goods, cosmetics, perfumes and all the media that surrounds the fashion and beauty industries. They were a major target of the Hawaiian, Australian and European tourist boards in the 1980s. Women in Japan had excess cash for the first time and they spent wildly. They became highly body-image and hygiene conscious and spent increasing amounts of time enjoying their own company. Many rejected the traditional route of marriage altogether, or at least postponed the experience. They were a familiar sight across Asia on package holidays and shopping sprees.

In Korea women are still opting for marriage but delaying it in order to enjoy themselves among their own sex for a while. In South Korea the phenomenon of the single office ladies (SOL) is a backbone of the domestic travel industry. SOLs travel in female-only groups, often to Europe and on more local weekend activity breaks. Typically they are single women in their mid-twenties with good white-collar jobs. They have become a major growth sector in the country's travel industry.

Dina Ponsel is typical of the growing number of Asia's young bachelor girls. She is Indonesian, well educated and has a well-paid job in advertising. She is a professional but does not like being called a yuppie. In June 1997 the *Jakarta Post* asked her if she has time for a boyfriend. 'No, I don't have any boyfriend,' she replied and went on to say: 'We broke up almost a year ago. I don't have any time to think about a new boyfriend. Most of the women in my office are not married ... My parents fear that I might not get married. Of course I will get married, but not now.'

This reflects the growing perception that marriage is an option, a choice to be made when the time is right. Ultimately most Asian women are still getting married eventually and most are dating in between studying, forwarding their careers or building their businesses. The single women of Asia have several things in common:

- ✦ high levels of education and career success
- ✦ financial independence and security
- ✦ rejection of the stigma that being single in their thirties is a disaster
- ✦ the desire and financial ability to travel
- ✦ higher spending on fashion, cars, technology and their own apartments.

In Taiwan, single women are called *dan shun gwei zhu*, single nobles. They are becoming major travelers, touring southeast Asia, the US and Europe. The economic crisis has curtailed some of this travel but it is still occurring. A taste of the consumer life is something that many women don't want to lose in marriage. Clever condo builders in Taiwan have copied the Japanese who developed apartments tailored to what they saw as the needs of single women, with central city locations and bigger bathrooms. And financial services companies have brought out policies to suit the single person. The bachelor girls are big business, whether it be the Prada bags (or very clever copies) they buy or their pensions.

In Singapore, the authorities have become alarmed at the level of women choosing to remain single and at the idea that being single is now considered *chic*. In response to this, the country has probably the only state-run dating agency in the world, Cupid. This looks at ways of promoting marriage, matching partners and organizing social events for singles to meet. The government has introduced tax breaks for working mothers, childcare and incentives for families having more children. However, women are not necessarily thankful for the government's efforts and opposition politicians have attacked the approach as callous social engineering. Government-sponsored adverts also fill the airwaves. Singapore's Channel 5 carries one ad with a busy executive whose work apparently makes life worth living and is keen to get home to the wife and children. 'Marriage – Save the Bond' proclaims the final screen.

Of course, women are still getting married. In fact, as wealth grows throughout the region, weddings remain big business. In China, as incomes have risen and open displays of affluence are becoming increasingly acceptable, families are spending more and more on marriage. Hotels, restaurants and the obligatory photographer are all reaping the benefits of this growth market. In the boom towns of Guangzhou and Shanghai, a growing number of families have been reported to be spending in excess of US$10,000 on their children's weddings.

Still a way to go

Though Asia's women have undoubtedly made significant strides over the last decade, large areas of the continent remain seemingly unaffected by the advances made elsewhere. Take India as an example. It is a divided country. On one side are women who have become internationally known and are seemingly able to compete with men, such as former Prime Minister Indira Gandhi and Booker prize-winning novelist Arundhati Roy. On the other side are the women of states such as Rajasthan with an 89 percent female illiteracy rate in rural areas and in Gujarat where only 55 percent of girls attend school. In other less developed nations such as Indonesia or Vietnam, there exist similar problems. But throughout the continent things are changing.

The question of what constitutes Asian beauty has been raised as women across the region become more image conscious. They want to be presented with a wide range of Asian beauty types through advertising and magazines. Yui Phetkanha, Thailand's supermodel profiled earlier, was not originally considered beautiful in her home country – international exposure not only propelled her into the world spotlight but changed many attitudes among Thais regarding darker-skinned women. The increase in gyms and health centers alongside hairdressers and beauty parlors is sign enough that women are paying attention to their image. In China, waiting lists to gain membership of fashionable fitness centers are long and women pay a high percentage of their earnings to join. Beauty contests are big business in Asia, especially in the Philippines, and the 1997 Miss World was Indian.

During the Miss Thailand competition in 1996 won by Sirinya Vinsiri, some accused the winner of being *farang* or caucasian. This sparked a debate over what was 'Thai beauty' and whether Thai women, and men (who were after all the majority of the judges), were worshipping the western look. This is not an exclusively Asian minefield, as witnessed when a woman of African descent won the Miss Italy crown and sparked a national debate about Italian beauty. Whatever the answer, it is another question for Asian women in their changing role.

Caught in the middle

Asia isn't quite sure what to do with its women right now. In so many ways they have contributed to the economic miracle that has created modern and growing societies. They provide labor power and the future workforce, they are the backbone of the service industry and cheap labor for manufacturers. They have built businesses and families and become consumers, helping to drive their domestic economies.

Yet now they find themselves blamed for the breakup of the traditional family unit, for letting their countries down by not having enough children, for seeking too much independence. Asian women are caught in the middle.

Many women claim that they are disadvantaged at work when the very boss who thought it proper that they should marry will not promote them and cites divided loyalties between firm and family. The result has been that growing numbers of women are opting for firm and putting off family. They are spending their time looking for a joint-venture partner rather than a life partner.

The saving grace for these women may be the fact that it appears a growing number of men are doing the same. The average age at which Asians are marrying is rising for both men and women. In Hong Kong men now get married at an average age of 31 as opposed to 28 in 1970, women at 29 now as opposed to 23. The pattern is the same throughout the region: men marrying at between 27 and 31, a few years later than in the 1970s; women in their mid- to late twenties rather than their early twenties. There is still a stigma, however – an unmarried 30-year-old woman in Hong Kong still dreads the slang term of being compared to an old teabag.

What will be crucial in the next few years is how women's roles in Asia continue to change, now that the rapid economic growth of the past decade has flattened out. If radical change is needed in many economies, banking infrastructure and management practices, making industry economically more viable and competitive, then will women find that they have an ever-increasing and key role to play?

If, as seems likely, this is the case, then how will women change the way they live? And how will their relationship to the rest of society change? Likewise, how will society's (and, more to the point, men's) views of women change? All these developments will be reflected in how women consume. Predicting consumption patterns in the future will be even more complex because of the change in women's status in society and will demand even more attention from those interested in selling in Asia.

How to market to women in Asia

✦ *Body and image consciousness* is rising, as mirrored by the growth in gyms, cosmetics and even plastic surgeons. Women, even those in non-professional occupations, are increasingly seeking to portray a professional image. Products that offer image-enhancing properties – skincreams, including skin-lightening creams, designer clothing both western and Asian, accessories including bags, mobile phones and jewelry – are likely to be more successful in post-turmoil Asia. Asian women may have had to forgo some luxuries, but products that enhance their image as professional and successful are still in demand.

- Women are increasingly consumers of *'big ticket' items*, or at least have a say in their purchase. Goods should be marketed at them as much as at men. Women are buying cars and single women are increasingly buying apartments and all the white goods that go in them.

- Asian women are major consumers of *women's magazines* and these are prime advertising locations. They are increasing their range of topics to include sex, financial planning, education, careers, travel and leisure activities. There is scope in these publications for advertising more than just clothes and shoes.

- Women are interested in a *widening range of products and services*. Pensions are a prime example – these are invariably targeted at men, but more and more women need their own financial products.

- *Direct selling and catalog shopping* are increasingly important as women have less time to go shopping because of their careers. The growth in women socializing together is also boosting the success of party-plan sales operations such as Tupperware, Avon and lingerie companies.

5

Here Comes the Middle Class

Asia's emerging middle class is built on brainpower and intellectual skill, capital and knowhow. It reflects Asia's growth from an assembly shop to an innovator, a region as likely to develop and invent as to make and assemble, a region with crucial stock and money markets, world-leading banks and investment houses.

The Asian 'miracle' may, as *Fortune* magazine claimed in August 1997, have been built on perspiration rather than technology, but as the region matures and develops, its nations have been directing investment into specific industries, technologies and services. With the success of that investment governments have created the breeding grounds of an entrepreneurial and newly rich middle class.

- ✦ Every country in Asia now has a middle class to a greater or lesser extent.
- ✦ In every Asian country the middle class is a growing section of society.
- ✦ The monetary definition of middle class differs from country to country.

- Across Asia the members of the middle class are becoming identified as possession cravers, keen to acquire everything from cars, to clothes, to investments.

What is the Asian middle class?

The emerging middle class is the section of society that is now able to operate as entrepreneurs, businesspeople and highly skilled workers. The new centers of production such as India's silicon valley around Bangalore, the high-tech parks of the Klang Valley in Malaysia and the service industries of Hong Kong and Singapore have been its foundation. Now it is increasingly the coastal boom towns of China, the advanced manufacturing centers of South Korea and Taiwan as well as the new trade centers of the Philippines and Thailand that are spawning the emergent middle classes.

Invariably, they are the people who have filled the need that appeared for managers, technicians and engineers as the nations of Asia moved from sweated to knowledge-based economies. They can be found running the host of new joint ventures in China's cities and administering the massive infrastructure projects across Malaysia, the Philippines and China.

The new middle classes are the personnel who have stepped into the region's new service economies. They are mid- to upper-level employees and managers of banks, airlines, computer companies and hotel chains. They are working in the media, starting franchises and pioneering new trading opportunities and specialist manufacturing. And this managerial class is set to grow. China alone will need an estimated 100,000 new managers by the year 2000.

And the new middle class isn't just found at the higher levels of corporations or in the cities. The rise of the professional couple has meant that even relatively low-income employees can find themselves prospering when their joint earnings are taken into account. And Chinese farmers who have switched from staple crops to new cash crops such as flowers, wine grapes and duck farming have found themselves propelled into the middle class, turning their communes into corporations.

The middle class is increasingly the most educated, often multilingual and well-traveled group in society, open to and familiar with the latest management techniques, office and business technology. As the first generation to become familiar with new technology, they have also been the first to appreciate its value. They combine their work ethic with an appreciation of the lifestyle economy and the importance of leisure.

Additionally, the middle class is the sector of society that is putting into practice many fundamental changes such as more equal partnerships between the sexes, financial planning and modern childrearing techniques. They are also the social group best able to realize the aspirations of home ownership and the purchase of major items such as cars, overseas holidays and so on.

The Asian middle class has obtained, or at least reached the potential to obtain, home and multiple car ownership, foreign travel and widespread further education. Within their own societies they are the social group that has achieved advancement and risen above the majority. In terms of purchasing power parity they are those best able to look to the future and plan rather than living hand to mouth. Additionally, they are significantly more experimental and adventurous than their western counterparts. For most they are the first generation of their families to achieve a recognizable level of wealth. Unlike the US or European middle class they are not the bastions of conservatism but the group that is most open to changes in the introduction of new technologies and working practices. Their support for these changes is continuing to provide the catalysts that are modernizing Asian societies and economies.

The effect of the economic problems seen in Asia since mid-1997 has been felt most keenly by the middle classes. It is a major threat to middle-class prosperity and growth. To be comfortable, secure and middle class is now a difficult feat.

However, commitments such as mortgages, hire purchase and school fees can't be abandoned in an instant. So for manufacturers and retailers not involved in the provision of essential goods and services, the climate has become noticeably tougher.

But the situation is not all negative. There are still many potential opportunities to be exploited. The middle class continues to consume, but its consumption is much more careful and discriminating. This is a trend to which manufacturers, service providers and retailers must be increasingly attuned. They have to adapt their product and service marketing strategies to respond more closely to the new wise, value-for-money-seeking middle-class consumers.

Indonesia has been particularly badly hit by the recent economic troubles. While the country's emergent middle class is now feeling the strain, its foundations have already been laid. It is a clear and undeniable force financially, politically and as consumers. Right now in Indonesia:

- 27 percent of Jakarta's 13 million population is considered middle class
- 70 percent of the middle class are homeowners.

This Indonesian middle class is composed of younger people who have grown up in the wake of the country's economic boom. They have been educated, raised in the cities and gained well-paid jobs. Many have traveled abroad to Europe or the US, often in pursuit of educational qualifications. Many of Jakarta's professional middle class are torn between the west and the east. Those returning from periods of study or work abroad talk of the need to readjust culturally. They admit that western values have influenced them but that they still respect traditional morals. This theme is mirrored across the region.

In Hong Kong and Singapore the middle-class expansion was driven by the rise of these city states as financial centers of world renown and power. In Malaysia it was the technicians and professionals who created the silicon suburbs of Kuala Lumpur. Malaysian newspaper columnist Karim Raslan described it this way: 'Educated and hard working, there are Malay doctors, lawyers, scientists and accountants, a vast middle class that has carpeted the Klang Valley with housing estates, golf courses and shopping centers.'

In South Korea and Taiwan the professions, from engineers to lawyers and accountants, have built up the new powerhouses of

THE MIDDLE CLASS EMERGES

Asia's emergent middle class is reshaping the continent. Its power is reflected in the shift in the pan-Asian economic system from one of conspicuous exporting to an increasingly mixed system of exports and growing domestic demand. As the middle class grows so Asia's economies will become more geared to supplying their own needs rather than those of the rest of the world.

1996	million	% of population
China	64.0	5.3
India	45.9	5.0
Indonesia	16.0	8.5
South Korea	10.1	23.0
Malaysia	4.9	26.0
Thailand	3.1	5.3

Source: National statistics

Seoul and Taipei. Now in India, Vietnam and China it is the entrepreneurs in manufacturing, the property developers and import/export specialists who are the backbone of the middle class.

Wherever they are in the continent, this new Asian middle class has certain things in common:

- *Better education* – increasingly university educated, often having studied abroad and technically skilled with knowledge of modern management and business techniques.
- *Urban lifestyle* – the Asian middle class is overwhelmingly urban, almost exclusively so in many countries such as India and China.
- *Marrying later in life* – with the expansion of educational opportunities and careers many Asian professionals are postponing marriage and childbirth until their thirties.
- *Having fewer children* – birth rates are falling across the region, particularly among higher-income, urban-dwelling couples.

- *Having no children* – the number of DINKY couples (dual income, no kids) is rising. They prefer to spend their money on traveling, clothes and entertainment.
- *Living longer* – better diets as children combined with greater awareness of health and improved access to private medicine are helping the rich live longer.
- *Demanding efficient private and public services* – they have become the main advocates of civic change across the region.
- *Pro-democracy and civil liberties* – they have championed the moves to greater democracy, whether in Hong Kong, India, Taiwan or Indonesia.
- *Demanding convenience* – the growth of the services sector is being propelled by the middle class's aspiration for convenience.

The new consumer culture

Certain elements of Asia's middle-class lifestyle are recognizably western. In South Korea, the young professionals who make up the middle class gather in Seoul's TGI Friday's restaurants to drink imported beer and talk shop. In Bangkok, they gather to sip imported malt whisky and assess each other's progress.

Despite the widespread western perception of the Philippines as a poor country, there is a growing middle class working for the multinationals who jabber away on mobile phones in air-conditioned shopping plazas. They have created gated communities with closed retailing, dining and leisure facilities based on similar US developments and protected from the Manila slums. In Indonesia they have built exclusive spa resorts in Bali and Phuket, not just for tourists but for the busy Jakarta executive's stress breaks.

In Kuala Lumpur's prosperous Golden Triangle, the city's middle class enjoys spending its new-found income in the plazas that line Julan Bukit Bintang and Julan Sultan Ismail. The KL Plaza is home to the region's latest branch of The Coffee Bean, a US specialty coffee bar and deli. On opening night in September 1997, KL's young professionals braved the haze that was enveloping the city and sat on the street sipping ice blended mochas and cappuccinos accompanied by biscotti and blueberry muffins. The Coffee Bean in KL is replicated along Singapore's Orchard Road where the country's numerous young professionals crowd the coffee bars.

In China, the success of the American Budweiser beer brand has been due largely to the newly emergent middle class. In 1996, Budweiser's sales exceeded company expectations threefold and the company's Wuhan factory was unable to meet demand. Sales are concentrated in the cities, among the 18–25 age group of young professionals and college students. Budweiser has become the major sponsor of the China National Basketball League, the sport of choice for many of the country's young professionals.

In the otherwise closed country of Brunei, the capital city, Bandar Seri Begawan, is starting to cater for the tastes of its professional classes. Its malls stock the latest European designer fashions and there is a cyber café and a Pizza Hut. Brunei's young professionals have taken to Pizza Hut in a big way along with the other favorites of Asia's professional class, McDonald's and Delifrance. When Pizza Hut in Brunei found itself unable to offer its popular chicken pizza topping due to strict laws demanding only *halal* chicken, the middle class turned their anger on the government for depriving them of their treats.

Tiny but visible

China has to be the most extreme example of the rapid development of a prosperous professional middle class, its society having made the leap from totalitarian communism to western-style consumption in less than 20 years. Although the middle class is still small in relation to the total population, it is the focus of most of the country's advertising and thus is having a strong indirect influence on the outlooks and aspirations of the entire media-literate population.

Proof of a Chinese middle class is offered by the appearance of shopping malls and supermarkets, selling convenience foods to put in computerized fridges, home computers and educational software, private car dealers (even Ferraris are available in Shanghai and Beijing), fashionable Italian designer boutiques, DIY stores for the new generation of homeowners – the list goes on.

Notable examples include French retail chain Carrefour which has opened three hypermarkets in China, all of which have been, so far, very successful. Success has also come to US DIY retailer Home Depot, along with Sweden's Ikea, both of which have set up stores to meet the new demand for home-improvement products.

The middle class consumes

Those in the Asian middle class are keen to acquire the trappings of success owing to their professional stature and income. The new professionals are seeking gratification and solace in consumption, manifested in their purchases of expensive meals, designer clothes or imported cars, or their lifestyle tastes for foreign television, overseas travel or fondness for adult-oriented rock (AOR) music. Retailers and manufacturers of consumer goods have not been slow to tap this new market.

Dickson Poon was perhaps the first Asian retailer to make a million out of the region's yuppies, although others have followed, such as David Tang. Poon is founder and chairman of Dickson Concepts, which owns the retailing and wholesaling rights in Hong Kong and much of Asia to luxury brands much beloved of the new middle classes such as Ralph Lauren, Rolex and Hermès. His boutiques were the first outlets to cater specifically to the new professionals and his subsequent career has been largely dedicated to bringing to Asians the world of luxury brands and the status they convey.

Luxury Hong Kong retailer Joyce launched its own credit card in 1991. There were 27,000 takers, overwhelming the company. In Jakarta, the queue outside the Hard Rock Café and Tony Roma's got longer as the middle class grew. Major Filipino property developer Ayala is building whole communities for the middle class complete with malls, sports clubs, schools and everything the newly wealthy consumer could want.

The mushrooming of chains such as 7-Eleven and Circle K shows that the convenience lifestyle is attracting those in the middle class willing to pay a little extra and conscious of time and relaxation. The same is true for supermarkets, fast-food joints, car-valeting services and dry cleaners.

The numerous plazas, malls and shopping centers that have opened their doors and switched on their vicious aircon systems in the last decade have become the meeting places for Asia's professional classes. Singapore's Park Mall on Orchard Road is a maze of designer furniture and homeware stores with everything the young professional could desire to fill their apartment. In Kuala Lumpur, the Star Hill Center and Lot 10 plaza have moved beyond the concept of an indoor market to be collections of designer boutiques populated by international brands such as Hugo Boss, Ralph Lauren and Calvin Klein, each anchored by a luxury department store such as Isetan or Tangs.

Trendsetters

The middle classes have become trendsetters of the Asian lifestyle.

In South Korea the middle-class demand for light beers has prompted strong growth in that sector of an already large beer-drinking market (valued at US$1.1 billion in 1995). The domestic manufacturers, including the major players Chosun and Oriental Brewery, have launched a series of look-alike bottled beers in an attempt to retain market share from successful importers such as Anheuser Busch and Carlsberg.

Throughout Asia the quality of local airlines, the food they serve and the promotional offers they present has risen dramatically in line with the number of travelers. Asian airlines such as Cathay Pacific, Singapore Airlines and MAS have begun to go after the middle-class market with campaigns stressing sophistication and comfort. Nor have foreign carriers like British Airways been slow to capitalize on this new market, emphasizing the 'stress-free' nature of their services that can whisk tired and overworked Asian executives away from it all.

Environmental concerns are increasingly important to the middle class. Surveys across the region have found that middle income

WHAT THE MIDDLE CLASS IS BUYING NOW (AND WILL BE BUYING NEXT CENTURY)

	Now	2000
China	TVs	Cars
	Telephones	Mobile phones
	Fridges	Property
Hong Kong	Insurance	Private medicine
Singapore	Insurance	Private medicine
	Property	Overseas travel
	Mobile phones	
Malaysia	Credit cards	Property
Thailand	White goods	Consumer electronics
	4WD trucks	Luxury cars
	Imported spirits	Holidays
Indonesia	Mobile phones	Property
	Branded cosmetics	Medical care
Philippines	Packaged foods	Insurance
	Cars	Travel
	Telephones	Mobile phones
Vietnam	TVs/VCRs	Computers
	Telephones	Mobile phones
	Motorbikes	Cars
India	Bicycles	Motorbikes/cars
	Property	Technology

earners are particularly concerned about growing numbers of incidents of environmental damage and pollution, brought home most pointedly in the 1997 haze. It is this group that is starting to demand environmentally friendly products.

In Thailand the upwardly mobile middle class have developed a taste for wine, especially Californian whites. The market is booming by 25 percent per annum, with wine increasingly being given as a gift more frequently than traditional spirits. The craze for US wine symbolizes that country's image to Thais as 'casual, young and lively'.

Upward and onward

Middle-class families are increasingly moving out of the cities – they no longer have to be there.

First, the cities have become increasingly crowded, polluted, expensive and crime ridden. Secondly, modern telecommunications are reducing the need to cluster around the central business districts. And transport, both private and public, is boosting a commuter culture. The cost of renting in the city centers has increased dramatically, while environmental sensitivities are creating out-of-town communities for those literally seeking greener pastures.

Many of Asia's new cities such as Subic Bay in the Philippines and Suzhou in China are largely middle class, high-tech and centers of new industry. They are not like Guangdong with a million people sleeping on the streets or Ho Chi Minh City where thousands of unemployed men arrive every month with little more to hope for than a manual job in the construction industry.

Middle-class ghettos

As the middle class opts to concentrate on careers and postpone starting families, it is helping to reduce the size of Asian households. The move away from the extended family and the search for individual accommodation has created a greater demand for housing. Much of the housing that has been built in the last 20 years has been small and functionally designed, simply to ease the strain temporarily. The new middle class has demanded something more. Aspiration and expectation are outstripping supply in many countries, though in others such as Thailand property developers who have misjudged middle-class tastes have found themselves with empty buildings.

Members of the new middle class are increasingly moving into modern developments complete with their kind of people, shops, leisure activities and services.

The Tampines in Singapore is a prime example of this sort of development – 60 percent of its residents have a gross monthly salary of S$4000 or more. It has 17,000 residents in five-room and bigger apartments and nearly 80 percent of inhabitants are aged under 45. Shops have moved closer to Tampines in order to extract the locals' disposable income from their wallets, including department stores such as Sogo at the foot of the Tampines MRT station, and employers are following suit. Two new high-tech developments literally on Tampines' front doorstep include Finance Park and Telepark.

The development's residents jog, swim and exercise – not traditional Singapore pastimes – and retailers are pursuing them and their cash. As part of its plan to open 500 new franchised shops in the Asia Pacific region in the coming five years, The Athlete's Foot, a US-based retailer of sports footwear, has launched its first megastore in Singapore at Suntec City Mall. The 8000 sq. ft store, built at a cost of US$168,000, consists of a 'fit analysis' zone, with video cameras and treadmills to analyze feet conditions, an in-house foot specialist to provide advice and an area with computer terminals on the latest games and happenings.

And The Athlete's Foot is not the only major US retailer to eye up the residents of Tampines. Toys 'R' Us, the biggest toy retailer in the world, opened its fourth Singapore store in Tampines in 1995, targeting the new generation of middle-class families.

In Thailand, the country's two largest retailers, The Mall and Central Group, are expanding into the middle-income enclaves in the provinces in order to tap the potential of this new group. Bangkok is the centre of activity right now. The average family income in the city is approximately US$8000 per annum compared to US$4000 for the country as a whole. But many retailers are starting to think ahead and anticipate the trend.

In South Korea too, large retailers are opening in developing cities such as Bundang, Ilsan and the Seoul suburbs, increasingly home to the newly affluent middle class.

The retail rush for China is even more frenetic than the last century's imperialist onslaught, with nearly every major international retail company setting up shop in a market that promises over a billion potential consumers (though this is somewhat of an optimistic view). Everyone wants in on the Chinese middle class, not least the international retailers. The best illustration of this is that even Harvey Nichols, the exclusive retail outlet based in London's Knightsbridge (though owned by Hong Kong-based *taipan* Dickson Poon), has set up a department store on a street corner in Shanghai.

Supermarket chains are popping up all over the major urban centers in the country, bringing new 'exotic' foods and other fast-moving consumer goods (FMCGs) to the unsuspecting, but often brutally critical, Chinese consumers. DIY stores have opened up to meet the demand for home-improvement goods, electrical stores now sell the latest Japanese gadgetry and even car parts suppliers are reporting brisk business.

Magazines target professional consumers

Regional business magazines are competing for advertising revenue. They largely have one target: the young, upwardly mobile, high-earning professional person. The growth of pan-regional business has driven the need for pan-regional magazines. Asian businesspeople are as interested in Asia as are their European or US counterparts.

Throughout Asia business magazines, whether international or regional, have experienced strong growth in both circulation and advertising revenue. Professionals are still keen to learn all they can about international management techniques (gurus such as Peter Drucker and Tom Peters are as popular in Asia as elsewhere). They are generally considered more open to ideas than are their western counterparts jaded by the glut of self-help tomes. Advertisers seem to agree that the regional business titles are the best way to reach the professional elites in Asia. Surveys have found that their readerships are generally those earning in excess of US$100,000 annually, with 75 percent flying regularly on business.

The traditional business magazine publishers are keen not to be squeezed out of the burgeoning Chinese market before they've even had a chance to dominate. From November 1996 *Fortune* magazine began publishing five times a year in China through a licensee. Initial circulation was expected to be 51,000 with a one-time color page ad rate of US$11,000.

SRG's *Asia Pacific Adex* reveals how important regional business magazines are becoming. It took just four years for *Asian Business* to increase its ad revenue by 33 percent, with circulation growing by 13 percent over the same period. *Far Eastern Economic Review*'s ad revenue shot up by 74 percent in 1996 over 1993 and circulation by 9 percent, while the Asian edition of *Business Week* saw a 56 percent growth in ad revenue over four years and a 39 percent increase in circulation.

Publishers have been keen to tap the cross-culture that is emerging as Asia becomes a key component to world trade. Thomas Wootson set out to tap that potential with *AsiaMag*. He surveyed the various markets and noted the obvious desire of a new generation of consumers for US-made products and services. He also realized that there was a need for native-language media to connect western goods with Asian consumers. Hence *AsiaMag*, printed in Chinese and distributed eventually throughout Korea, Singapore and Malaysia as well as China, and providing contacts, exposure and networking opportunities.

The growth in the number of publishers targeting the Asian middle class is not just confined to foreign publishers repeating their successful western titles with an Asian slant. The last five years have seen the rise of a number of domestic titles and media barons riding the wave of the middle class's reading habits.

This fascination for business titles has spilled over into the more conventional book-publishing industry. Most Asian bookshops are noticeable for the prominence given to both business titles and self-help books. MPH bookstores in Malaysia, the country's major chain, and Berita Book Center reflect this in their bestseller lists. In September 1997 Berita's top 10 sellers for Malaysia and Singapore included a plethora of self-help and business titles such as *God Wants You to be Rich* by Paul Zane Pilzer, *Human Relations and Interpersonal Communication* by Tan Tuan Hock, *Overdrive: Bill Gates and the Race to Control Cyberspace* by James Wallace, *The Power Principle: Influence with Honor* by Blaine Lee, *Soros on Soros* by George Soros and *The New Maharajahs* by Claudia Cragg.

And broadcasters too...

TV – terrestrial, cable and satellite – is also being directed towards the region's growing middle class. We discuss the growing media empires, both domestic and foreign, in Chapter 10, but without doubt it has been the emergence of the middle class that has spurred broadcasters such as CNN to move heavily into Asia. There is now a bewildering array of channels to surf but it is not always the foreign stations that are watched the most.

The middle class in Asia has shown heightened international awareness and an interests in news and current events including fashion, new technologies and ideas. Channels catering to this market include pan-regional satellite channel Asia Business News. But there are also regional terrestrial channels such as China Central Broadcasting, the main national channel which has bought rights to various programs including the UK Premier soccer league, international wildlife documentaries and dramas, reflecting a broadening of interest among the viewing public.

The fact that television viewers in Vietnam, as well as more obviously middle-class countries such as Singapore, can watch US shows such as *Seinfeld* reflects a new world appreciation and interest in foreign programming. This is indicative of a growing sophistication and broadening of interest.

The Lopez family are the owners of Benpres Holdings Corporation, a one-time sugar-rich dynasty that has now become the most powerful television operator in the Philippines. The corporation owns ABS-CBN which operates Channel 2 and holds 62 percent of the Filipino television-watching audience and 45 percent of the crucial Metro Manila audience. ABS-CBN also operates national and local radio networks with 10 percent of radio advertising in the country. The Benpres empire also includes 20 percent of Sky Cable, the largest cable TV company in the Philippines with 80,000 subscribers in Manila alone, mostly in upper- and middle-income households. With 40 channels Sky Cable has become the way to reach Manila's affluent couch potatoes.

Pleasure and leisure

As more and more young people earn more money and, thanks to delayed childbirth, have fewer family responsibilities, a new era of leisure is opening up to them. They have the disposable income to enjoy themselves, but how exactly are they doing it?

As Asia's professional middle class saw its standing in society grow so they began to spend with a little less caution, even indulging in treats. Be it pints of luxury ice cream or first-class travel, Asia's yuppies were starting to relax and enjoy life a little more. After the economic crisis in 1997 the middle class was forced to think more about their financial outgoings. It has acquired a taste for life's little luxuries but is now acting more selectively and being more cautious.

For instance, family restaurants have become a growth industry in southeast Asia, not simply small independents which have long dominated the consumer-catering industry, but chains with names recognizable from Pittsburgh to Paris to Tokyo. While traditional restaurants have been severely affected by the economic downturn (with record bankruptcies across the region), family-style restaurants appear to be weathering the storm. This is because many middle-class families perceive them to offer value for money, the ability to budget expenditure while still providing a night out.

In South Korea, family-oriented restaurants have become the vogue. The country is the largest single consumer-catering market in southeast Asia, valued at US$10 billion in 1995, a growth of 40 percent since 1991. Seoul's vibrant restaurant scene includes international brands such as Sizzlers and Planet Hollywood. Increasingly the new middle class thrown up by the Korean economic miracle is passing over the traditional *chap chee* and *chigae* and opting for international brands such as Pizza Hut and TGI Friday's. In 1992, TGI Friday's Korean sales were US$5.8 million; by 1995 turnover had grown by 300 percent to US$22.5 million, an average day's take of US$15,000 per branch. TGI Friday's is not alone. Sizzlers successfully sells steaks to Seoul's professional crowd as does US-based steak-and-salad chain Ponderosa. Most of these western family establishments are franchised to local operators such as the

Tongyang Group and Taihan Sugar Industries. Now Korean restaurateurs are copying the formula for themselves. Not just in South Korea but in Malaysia, Singapore and Hong Kong, family-style restaurants are emerging and becoming profitable.

With Asia's professionals willing to spend a little extra for the good life if there is a return in terms of value for money, entrepreneurial ideas have found willing customers. One example is Hong Kong's Citybird commuter coach. The service covers the route between Central and Shatin, a town in the New Territories. Shatin to Central used to be a nerve-racking journey, but thanks to Citybird commuters willing to pay a little extra can enjoy 49-seater coaches with reclining seats, fold-down tables, breakfast served by hostesses, televisions, toilets and mobile phones.

Across the region young professionals have been displaying pride in their cosmopolitanism. They travel more often and further afield, they watch western TV programs and read western magazines and novels. In Asia's major cities they gather at European-inspired cafés such as the Dome chain and Delifrance. Delifrance has been massively successful in Asia, increasing annual profits by 33 percent and pre-tax profits by 42 percent in 1996. Singapore accounted for 54 percent of the profit and Hong Kong for another 22 percent. The company now operates over 150 outlets in Asia with franchises in Malaysia, Philippines and Indonesia. Delifrance is planning its next expansion drive for China and Indonesia.

Luxury snacks

With greater disposable income Asian professionals are treating themselves more and more. They are spending not just on designer clothes and fast cars, but on easily attained, everyday luxuries such as a premium cup of coffee in nice surroundings, or a scoop of luxury ice cream in a well-appointed parlor. There is a greater need to supply oneself with regular perks as the pressures of the workplace have increased, leaving most Asians with little in the way of free time during the working week, exacerbated by the recent economic turmoil where working harder means more job security.

Diageo's Haagen-Dazs premium ice-cream chain has been spreading the word about luxury pints of fattening flavor for several years now. The company has outlets in Hong Kong, Indonesia, Malaysia, Korea, Singapore, Taiwan and elsewhere.

And Haagen-Dazs isn't alone. Baskin-Robbins has entered the market and Ben & Jerry's is also competing to be flavor of the month with the Asian middle class. Baskin-Robbins has even found a market in Vietnam where a pint of ice cream can cost the equivalent of a week's wages for an unskilled laborer.

International ad agency Leo Burnett has launched a series of ads in China for Sprite – Coca-Cola's lemon-flavored soda drink. The TV ads clearly target newly affluent males. The advert shows a young man gazing into a bank of TV screens imagining his future life: college, water skiing, tennis and beautiful women. The ad poses the question 'Right Now?' and answers with the Sprite slogan: 'Obey Your Thirst'.

This ad reflects the typical aspirations and aims of the newly wealthy man while emphasizing notions of hard work and patience. It ran on local channels in Shanghai and other regional cities.

Luxury boom bust

Luxury had become a watchword for Asia's new professionals and the world's manufacturers had found profitable markets across Asia. However, luxury goods manufacturers, be they purveyors of salmon-colored designer dresses or fresh salmon, have to be alert to changing moods and tastes.

The change in economic fortunes arising from the events of 1997 has put an end to the large-scale consumption of luxury goods in Asia. Retailers have seen their sales plummet across the region as consumers have decided that they can no longer justify their luxury purchases.

Luxury brand owners and retailers need to remember a few basic points about their products:

- Consumers in Asia are having to watch their pennies more closely, which means that in the luxury market there has to be an even better reason for a consumer to buy. Just being expensive/exclusive is no longer the criterion by which goods are judged. The crunch word here is quality, both of product and service. Manufacturers and retailers must pay particular attention to aspects of their products or services which justify the outlay.
- The definition of what is or isn't a luxury brand can change as a one-time luxury becomes overexposed through advertising and licensing. For example, a visitor arriving in Singapore from London could be forgiven for thinking that Dunhill, though up-market, is not all that exclusive. The company does little mass-market advertising in London, preferring to remain closeted in its exclusive Jermyn Street store. However, in Singapore its advertising seems to be everywhere, from sponsoring the movie of the week to billboard hoardings. The brand appears diluted and far less exclusive.
- Luxury brands can age overnight, leaving them lacking in *cachet*. This can particularly affect clothes brands, as every week seems to bring new designers not previously available to Asian consumers into the department stores and plazas.
- Luxury brands do not necessarily have to come from old-established manufacturers. Indeed, the definition of a luxury brand is more often to do with mood and canny marketing. An example of this is Casio, traditionally a manufacturer of fairly ordinary watches that inspired little aspirational greed. However, the popularity of its G Shock and Baby G range in Asia proved that a catchy design at a reasonably high price, for what is essentially a plastic watch, could prove successful.

US influence

Without doubt the US influences Asia, partly through movies, partly through TV, but also because of more tangible links. In the last decade the old ties of imperialism have steadily slipped away as

ASIAN IMMIGRANTS IN THE US

Chinese	1,645,472
Filipinos	1,406,770
Asian Indian	815,447
Korean	798,849
Vietnamese	614,547

Source: US Census Bureau

Asia has become more sure of itself, as witnessed by the coolness between Malaysia and Britain over the Pergau Dam affair, or the public relations disaster of Queen Elizabeth's Indian visit in October 1997. The handover of Hong Kong to China in July 1997 was obviously the most ostentatious example of the decline of British influence over life in Asia. An informal policy of self-assurance and rejection of the old colonial manners had been occurring in Malaysia and Singapore for years. The French now have little more than a passing interest in Indo-China, the Portuguese cede Macao back to China in 2000 and India is now 50 years into independence.

The US has a total Asia-Pacific population of 8.9 million, projected to grow to 11.9 million by 2000. There are a host of daily flights between the regional hubs of southeast Asia and the US as travel restrictions are eased and disposable income allows for frequent visits.

The US, Australia and Canada have become the destinations of choice for Asian immigrants. Changes in immigration laws in Europe have meant that Indians and Pakistanis are now becoming as familiar on the streets of New York and New Jersey as in London or Birmingham, and just as successful in business.

US sports and filmstars attract large followings among affluent Asian teens and young professionals. When US golf star Tiger Woods arrived in Thailand for a pro-am event in 1997 he got a bigger reception than either Bill Clinton or Queen Elizabeth, according to the press reports of his arrival. All five national TV networks covered the arrival at Bangkok airport of the half-Thai golfer and

Tiger walked off with a reported US$500,000 in appearance money during his stay.

Asia's middle class appears comfortable moving between different continents. It is being boosted by a large number of Asians who had left the continent to study abroad and never came back, until now. In the last 20 years China alone sent 200,000 young people abroad to study. The rate of return wasn't great – just 10 percent came home directly after their studies. It seems that a couple of years at Stanford or Yale was a difficult journey to return from. Now, however, they are coming home to build careers in the newly prosperous regions of southern China. Hong Kong's newly formed Federation of Mainland Professionals features experts in joint-venture law, tax havens and public relations.

Many of these returnees are uniquely placed to command huge salaries in the new China. Most were the sons and daughters of senior government officials and have influential contacts or *guanxi*. And they are demanding the same standard of living in Shenzhen or Guangdong as they enjoyed in California or New York.

Tomorrow's middle class

Vietnam is one of the poorest countries in the world, according to the World Bank. But that does not take into account the massive black economy that makes any accurate study of per capita income impossible. The size and wealth of the middle class varies greatly across the region, but in Vietnam, as in China, a group of consumers is emerging who can begin to aspire to a greater range of goods, even if at first sight it appears that just about everything is beyond their reach.

Every mattress in Vietnam is a bank and beneath every floorboard lurks a secret cache of cash. The race is on to get it. The government wants it so it can use domestic capital to fund development and it can't get away with increasing taxes. Everyone else just wants Vietnamese consumers to start spending it.

The World Bank assesses Vietnam's per capita wealth at around US$200 per year. Of course, there are regional disparities. Rural incomes can be as low as US$10 a month and the nouveau capitalist riche in Ho Chi Minh City and Hanoi have significant wealth. However, while disposable income is low by southeast Asian standards, it is boosted by the fact that mortgages are rare, utility costs are low and fresh food is cheap. The real problem is that very little or any of it is in the bank. This need not concern those with consumer goods to sell, as all they need to do is persuade consumers to lift their mattresses.

Ho Chi Minh City has become the beacon for Vietnamese youth. This is where the trends hit first and grow. Baskin-Robbins started selling ice cream here, the drinks manufacturers have piled in rapidly, the fast-food giants, led by Kentucky Fried Chicken, are eyeing up the city. Ho Chi Minh City *is* the consumer market in Vietnam at the moment:

- ✦ 96 percent of households own a TV set
- ✦ 69 percent have a VCR
- ✦ 85 percent a motorbike
- ✦ 46 percent a refrigerator
- ✦ 11 percent a washing machine
- ✦ 76 percent a stereo
- ✦ 89 percent a radio.

If per capita income in Vietnam is as low as US$200, then how can it be possible for 96 percent of households to own a TV set?

Vietnam is a problem for marketing people but also a challenge. The seventh most populous country in Asia, with a population set to double by 2025 – it can't be ignored.

New consumers in Thailand

The Thai National Housing Authority (NHA) acknowledges that 2.29 percent of the country's population live in slum communities, 80 percent or more in the Bangkok area. It has developed a scheme to improve conditions. New residential projects are to be constructed by moving the slums to new sites. Despite the poor conditions, many of these two million people are already consumers and are taking on middle-class characteristics. Television aerials and motorbikes are familiar features of the slums.

On average Thais are getting fatter as they get richer. The number overweight in the country increased from 5 percent in 1985 to 15 percent in 1995. According to the polls, however, Thais don't care. They've gained a taste for fast food and convenient ready-to-eat meals that mean they don't have to cook. The man of the house is looking a little fatter and that's partly due to the fact that his wife hasn't got time to cook for him now she's working as well, nor do his daughters who have work of their own or are off at college.

As a consumer society has grown in Thailand, so there has been a complete overhaul of the financial sector. Economists are panicking, but not so the retailers. Thais now think nothing of slapping down the plastic for that new wide-screen TV or designer suit, even a holiday. Savings are being eroded, true, and the savings to investment gap is becoming a problem, but not enough to stop credit-card applications from pouring in.

The use of credit cards in Thailand has prompted the Finance Ministry to curb spending by those traveling overseas. Total credit-card spending has reached US$320 million a month with about two-thirds on international cards (Mastercard, Visa and American Express) and the rest on locally issued plastic.

How to keep winning the middle class

✦ *Break them down* – In Malaysia and Singapore segments such as cappuccino, espresso and decaffeinated are breaking the coffee market open all over again. Retailers like US-owned The Coffee Bean and Starbucks are not slow to exploit this trend. In South Korea, near beers, dry beers and micro-breweries are segmenting the massive beer market. Clothes retailers who have introduced workwear, casualwear and sportswear into their collections have found appeal to the new multifaceted middle class. The rise of the western taste for dress-down Fridays is also forcing the Asian middle class to pay attention to its wardrobe.

No sooner has the middle class found a taste for something than the market segments in a process of extremely rapid diffusion.

- *Luxury and value* – These appear to be mutually exclusive, but look at the winners in the retailing stakes, for example discounters such as the Dutch-owned Makro chain. Before the economic downturn the new middle class liked to enjoy its wealth in department stores such as Sogo, Isetan and Tangs. In post-meltdown Asia the middle class is seeking additional value on regular purchases. Hence Makro's continuing success while the department store chains admit to feeling the pinch.

- *Get them young* – The newly expanding Asian middle class is never too young to have a credit card, insurance policy or private medical scheme. Those manufacturers and retailers targeting teens are realizing the benefits that brand loyalty can bring over time as teens become young professionals with high salaries.

6

Moving On, Moving In

Asia is the world's most densely populated region, so its cities are some of the world's most overcrowded. Providing housing for urban populations, which are growing at much faster rates than national populations, has therefore become a major planning concern of most Asian governments. In the poorer countries of the region the situation is drastic – Mumbai has five million people living in shantytown conditions, Manila 40 per-cent of its population in slums. However, in the more developed cities it is a question of upgrading rather than moving people out of utter poverty.

In Asia's growing consumer-driven markets, demand has appeared for a wide range of housing, varying in price to meet the needs of different income groups and tastes. There is the extra concern of where residents can store the increasing number of private belongings and vehicles at their place of residence.

Across the region new housing is appearing, both public and private, in an unprecedented wave of building. This housing is highly targeted: condominiums for the professional middle class, new public housing at the lower end to reduce overcrowding and luxury mansions for the region's new rich.

Whole new styles of housing have appeared in the emerging markets of Asia, China being a prime example. Beijing residential and business floor space rental prices topped those of London or New York in the mid-1990s, due to the increase in demand overtaking the supply of new and existing space.

This has meant that those with enough money in Beijing are able to buy into the few luxury apartment blocks being built in the city center, but also into new edge-of-town housing developments made up of luxury houses, often with gardens and garages. This is a type of housing that would have seemed impossible in the more rigidly communist China of only a few years ago. In Shanghai, a survey of savers found that 11 percent were saving to buy or build their own houses, twice the percentage of a previous poll where only 5.7 percent were doing likewise.

These new types of housing can only be afforded by the very richest at the moment, but this segment of the population is increasing rapidly. In the countryside, such housing is becoming quite common, often self-builds put up by richer farmers who have made good by switching to lucrative cash crops early on during Deng Xiaoping's economic reforms.

With growth in house ownership comes growth in demand for new types of products. Garden supplies, DIY equipment, furniture, carpets and decorative lighting have all become boom areas in the retail industry in China, as they have in such countries as Taiwan, Malaysia and Singapore, all for much the same reasons.

These changes in living conditions have therefore had a profound effect on consumer attitudes and expectations. The new lifestyles have become the aspirational peak for many people lower down the income scale, and demand for DIY materials, new furnishing and carpeting has also risen among these consumers.

- ✦ Asia's new homeowners are becoming increasingly 'house proud', boosting the market for housewares and everything from table linen to hose pipes.
- ✦ Many of the new homeowners are first-time gardeners on the market for seeds, garden tools and shrubbery.

- ✦ DIY is an increasingly popular pastime as homeowners want to improve their homes with help from the new DIY superstores.

Greater wealth in society has created demand for a better quality of life, especially better housing. This continued desire will ensure that new home building will carry on at a rapid rate for several years to come, and this will have a knock-on effect on the development of new roads, new retail parks and business centers. These developments will in themselves cause the continued spread of city boundaries to incorporate smaller satellite towns and villages.

Governments across the region have urged citizens to buy their own homes and the banks have all developed starter packs and mortgage offers. The Chinese government allocated US$11.8 billion in 1998 solely for housing loans to encourage home ownership. This is intended to boost the Chinese market for homes which in 1997 saw over US$5.4 billion invested in house buying, a rise of 40 percent over 1996. While some commercial banks in China have been allowed to offer mortgages, the state still retains the role of major lender.

The rush to be homeowners

Private flats are being snapped up every weekend in Singapore with buyers clamoring for properties around the US$1 million mark. One weekend in April 1997 the *Singapore Business Times* visited Springbloom, a condominium project built by MCL Land. This is how it described the scene:

'In the lobby outside the show flats, groups of buyers were seen talking deals. Other would-be buyers spilled over into the show flats themselves, doing their sums with agents and bank executives at dining tables or, in the case of one family, the kitchen counter. The same scene was repeated yesterday afternoon, with cars lining both sides of Lorong Chuan and spilling into Serangoon Ave 3. By evening, 60 of the 248 units were sold. All units at Springbloom are priced at under S$1.2 million.'

Property speculation reached epidemic proportions in Singapore in 1996 and forced the government to introduce anti-speculation measures. Executive condominiums are a new development which have become big business, hybrid creations formed by a mixture of public housing and private flats. Exec condos are built on 99-year leases on state land and sold at a third less than private flats. Buyers are required not to sell for five years, after which they can sell only to local people for another five years. A decade after construction, exec condos can be bought by foreigners.

Condo crazy

'Wake up every morning to panoramic views of undulating landscaped gardens or rolling golf greens, dotted with shimmering lakes. Enjoy a gracious lifestyle in our Mediterranean inspired condominiums, that come equipped with modern amenities and recreational facilities. Revel in the benefits of resort-style country living all year round, while only being 25 minutes away from the capital city. Come live in this tranquil haven, away from the frantic hustle and bustle of city life. Come live at Garden Condominiums – your home amidst nature at her very best.'

The marketing blurb above is from an advert in the Malaysian *New Straits Times* for Hong Leong Properties' The Gardens situated near Kuala Lumpur with 458 units due for completion in 2000. Asia's newspapers are full of adverts with copy like this and artists' impressions of new condo constructions.

Much of the new building in Asia has been of the condominium type. Singapore and Thailand have gone condo crazy and the Philippines is following suit, as is Malaysia. A typical example of Malaysian condo building is a development in Luyang, Kota Kinabalu, which is being constructed by the timber manufacturer TimberMaster Industries. The project combines low-rise and high-rise condos which, according to the brochure, come with 'a lush and tropical ambience for a leisurely lifestyle'. Condo prices in Malaysia start from around US$60,000 for a two- or three-bed suburban apartment.

THE LAP OF LUXURY

Hong Kong has never been a bargain center for houses, but in a city where paying US$10,000 a month for a modest flat raises no eyebrows, continuing sales of homes for up to US$120 million *are* a talking point. The uncertainty over the reunification with mainland China also did nothing to dent prices for luxury properties and ensured Hong Kong's position as the most expensive and exclusive property market in the world. To get the figures into perspective, it is worth noting that the most expensive house ever to enter the US property market was around US$50 million and that had nine acres along with it, an impossibility in the crowded special administrative region.

Malaysian home buyers are more fortunate than many other Asians. At least space is not such a problem. In Hong Kong it is another story. Newly completed condos attract long lines of potential buyers who sign up for coupons allowing them at least a chance to buy. These coupons alone change hands for large sums. All this for apartments that invariably afford no stunning views, no balconies and low ceilings. Typical of this type of construction would be an 800 sq. ft apartment in a tower block with no nearby public transport, remote from the central business district and a lack of shopping facilities. People queue up to pay US$550,000 for such a property.

Apartments targeted at Indonesia's middle class have been springing up throughout the DKI area (Greater Jakarta) but supply is still lagging behind demand with a shortfall of about 40,000 units. That there is demand from the middle class for suitable housing in the DKI is clear. PT Satwika Permai Indah (SPI), a subsidiary of real estate developer Putra Surya Perkasa (PSP), sold 100 percent of its middle-class apartments in the Taman Surya housing complex in western Jakarta. The target market is young professional couples earning between one million and one and half million rupiah a month.

Overestimating the demand

While it is true that the demand for good-quality housing is massive throughout the region, developers are having trouble synchronizing their building timetables with consumers' ability to pay.

In Thailand property developers have been left licking their wounds after yields on condos and apartments dropped well below interest rates. The glut first became apparent in 1994 when Thai builders put up 45,000 condos and sold only 20,000. By summer 1997 vacancy rates were running at 35 percent, developments were being put on hold and construction staff laid off. Property analysts do not expect the oversupply to be corrected until at least 1999.

But the property slump is the fault of overenthusiastic developers, not consumers. Though consumer spending has rocketed in Thailand, the oversupply of housing has meant that prices have remained stable and developers are offering discounts to stimulate occupancy as they are faced with billions of baht in loans they can't repay.

Meanwhile in the Philippines, the largest real estate firm, Ayala Land, has taken note of the Thai debacle and restructured its plans to target middle-income housing only, most of that situated outside of the Metro Manila area. Ayala Land is afraid of a glut in high-end property but is keen to expand its portfolio of mixed-use residential developments. The Philippines has seen a massive rise in the number of property developers in recent years as large tracts of land, much of it former US naval bases, have become available. This new industry in itself is a sign of the changing times in the country – Filipino 'new money' is funding much of the construction rather than the traditional source of finance, the *mestizo* old money of the Spanish-derived population. And new money is often buying the homes too as they are snapped up by those able to call on remittances from abroad, including the thousands of Filipinos still working throughout Asia as domestics and laborers.

Residential development is following industrial development. New house building is springing up in the Calabarzon area where low- and medium-end housing projects are being built in anticipation of the industrial boom. A similar route is being followed in

Indonesia where developers (many of them Singapore based) are investing in new housing in the Bumi Serpong Damai area of Tangerang, 25 kilometers west of Jakarta. Singapore construction giants like Hong Leong are often the driving force in areas such as Tangerang and Bandung where industrial estates are thriving.

Urban living

Most of the new condos being built in Thailand are in the Central Business District (CBD) of Bangkok. The reason many professional people are moving into the CBD is simple: traffic congestion has made suburban living difficult. Bangkok has no mass rapid transit system like Singapore or Hong Kong where the growth has largely been out of town. In Bangkok journey times are horrendously long, hot and bothersome.

Many of the out-of-town developments have become ghost towns with occupancy rates below 20 percent. Unfulfilled tenancy expectations have led to half-finished drains, poor security and, of course, no services. According to Thailand's Finance Ministry, the result is 850,000 unsold housing units, of which 450,000 are in Bangkok. The Ministry predicts that demand for new homes in 1997 was 120,000 for all of Thailand and this figure will undoubtedly be lower for 1998/9.

Take for example Muang Thong Thani, a large housing development near Bangkok airport. This was developed along the lines of the satellite towns that have sprung up in Hong Kong to ease overcrowding. But Thais didn't take to the concept and the development has remained virtually empty.

Hong Kongers themselves are finding that their aspirations to home ownership are often thwarted not due to lack of cash, despite the continuance of astronomical prices, but lack of available properties. The Hong Kong Ratings and Valuations Department estimates new housing supply to be between 22,000 and 33,000 annually but demand to be for 88,000 apartments. Prices rose by 30 percent in 1997 despite the uncertainty of the handover to China and, with the population growing daily, numbers needing accommodation are swelling. At present about half the SAR's population live in rent-controlled public housing estates with a waiting list 150,000 people long.

The Hong Kong Government Property Agency is selling former government-owned flats off to individuals. Prices start from approximately US$489 per square foot including a parking space. These government tenders are popular events for would-be home owners. Typical of the sort of property available is Baguio Villa on Hong Kong's Victoria Road. The building is a high rise built in 1975 and not particularly attractive on the outside, but it does have four-room flats with reserved prices of US$1.1–1.6 million.

Much of Asia's large, cramped urban population is clamoring for new housing. In China, luxury houses on new estates are one answer. Often built outside city perimeters, due to lack of space in the center, the new occupants of houses on these estates are almost automatically in the market for cars (the only transport) and shopping malls with parking facilities in which to stock their larders, leading to the building of hypermarkets and out-of-town cinema-cum-bowling complexes for entertainment.

In Singapore, the Land Transport Authority has coordinated its actions with builders and developers. Residential, commercial and transportation property and facilities are combined in several planned projects. One involves 800,000 square feet with two levels of new retailing space beneath a transport depot and MRT station with 200 homes above. From house, to train, to office, to shops and an investment by the developers of US$238 million. What more could the hard-working, heavy-consuming Singaporean professional require?

This mix of residential and commercial is the hallmark of much of the development across the region. It is generally assumed by builders that the targeted middle and upper middle classes want access to all their needs close by. It is this philosophy that has led PT Plaza Indonesia Realty to sink an additional US$225 million into expanding its Plaza Indonesia property in Jakarta. The expansion will increase floor space by 153,000 square meters with a shopping center, a 50-floor office building and apartment complexes.

Where will they put it all?

The relationship between living space and consumption is one that is taxing the minds of every interior designer in Asia, professional and amateur. As people move into their new homes or redesign their existing ones in a world of growing disposable income and wealth, so they are faced with the question, 'Where will we put all this stuff?'

Expectations are changing. Parents want their privacy, as do grandparents. Children want their own toy-filled rooms, teens their own dank pits and students space to study. Mum wants her kitchen, Dad his den, everyone wants a bath, shower, WC – one each – and plenty of storage cupboards. Increasingly families want gardens, or at least balconies, and a garage for the car would be nice.

People are starting to acquire stuff that takes up room: computers, TVs, videos, hi-fis, lawnmowers, toys, books and, of course, furniture. Kitchens are bursting with microwaves, fridge-freezers and blenders. Walls strain with art, air conditioners and framed certificates of educational achievement. And all the time parents remember, partly with fond nostalgia but mostly with horror, the overcrowding of their own childhood.

This is the central conundrum of modern Asian homesteaders. No sooner do you get your new dream palace than it becomes full of your stuff. The new homes are undoubtedly nicer, airier, free of damp and dry rot, but not necessarily a great deal bigger.

Additionally, many of the new homeowners in the middle class are doing things differently to their parents' generation. Hong Kong's professional classes are entertaining at home more, rather than as traditionally at restaurants. This has increased demand for silver, china, crystal and linen for entertaining which had not previously been required. This new trend of showing off your home and using it for dining has also reportedly boosted sales of wine and pushed up prices of the most popular Margaux, Latour, Le Pin and Château Lafite. These changes are starting to be echoed by other new middle-class homeowners across the region.

Cashing in on the new homeowners

Across the region professionals are getting their mortgage applications in, arranging completion dates and calling the movers. Once they're in their new houses, no sooner do they sit down than they have to go shopping (although increasingly they just flip through a catalog and use the phone). And in the last five years the range of DIY, furniture, home furnishing and textiles stores across the region has exploded.

Home improvements and furnishings are massive growth sectors and as more housing becomes available the market can only grow. Cars and buses of couples, young and old, with children and grandparents in tow, pulling up outside home-improvement stores is becoming as familiar a sight in Asia as it is in Europe or the US.

When UK-based retailer BhS set up shop in 1997 in the Sunway Pyramid shopping complex in Petaling Jaya, Kuala Lumpur, Malaysians made a beeline for the store's home furnishings department. British pot pourri, cushions and lampshades were snapped up, as were ready-made curtains and crockery sets. The array of soothing pastel colours inherent in the BhS line found instant favor with Malaysian homeowners.

In Indonesia, a surprisingly large number of people own their own homes. However, as in some other parts of Asia, labor remains cheap and this has restrained the DIY craze for the moment. Still, stores such as the two 15,000 sq. ft Ace Hardware outlets in the Lippo Supermall and the Megamall Plaza are doing brisk business and have ambitious expansion plans.

In India, although the rising middle class can often afford to pay for the best paints and other decorative materials, there is still a fairly conservative taste in decoration, people being more concerned with covering walls to protect from the humidity. However, it is a large country and there is a general tendency for southern Indians to be somewhat more adventurous with their home decor.

The burst of construction activity across Beijing and China's other major cities is a sign that the urban middle class is buying itself new apartments to match its lifestyle. Not far behind has come Home Way. The first Home Way was built in Tianjin as a

100,000 sq. ft warehouse retail outlet stocking everything the new Chinese homeowner could desire. Home Way wasn't the only supplier to the housewares market for long. Britain's B&Q, Germany's OBI and US-based Sentry Hardware have all opened joint ventures in the PRC selling everything from kitchen sinks to cabinets to DIY tools.

And it's not just China. Across Asia, homeowners are spending their Sundays doing up their new homes, whether they be luxury condos in Singapore, high rises in Hong Kong's New Territories or a simple brick structure in Vietnam.

Asia's new towns

Whether it be new satellite towns around Kuala Lumpur or overspill on reclaimed shoreline in Hong Kong, villages turning into new towns along the Pearl River and leisure complexes-cum-cities in the Philippines and Thailand, or the complete relocation of ancient cities, 300 feet upwards along the steep banks of the proposed Yangzi Three Gorges Dam flood area – whole new townships are appearing all over Asia.

Building whole new towns, with more modern infrastructure and more space, will create better conditions for the inhabitants to become consumers of a wider range of products. Many of the people currently filling the new apartment blocks in these new towns are ex-rural dwellers, who have not had to endure the same kind of cramped conditions as their urban cousins and so arrive with new ideas.

Urban people will also come to live in these towns to escape the increasing pollution and congestion of the big cities, and so the mixing up of attitudes will bring about a new type of middle-town mentality.

New towns offer the opportunity for new stores to supply the population and their new mix of tastes and needs. They offer an opportunity to break from tradition and open up new types of retail outlet, with new product ranges, along with new leisure industries and so on. This is mimicked in the new suburbs, but in the established towns and cities the old style lingers on in the collective culture. It is often the new towns and cities which provide the biggest opportunities to break with traditional buying trends and to offer new ideas in home design and decoration – even in how the home is used.

Traditional Asian cities, with their small homes and many cheap restaurants, tend to make people socialize out of the home. In new suburbs and towns, the idea of home entertaining and leisure is much more practical. If people are entertaining both themselves and friends in their new homes, the drive increases to create a home habitat of which the owner can be proud, that reflects their success, values and is more inviting. This is in part why the urge to decorate is now so strong within many developing countries in Asia.

The Chinese Monopoly board

In China the process of new private-ownership house building is just kicking off and is therefore worth looking at in some detail due to the huge potential demand.

This demand stretches right across the income levels and is felt most urgently in the already overcrowded major cities. This often means that even poor housing – built during the height of communist dogma when uniform, concrete blocks of apartments, the utilitarian living quarters of a classless, worker society, were the norm – is still crammed with families, despite being badly maintained and poorly served by utilities.

For those who have made fortunes out of the economic boom in China, there is an opportunity to move upwards in terms of housing since developers spotted the demand early on for luxury flats and houses. These take many forms, but there are two main types of new development: the high-rise condominium-style apartment blocks in city centers and the estates of new, luxury houses in the suburbs.

Chinese cities lack space for new development and the high-rise condominium has become a common feature in Beijing, Shanghai and Guangzhou. Large billboard posters illustrate the utopian aspirations associated with these new developments which, from the evidence in the windows of newly opened estate agents, can fetch prices of well over US$120,000 each. When apartments are built in Beijing, with prices already this high, they tend to be bought up (cash on the nail) before the buildings are even complete, such is the demand and the amount of saved, expendable income.

Take the example of the Sanquan Apartment Building in Beijing's Chaoyang District. Located near the embassies and new five-star hotels in the Chinese capital, the development consists of three apartment towers and a list of amenities including tennis and squash courts, swimming pool, simulated golf driving range, fitness center, sauna, supermarket, beauty center, karaoke, satellite TV, European furniture and 24-hour security.

With the luxury of space comes the desire to decorate that space in an individualistic way. In a country of 1.2 billion people, most of whom wore Mao suits in one of three colors (green, blue and grey), the urge to express one's individuality is intense. At first it was colorful, often garish clothing, now, with the property boom well under way, interior design is all the rage.

Interior design magazines and books are among the most popular and bestselling in China, as the new rich experiment with every style conceived so far in the west and the east, mixing these up to arrive at something new and individual. China's new homeowners have so far opted for imported foreign magazines, but craftily titled domestic publications such as *Decoration* and *Furniture* have appeared on the market.

Condo developers have even incorporated some of the passing fashions for interior design into their buildings. In 1995, for example, the fad was for mock Imperial Chinese style, with plenty of gold and red trimmings, even gold-colored internal columns, decorated with relief designs of rampant dragons and phoenixes.

The second main type of housing in China is the estate house. New houses tend to be three storey, with a garage sometimes incorporated depending on demand. In southern China, most are flat roofed with a sun terrace on top, allowing for some privacy when drying the week's washing.

More significantly, these houses have gardens. Gardens are the supreme luxury in a country where private space is at a premium. They also hark back to an age when the scholar gentleman would write poetry in his formal, walled garden, an aspiration to which many Chinese are drawn.

Public parks have often been the only form of cheap, mass entertainment that many city-dwelling Chinese have known, but on a Sunday in most inner-city parks the joy of nature has to be shared with millions of others, all in search of peace and quiet – a self-defeating pursuit. A private garden, on the other hand, means that the desired peace is not only within the confines of the home but, more importantly, is private.

It is no wonder that more of these new estates with gardens are popping up increasingly rapidly on the edge of city centers, and sometimes in the outer parts of central districts. Ownership of a garden changes a consumer's outlook on their home in several significant ways:

- ✦ The outside appearance of the home becomes more important – who wants to sit in their lovely garden and look at a shabby house?
- ✦ A garden is to be cherished and so spending on decoration for the garden becomes significant.

One only has to see the size of garden ornament shops in Malaysia, where statues, fountains and urns are all for sale to a largely ethnic Chinese population, to see how demand for such goods will grow in mainland China.

Upkeep of buildings means learning about brickwork, plumbing, electrics and plaster, or learning about who can maintain these features and how to reach them at 3 am. Decorating and repair companies have begun to appear in China. Small-scale builders and tradesmen have increasingly seen potential away from the concrete dust of large-scale construction projects.

Lastly there is China's new rich town. An example is to be found just outside Qingdao, in Shandong province. Whole new town centers, with condos, housing estates, shopping malls, golf courses, marinas, the whole package, are being created in the richer parts of the country, such as Qingdao or in the Pearl River delta region. These are to be the playgrounds of those who have really struck it rich in China, including the wealthy of Hong Kong who have become fed up with that city's cramped conditions and are resigned to becoming an integrated part of communist China.

These places also have a ready market in expatriate executives, such as the Japanese managers of joint-venture companies, posted to China with initial reluctance, then loathe to leave when they discover that they can have a whole golf course on their doorstep, rather than just a driving range in a suburb of Tokyo. Such new towns tend to be set somewhere on the southern coast, much of which remains undeveloped but within the reach of the boom towns, and all will eventually have their five-star hotels.

This is only the first step in the development of a Chinese riviera, where the playboys of the east will come to spend their considerable amounts of cash. These new enclaves of consumers will be very different to the mass of Chinese, still stuck in clamorous cities or the impoverished countryside, and they will create a whole new consumer culture, more akin to the excesses of California than anywhere else, but with a distinctly Asian feel to it.

These developments are the pinnacle of the consumer ladder in China and will no doubt become the backdrops for popular soap operas (several are already planned), much as Dallas, Los Angeles and Denver were to the US in the 1970s and 1980s. The fact that China, still a communist state, will have such opulence will no doubt have repercussions, whether they be envy, emulation, jealousy, contempt or a mixture of all of these. The existence of such places will alter how the Chinese see their country and their place within it, and will have an inevitable effect on how they respond as consumers.

In 1989, there was already a locally made version of the globally popular board game Monopoly, called Qiangshou (literally 'strong hand'), with fictitious places replacing the famous London or New York landmarks. How long will it be before Chinese people can play at building hotels on Chang'an Avenue?

How to market to the new homeowners

- Home ownership is a new environment for many Asians. New homeowners are aspiring to new environments, often highly conscious of not replicating the tastes of their parents. They are very open to ideas – they are mixing modern and traditional, eastern and western.

- The developed markets of the region are more attuned to mixing styles and creating lifestyle images, whereas in China and other less developed countries style often happens spontaneously.

- Small is beautiful in Asia as most homeowners still lack large amounts of surplus space.

- Financial services companies are finding that people across the region are now seeing loans for home improvement as a worthwhile investment. Additionally, there is a growing market for interest-free credit in furniture stores.

- As people become more and more house proud so new markets appear and blossom such as dining room furniture, carpeting and wallpaper, all non-traditional accessories in Asia.

- As new homeowners increasingly count the pennies and still seek to make improvements, the market for DIY is growing. Self-assembly furniture, remodeling kits and tools are all becoming required items.

- Most new homeowners in Asia are first-time buyers and this is propeling the market for ancillary services such as estate agents, removal companies, insurance policies and, at the upper end, interior designers and home security.

Part Two

The Consumer Environment

7 Growth of the Megacity

Perhaps the greatest influence on consumer attitudes and habits is the environment in which a consumer lives. And of all the environmental elements that have an influence on human culture, cities are the most potent. The figures for urbanization in Asia are astounding: in the 1970s less than 40 percent of Asians were city dwellers, far fewer in China and Indonesia, but now the ratio is at least 50:50. Excluding China, between 1980 and 1990 over six million Asians moved to the cities. With the figures for China factored in, over 21 million Asians became urban dwellers each year, that's roughly 60,000 people a day moving from country to town.

Cities are the tropical rainforests of human society – as the rainforests are rich in biodiversity, so cities are the breeding places of the greatest variety of modern culture. They are also the epicenters of consumerism. They are locations for the great concentrations of retailing infrastructure, they set the trends, dictate the market and are home to the bulk of the active consuming population.

Asian cities are no exception. Even though the region is dominated by its historically rural culture, the urban has a long history in most of the region and Asia's major metropolises have been founded on trade and commerce. They are where the employment and earnings potential resides. Target the cities and you target affluent Asia.

The old tradition of movement from countryside to city is being witnessed across the region, though with a rapidity never before seen. Every minute of every day would-be urbanites are arriving in the cities, changing them from sizeable metropolises to megacities in the space of a few years.

The population movements now occurring in Asia are unique. They are not due solely to industrialization the way the English Industrial Revolution sucked agricultural communities wholesale into the teeming nineteenth-century production centers of Manchester, Liverpool and Leeds. Nor are they the result of economic and agrarian disaster like the great migrations of Americans from the mid-west to the emerging cities of Los Angeles, Chicago and Detroit in the 1930s. The new Asian urban dwellers bring with them new problems for city administrations charged with planning the growth and expansion of the booming conurbations. The responses have been radical, from closed cities in China (a largely unsuccessful policy) to widespread house building to accommodate the newcomers.

The urban influence

Cities in Asia are the main source of consumerism and the breeding grounds for most new consumer trends. These trends then filter out via the suburbs and provincial towns into the rest of the country.

A perfect example of this is the spread of modern retail outlets in countries such as China. At the beginning of the 1990s, it was possible to count the number of modern-style supermarkets in the whole of the country on one hand. By 1995, the figure was somewhere near 5000. These supermarkets started springing up in the main commercial cities of Guangzhou, Shanghai and Beijing, and were mostly Hong Kong or Japanese funded. As time went by, more of them began to appear in the city centers, then in the suburbs and

URBAN VS RURAL

By 2025, one third of the world's population will be living in Asia's cities. In the space of just 50 years, the region's cities will have turned from being largely devoid of running water and sanitation where non-motorized forms of transport were the norm, to metropolises complete with public transport systems, flush toilets and one-stop shopping malls. In the late 1990s, Asian cities are already the trophies of national success and the new consumerism.

% urban population	1997
China	32.0
Hong Kong	94.9
India	28.1
Indonesia	37.3
Japan	77.7
Malaysia	55.4
Philippines	56.1
Singapore	100.0
South Korea	82.3
Taiwan	74.6
Thailand	27.6
Vietnam	22.1

Source: National statistics

provincial cities, such as Hangzhou and Nanjing near Shanghai. Now the companies setting up these stores, such as Shanghai Hualian and Leduoduo in Guangzhou, are laying out plans for expansion into the Chinese interior, beginning with the larger cities, especially Wuhan, Chongqing and Chengdu, but eventually in most medium-sized towns.

Cities are porous, they leak at the edges and suburbs expand, taking the form of either middle-class enclaves as in Singapore or slums as in Bangkok. In Manila, slums grow in the shadows of glass-fronted tower blocks. Singapore already has more in common with the old Italian city states of 200 years ago than a modern US or European city. China's Special Economic Zones (SEZs) are essentially massive areas of settlement built around a cluster of cities, often less than a decade old, which form the economic core of the zone.

Zone living

With rapid new development come new towns, suburbs and even whole new cities. China's rapid economic growth over the past decade has fueled the spread of a whole series of new cities, especially in the SEZs of southern and southeastern coastal China.

Shenzhen is the epitome of the new city and is famous as a place of opportunity and the center of new economic development (it even has its own stock exchange). But what is it like? Is it really the ideal location for making capitalist dreams come true, for getting rich and living in luxury?

For a few this may well be the case. There are hundreds of new factories and office blocks in Shenzhen, which all testify to the fortunes that have been made in the city. Its streets also bear witness to the wealth of the city, its citizens dressed in smart suits, with mobile phones and drinking at bars serving expensive brandies.

But this is the life lived by only a few of Shenzhen's displaced residents. Nearly everyone is from somewhere else. Shenzhen was itself a tiny village until the SEZ was set up and construction of the new city took off. The workers, the managers, the street cleaners – all of them came from elsewhere in China, having left the security of the extended family unit, which brought them up with traditional Confucian values.

This displacement is a crucial feature of Shenzhen. Chinese society is based around the family unit, which begs the question: what is a Chinese without a family? Without a family the restraints of traditional values fall away, and selflessness departs in favor of the selfish pursuit of cash and pleasure. In a way, Shenzhen has become like the old prospecting towns of California at the end of

China's Chinatowns

Shenzhen is just one example of how people from all over China have congregated in the country's main urban centers. These places offer better economic opportunities than people's native counties or provinces.

Shanghai was like Shenzhen in many ways. Prior to the invasion of the European colonial powers in the nineteenth century it was a small fishing village (as was Hong Kong). As both of these cities grew, they attracted the more adventurous Chinese who set up businesses, trading with the foreign powers. These businesses grew and began to employ more people from other parts of China, just as is happening in Shenzhen now.

The people who arrived in these cities, including Wuhan, Tianjin and even Beijing, came from all over China and doubtless felt the same sense of being cut off from their ancestral homelands as many in Shenzhen do now. The new arrivals spoke different dialects from each other and the locals – many Chinese dialects being as mutually indecipherable as German is to Spanish. They therefore sought out the company of other people from their neck of the woods.

These small 'expatriate' communities grew as more people arrived and communities formed around certain areas within the cities. In these areas, local regionally representative clubs and societies were set up, mostly as mutual self-help societies. Restaurants and teahouses appeared serving local dishes and became places to go where people could speak their own dialect and still be understood.

Thus grew up what became Chinatowns within Chinese cities. Many of these communities have been dissipated by the tumult of China's recent history, but in certain parts of cities such as Beijing and Shanghai they still exist. In Beijing's university area, for example, many of the so-called national minorities (people not of Han Chinese descent) have chosen to live together, perhaps feeling more in common with the foreigners who come to study in this area than they do with the local Chinese.

the nineteenth century, filled with dispossessed men in search of some fabled fortune, facing the reality of crime, grime and the base pleasures of alcohol and prostitutes.

A frontier town indeed, Shenzhen ends, rather abruptly, at the border with the New Territories of Hong Kong, at the railway station, where most of its residents will have arrived, the airport still being rather basic. There are men with the false smile and platitudes of someone scheming how best to relieve you of your cash. Most of these men are single, or seem so. Their wives, if any, are a safe distance away, in some hinterland province, and the only contact is a monthly wad of cash and a letter, informing the parents (who will inform the wife) how the prodigal son is getting on.

Crime is becoming rife in some parts of China and Guangdong province is its hub – and the focal point of Guangdong's crime is Shenzhen, the center of smuggling operations into and out of Hong Kong. Prostitution is overt, even in the top hotels, feeding off visiting businessmen, Chinese and foreign. Other grim realities include the leprous beggars on the street, even on the overhead walkways linking the railway station with the best hotels. It is not uncommon to be mugged by a boy as young as seven. The locals seem able to remain unaware of the abject poverty around their feet – not so the foreigner, who is a soft and rich target for beggars.

From a distance, Shenzhen's glittering towers make an impressive skyline, these new skyscrapers glittering white, topped with brightly colored neon signs which light up the sky at night. What these monuments to the success of the few manage to divert your eyes from are the slums which they straddle. Slung around the factories are the temporary shacks, bare concrete dormitories and tin toilet cabins of the poor. There are no services, little in the way of clean water, and rubbish is everywhere.

Most of the workforce in Shenzhen live in such places, especially the many who come in from outlying provinces, lured by the prospect of wages double what they can earn at home. In the factories conditions are atrocious, hours are long and safety is a taboo word. Those who have been there for a while and have moved up the work ladder can afford to rent small apartments in high-rise concrete blocks. These are less than 15 years old, yet look as if they have been there for half a century: badly maintained, with poor electrics, badly ventilated, rubbish collecting in stairwells and, wherever you live, a stone's throw from a 24-hour building site, the thump of pile-drivers beating just irregularly enough to be really annoying.

Things are improving. The numerous factory accidents have forced some changes in working conditions. New housing continues to go up, so at least there are opportunities for people to move out of the slums.

However, Shenzhen seems soulless in comparison with older Chinese cities, even the last wave of new cities such as Shanghai, Qingdao and Wuhan, all of which have the romance of the last century about them. It is no wonder that one of the Hong Kong people's greatest fears about reunification with China was the inevitable spread of Shenzhen's rapidly expanding conurbation in their direction, bringing with it more of the violent crime which has already manifested itself in the form of armed raids in Hong Kong shopping malls.

Asia's cities are still forming, still growing, they are in a state of flux. It is too soon to draw any permanent conclusions as to their long-term effects on the region's social and economic fabric. The new cities are based around migration, new industries and fresh areas of potential as once remote regions find themselves located on the new trade routes of the late twentieth century, just as Hong Kong and Singapore found themselves on the trade routes of the eighteenth and nineteenth centuries.

Engines of growth

Cities are the engines of Asia's growth. The Asian countries with the highest per capita wealth are also those with the most developed urban centers – Hong Kong, South Korea, Singapore and Taiwan.

Perhaps the new metropolises best represent the economic miracle that has hit the region. They were also where the economic downturn was most keenly felt. Just as the skyscraper culture of US industrial cities represented a booming new confidence (albeit

ASIA'S MAJOR CITIES

Of the world's 25 largest cities, 13 are in Asia. The region's megacities are growing at a rate in excess of 2 percent per annum. The number of Asian cities with populations exceeding 1 million will have doubled by 2015. By the year 2005 in excess of 4.2 billion Asians will be urban dwellers.

	1996	2005	% growth
Chongqing	30,020,000	32,121,000	7.0
Mumbai	15,093,000	21,208,000	40.5
Shanghai	15,082,000	19,435,000	28.9
Jakarta	11,500,000	16,748,000	45.6
Beijing	12,590,000	16,086,000	27.8
Calcutta	11,673,000	13,960,000	19.6
Delhi	9,882,000	13,561,000	37.2
Seoul	11,641,000	12,719,000	9.3
Metro Manila	9,280,000	12,354,000	33.1
Guangzhou	7,160,000	10,200,000	42.5
Bangkok	6,566,000	8,210,000	25.0

Source: National statistics

somewhat dampened by the 1929 Wall Street Crash), so skyscrapers such as Kuala Lumpur's 445 meter high Petronas Twin Towers symbolized Malaysia's growing self-confidence. Cities engender national growth through the networking of investment, innovation and finance within their boundaries. Ultimately, it is the ability of the cities to recover from the turmoil that will determine Asia's future.

Cosmopolitanism

Cities are the first points of entry not only for foreign goods, but also for foreign culture and fashion. The major cities are where new influences on Asian culture are concentrated, assimilated and often altered to comply with local tastes.

City dwellers in Asia see themselves as cosmopolitan. They are well educated, well informed and, more often than not, wealthier. They are the shapers and the innovators of consumer culture in each country.

The fact that city dwellers are so significant has not escaped the attention of foreign companies moving into Asian markets. Not only do most enter via the cities because average incomes are higher, but even before they begin trading most avail themselves of market surveys and research focused on the attitudes of consumers in the main urban centers.

Megacities

A megacity is an urban conurbation with 10 million people or more and is undoubtedly a complex organism. Large cities tend to fill politicians with hope and dread: hope because controlling a major city is immediate political power, and dread because city populations are notoriously uncontrollable and volatile.

The megacities become repositories of wealth, consumption and inward investment. They become the home bases of the domestic advertising, marketing, retail and broadcasting communities. They attract the young and the ambitious. By 2010 hardly an Asian country will be lacking a megacity.

This raises problems for urban planners. Asia's megacities already exhibit the effects of rapid growth – pollution, traffic congestion and housing shortages. Problems of waste disposal, sanitation and disease will need to be tackled if they are to remain liveable and vibrant. Additionally, the continuing inmigration is a disrupting experience for some. The World Health Organization (WHO) has argued that one of the main causes of the growing use of tobacco and alcohol in Asia is increased urbanization. It claims that: 'urban migration uprooted people from their cultural traditions encouraging new lifestyle patterns and promoting detrimental habits such as smoking and excessive use of alcohol'.

The megacity network

The emergence of the new economic centers that are the Asian megacities is creating whole new prime trade routes, channels for the flow of goods to supply the ever-increasing consumer demand. Historically, trade in this region was governed by the trade routes of the South China Sea and the Malacca Strait between Malaysia and Indonesia. However, these traditional routes were developed in order to transport goods between Asia and Europe, whereas now the bulk of trade is within the east Asian region.

The need to process increasingly large quantities of goods as they enter and leave each country has created the demand for ever bigger container ports, capable of shifting vast amounts of goods very quickly and of accommodating the massive bulk-carrying ships which now account for most of the region's physical trade. New ports and expanded docking facilities are being built throughout the region.

In China, the need for better goods handling has been met by the development of new container ports all around the SEZ cities of the Pearl River Delta, in Xiamen, Shanghai and Tianjin, as well as in Liaoning in the north. Hainan Island, previously part of Guangdong Province but now a Special Development Province in its own right, has become the center of new shipping-handling activity and the whole east side of the island is set to become one of the largest bulk container-handling ports in the world.

It is no coincidence that the new container-handling ports are being established in close proximity to the largest of the new developing megacities.

The physical city

The structure of any city is a crucial factor in how the consumer attitudes of its citizens are formed and develop.

One of the most influential physical aspects of many Asian cities is their sheer size, both in terms of area and population. As well as the megacities, the development of megalopolises such as Tokyo,

Shanghai and the confluence of urban centers around the Pearl River delta, from Hong Kong through Shenzhen, Guangzhou, round to Shantou and Macao, has been a feature of the importance that cities have in the emerging market economies.

These physical entities draw attention from people within these countries, but also from those abroad. Conscious of this, the administrators have become aware of their cities' political importance, as have the citizens who live there. This awareness has begun to emerge as a new form of regional patriotism, an example being the view of many Shanghainese that their city should be the financial center of Asia, rather than Hong Kong or Tokyo and certainly not Beijing.

Another effect of the attractive draw of the major cities is that people from all over a country, and also from outside, become mingled together in one place. They are sharing and swapping experiences, influencing changes in each other's attitudes about other people and places and heightening understanding of what these places have to offer.

This shared experience is all part of the larger process of what is nowadays known as globalization. It is creating greater homogeneity between regions and countries. How else could McDonald's now exist throughout Asia and why else would so many Asians be learning to speak English and other European languages, so they can communicate on a common footing with people in countries they may never get the opportunity to visit.

It is this sort of process that has allowed many western educational establishments to set up courses in Asian countries, an example being the University of Leeds which has established a whole business studies department in downtown Singapore. This has become even more important as currency exchange rates preclude many students from studying overseas in the post-turmoil environment.

The development, size and success of Asia's cities vary from country to country, but one thing is for sure. The new metropolises are changing the demographic and social map of the region irreversibly and therefore are also having a major impact on the development of patterns of consumption.

The cost of living

However, large cities, especially megacities, become expensive places to live. A *Washington Post* survey found that Beijing, Hong Kong, Seoul and Guangzhou all fell into the top 10 most expensive cities in the world. Others making the list were the Japanese cities of Tokyo and Osaka, along with the special cases of Moscow (the cost of security pushing up overall living costs) and the Swiss cities of Geneva and Zurich (bankers tend not to welcome those with less cash than them inside the city limits).

Locating in Asia's cities is not cheap either. Asia is on average 95 percent more costly than the US to locate in and 57 percent more than Europe. Hong Kong and Singapore joined Tokyo at the top of the list for expensive office space, with Beijing, Shanghai and Taipei not far behind. In Beijing foreigners have always paid more and apartment rents are still rising. Two- and three-bedroomed apartments for non-Chinese in the Jianguomen Wai area start at US$2500 per month but US$6000 is not uncommon. Finding a three-bed flat for under US$3500 per month near the city's Lido Hotel is a difficult proposition. And these prices are for apartments averaging just 150 square meters.

City planning

The stereotypical, but often true, picture of Asian cities is of over-populated, bustling streets, filled with wet markets and festooned with brightly coloured shop signs. What sets them apart from cities in other parts of the world is the almost tangible nature of their commercial vitality. Asian urbanites all seem to be very busy, rushing about looking for a viable niche to fill, and are unabashed about displaying their success in doing so.

It is this commercial vitality which not only shapes the attitudes of these city's people, but is also the shaping force behind the physical design of the urban environment. Hong Kong is a prime example, and perhaps the best known, but the model has reappeared throughout Asia, not merely as an attempt to copy the colony's success but as a direct result of the urge to develop felt quite independently in each of the developing nations of the region.

Asian cities are also historically well planned and ordered. Most are there by some imperial design, Hong Kong and Shanghai being the prime exceptions thanks to their colonial past. Cities were traditionally the centers where the intellectual bureaucrats, tasked with the running of state, congregated, with others gathering there to serve the needs of ministers.

The cities therefore attracted satellite communities of traders and artisans who supplied the expensive needs of government, just as medieval European cities grew up around the castles of power. Thus the planning of cities has been a key feature of Asian politics for many centuries and their design was often based around segregation of the political (high) and the commercial (low). Now commerce is king and city centers are being transformed from political power bases into commercial money-processing machines.

One only has to look at the centers of Hong Kong, Shanghai, Singapore, Tokyo, even Beijing, to see how the new god of wealth is paramount. Consider the fact that in Japan, until very recently, no buildings could be built over a few stories high, lest the inhabitants were in the position of looking down on the emperor's palace and by extension on the emperor himself.

Many of east Asia's imperial cities, such as those in Japan, Korea and China, were designed around a grid structure, with the central administrative areas surrounded by residential areas and most commerce being conducted in separate 'ghettos', many of which were based around markets on the outskirts of the cities.

In China, as imperial power waned, the areas around the administrative locations became occupied by rich merchants, who brought commerce into the city centers and encouraged the growth of entertainment such as theaters, hotels, teahouses and wine shops.

This commercialization has continued, but recent developments in modern retailing, especially for larger outlets such as supermarkets and hypermarkets, have meant that the lack of cheap retail space in the center has forced many developers to move away from the inner cities.

The result has been that most of the new supermarket and hypermarket stores being built in Asia are going up in suburban areas, in purpose-built retail parks, while in the city centers there has been a greater focus on updating the existing retail sites, especially department stores.

Suburbs versus the center

The result of the shift in large-scale retailing out towards the suburbs has changed the way consumers are doing their shopping.

Having been served by small, local, specialist retailers for most day-to-day needs, consumers have tended to travel out of their own local area to do their shopping only on a once-a-week basis. This is now changing, thanks to the development of large hypermarkets which supply both day-to-day and infrequent purchase items. Through competitive pricing, these stores are seeing the same customers visiting day after day as well as weekly visits by people who make purchases for the following seven days.

The outcome of this is that the retail situation in many of the more developed of Asia's cities is becoming more like the current situation in western Europe and North America. This trend is still in its infancy and has only occurred in the largest cities. Smaller towns still tend to be served mostly by small local, specialist and general stores throughout the town, with larger department stores in the town centers.

Urban transportation

As Asia's cities have increased in size, the need for better urban transportation networks has become apparent.

With many more people to supply, and the need to move greater numbers of people into and out of city centers on a daily basis, transport has become one of Asian governments' worst logistical headaches. This is a problem not helped by people's increasing wealth encouraging them to own private cars.

Throughout Asia, huge amounts of government money are still being invested in new roads, especially multilane highways, railways and subway systems. These developments have accelerated the increase in size of most cities, creating whole new residential and business areas.

Such changes in the way people get about their cities have also altered their lifestyles. New highways don't necessarily mean that people get to and from work quicker – in fact because the volume of traffic in most cities outgrows the rate of new road building, many new roads have become regularly gridlocked almost as soon as they are opened.

Urban vs rural

The relationship between city and countryside in the emerging Asian economies tends to go through several clear stages of development. Initial economic development is focused on the cities, but for such development to be sustained there has to be a spread of wealth back out to the rural regions, enabling the urban industries to remain well supplied with the raw materials of production.

China's breakneck economic growth has left many rural areas behind, causing the economies of these areas to decline, forcing people to begin to move away from them in search of more lucrative earning opportunities. This has lead to a general migration of labor from the countryside to the main urban centers. This has altered the shape of the cities' populations.

Rural workers who have been successful in finding work in the cities have tended to send the greater part of their earnings back to their home towns, helping to bolster their families' incomes but also injecting much-needed cash into these economies. Absent workers are also acting as transmitters of the new consumer culture out to the rural areas, introducing new products to outlying locations.

People are still living in rural areas, although fewer every day. An anomaly of the growth of urban population has been that birth rates fall in the cities while remaining constant, or even expanding, in the countryside. The cities grow, the countryside continues to replenish itself with candidates for migration, the cycle continues. However, the rural population is beginning to age.

Megacity problems

With the growth of cities and the number of people living in them have come all the problems associated with cities around the world – overcrowding, squalor, inner-city decay, pollution and crime.

These problems are visible across Asia, as are a variety of solutions to combat them. Controlling such huge populations, especially those packed into the large cities, has become one of the main concerns of municipal governments and the methods chosen have tended to depend on the extent of the governmental infrastructure in each country and how much these infrastructures have become strained by the speed of economic development.

The fact that many of the countries of east Asia have developed very rapidly over recent years has meant that their cities have grown very rapidly, as have the social problems connected with these changes. In many countries the authorities have struggled to keep up with the rapid pace of social change, resulting in the adoption of draconian, authoritarian methods to maintain control of increasingly sophisticated social problems.

Western onlookers have often shown scorn for such dictatorial methods of governance. However, in most cases these hard-line stances are necessary. Asia has not had the luxury of developing its commercial and infrastructural organs since the beginning of the industrial revolution, as in western Europe and North America, and in countries such as China, cities like Shanghai and Guangzhou have made a leap over the past 10 years that compares to 200 years of development in such cities as London or Paris.

These dramatic changes are bound to upset the fabric of society and social problems have been an inescapable side effect. Keeping law and order in populations undergoing such fundamental changes is therefore much more difficult and authoritarian measures are more applicable in these situations.

Despite the differences across Asia there are similarities too – the old Asian conundrum of same yet different applies once again. Retail outlets along Orchard Road in Singapore and in the malls of Shanghai, Bangkok and Manila stock many of the same labels and brands, even the retailers themselves are becoming pan-regionally recognizable. All Asian cities have their enclaves of privilege with the new rich and political and professional elite driving the same imported Mercedes and installing the same burglar alarms and CCTV systems. Likewise, all Asian cities increasingly have their no-go areas where the social evils of unemployment, poverty, poor housing and crime are centered. The evils so long associated with western urban living – drugs, murder, organized crime and ghettoization – are becoming apparent social phenomena across the region to varying degrees.

The differing agendas of the modern Asian urban dweller are also appearing. The middle class is concerned about taxes, about schools, hospitals and the pace of urban sprawl. The urban wannabes, those who come to the cities seeking prosperity, have a different agenda, one of housing, sanitation, jobs and opportunity. Subjects such as property prices, zoning, residential growth and even local democracy have now entered the minds of urban dwellers.

Asian citizens seem to prefer to have the law and order necessary for them to work hard and improve their material lives rather than enjoying many political freedoms, but political awareness also increases as people become more financially powerful. Cities have been the central points for the development of political movements the world over and Asia is no exception – the Chinese Communist Party (CCP) is a prime example, having emerged from 1920s Shanghai. Knowing this tendency, it is no wonder that control of law and order in the cities is of paramount concern to most governments in the region.

Where is Asia's capital?

Competition between Asia's cities has become furious over the last decade. The models have been Hong Kong and Singapore, powerful metropolises that have seemingly avoided the urban decay of too many western cities and built their power on investment, labor productivity and geographic locations at the apex of trading routes. But in the late 1990s, with Hong Kong subsumed into greater China and Singapore openly struggling to maintain its lead, a new tranche of cities are entering the battle and each, in their own way, is a contender for the title of Capital of Asia. The list includes Shanghai, Kuala Lumpur, Taipei, Seoul, Tokyo, Singapore and Bangkok.

When it comes to arguments over a capital for Asia, size is not necessarily a determinant. Singapore is far from being a megacity, so is KL, but both are challengers. Big cities come with problems that hamper them. Take Beijing: 12.59 million residents but 14 percent over 60 years old, 250,000 made redundant in 1996, 226,000 unemployed and 175,000 new workers entering the city annually. With figures like this it may not be an attractive center to many. The same is true of Shanghai with a migrant population of three million and poor, though improving, healthcare facilities that have meant high rates of infant mortality.

Singapore

The pundits have been heaping praise on Singapore for years now – the Rolex of cities for its smooth operations, Asia's Switzerland. No doubt Singapore is an oasis of calm compared to down-town Manila or the shanty towns of Jakarta. It is very much a planned metropolis (down to the level of banning bubblegum!) thanks to its small size, lack of surrounding regions and wealth. Despite small rises in the crime rate, it remains one of the safest cities in Asia, education and healthcare are praised, the environment is relatively clean and accommodation well built. However, Singapore is expensive and its unique geographic location and history mean that the city can control entry to its environs in a way no other city in Asia could hope to.

The rapid growth of alternative urban centers of power in Asia, proven by their abilities to attract inward investment, has alarmed Singapore, which is desperately trying to retain its position as the

Falling down, KL style

A British newspaper reported in 1996 that sales of baseball bats had grown phenomenally in KL despite the fact that few people actually play the sport in Malaysia. The reason apparently was that bats had become the weapon of choice for road rage instigators and victims alike in the city's choked streets. A particular black spot is the Klang Valley motorway on which 1.3 million cars struggle into KL daily.

Newspapers have tried to help alleviate the road rage problem. The *Star*, a Malaysian daily, prints a Road Beasties Poll which has even suggested that drivers should be allowed to carry weapons legally despite Malaysia's strong laws against knives and guns. Car sales are rising by 50 percent a year in Malaysia itself and throughout Asia the number of vehicles on the road will at least double by 2000 due to locally made cheap vehicles such as the Malaysian Proton. This growth in car sales means that baseball bat manufacturers are strongly urged to enter what will undoubtedly become a highly competitive car accessories market as soon as possible.

region's hub for electronic commerce and trade. Its traditional role as 'middleman' in international trade and as a re-export center is clearly threatened. Now Singapore is attempting to reposition itself as a global trade city, leveraging the nation's expertise in information technology. But it has competitors, not least neighboring Malaysia.

Kuala Lumpur

The Malaysian census found that 51 percent of the country's population – one in four – were living in the urban areas, compared to 34 percent in 1980. The top five urban areas are Kuala Lumpur, Ipoh, Johor Baru, Klang and Petaling Jaya.

As if having the tallest building wasn't enough, KL will eventually get the longest building too. Malaysian authorities have granted approval for Gigaworld, a 1.8 km long cylindrical structure to be built on stilts above the River Klang. The plan includes a pledge from the developers to clean up the notoriously dirty river and relocate 1000 squatters. Just outside the city limits will be Putrajaya and Cyberjaya, Malaysia's bid to build Asia's Silicon Valley and become the dominant force in IT.

Certainly, the city's multiethnic feel lends it the air of a representative of the region, but despite all the building KL remains a minnow by Asian standards.

Jakarta

Following the events of 1997 and 1998 Jakarta has really written itself out of the running for Asia's capital, yet it remains one of the region's largest cities. The diverse breadth of life on the Indonesian archipelago has meant that the government has long instituted national policies aimed at unity. Perhaps, if current trends persist, that much sought-after unity will be achieved through urbanization.

By the turn of the century an estimated 200 million Indonesians, or 36 percent of the population, will be living in urban areas. Cities with populations over a million will include Jakarta, Bandung, Surabaya, Semarang, Bogor, Medan, Palembang and Ujung Pandang. The bulk of this urban growth will be the result of migration from the rural areas to the cities as the economy expands.

Jakarta has certainly been gearing up to become a business center. During 1996 over 363,000 square meters of office space became available and an additional 1.2 million square meters was planned for completion by 1998.

Taipei

Taiwan's capital city is a fast-paced, heady mixture of Chinese culture, western capitalism and the strong influence of nearby economic superpower Japan. Wealth is visible all over Taiwan and in Taipei it is concentrated and overt. Even the shabbiest of downtown bars will have a TV in a prominent corner, often showing the financial news and stock-exchange prices, when it isn't being used for karaoke videos. With so much wealth created by the Taiwanese genius for manufacturing and trading, playing the stock exchange is to the Taiwanese what betting on horses is to the English. However, despite its wealth, Taiwan is fraught with insecurities, foremost of these being mainland China.

Perhaps Taipei is doomed always to be the outsider. With no one in the region keen to annoy the Chinese mainland, Taiwan has largely been left to get on with things itself. Despite this it has become a glittering metropolis, home to a substantial middle class, some extremely wealthy residents and swathes of development. Like most other Asian cities Taipei has been rebuilding itself. The city's monorail glides silently over the roads which cover its new subway system – its construction has allowed Taipei to avoid the gridlock that never seems to end in Kuala Lumpur or Bangkok. The rail system is perhaps Taipei's *leitmotif*. A problem occurred – traffic congestion – so the city administration dealt with it – US$18 billion worth of new transportation infrastructure.

Taipei was a city built on low-cost manufacture: assembly work boosted the economy tenfold between 1955 and 1985. Now Taipei is welcoming home its foreign-educated sons and daughters who went to US colleges and didn't come back. This injection of intellectual capital combined with home talent is building the city's financial reputation as an investment center. But the shadow of China's mainland looms large. Direct trade is still outlawed and the missile crisis of 1996 did little to ease tensions between the island state and the mainland. Despite the lack of a formal relationship it is still the case that if Beijing catches a cold, Taipei gets pneumonia.

Taipei and its 2.6 million residents may be one of the more relaxed capitals of Asia but it stays at second place, sometimes for good reasons – low crime, cheaper rents than Tokyo, less pollution than KL – and other times for the wrong reasons – not the financial center that Hong Kong is, not the investment magnet that China is.

Seoul

Seoul has grown too fast for its infrastructure to keep up and gridlock is an everyday occurrence. The rapid growth of the Korean economy has also made the population stock-market entrepreneurs, but Koreans have less of the brashness of the Taiwanese, perhaps because of their long history of isolation which helped crystallize a highly formalized culture. Insecurities also abound in Seoul and if students aren't demonstrating about some corrupt official or general, they are debating about the threat of their northern, communist cousins.

Koreans are rightly proud of their independence and resistance to all attempts to colonize them. However, a downside has been that Seoul lacks the diversity of other Asian cities. With 99 percent of the population Korean and spoken English rare, the multinationals have settled for branch offices rather than HQs in the city. Seoul is a major consumer market in its own right – 11.6 million people, a burgeoning middle class and a developed retail infrastructure. Despite the difficulties, it is arguably one of the three main gateways to the region, a link between China and the rest of southeast Asia.

Affluence is familiar in Seoul. South Korea's imports of consumer products have grown by 25 percent a year and most of the big-ticket items are sold in Seoul's Kangnam district where luxury cars, watches and clothing didn't linger for long on the shelves or in the showrooms. But Seoul's bid to be the capital of Asia is hampered by national issues: the plodding, top-heavy bureaucracy of Korean business and the recently exposed questionable organization of the national political situation and finances. The *chaebols* rule and unless you can do business with them, operating in Seoul is difficult to say the least.

Metro Manila

The term 'the sick man of Asia' was a little overused in the 1970s and 1980s when describing the Philippines. But development is moving ahead in Manila. New shopping plazas have sprung up across the city, which is also starting to tackle its congestion problem. Construction has begun on a new 18 kilometer 'skyway' road costing US$550 million. It will eventually charge a toll and bisect the city, linking the growing port of Pagbilao to the Central Business District. Other expressways are being built linking Manila with Clark Airbase and Subic Bay Freeport. At least it will soon be in touch with its hinterland, if not the region as a whole.

Hong Kong

Hong Kong is not yet a megacity, with a population of some six million, but its reunification with mainland China means that the border which has held back the southern expansion of Shenzhen will fall, and the former colony will doubtless become engulfed in the rapid urbanization of the Pearl River Delta region. Following the handover of Hong Kong to the Chinese, a rash of articles appeared in most major newspapers and journals claiming that the SAR was taking over China and not vice versa.

In Hong Kong the Chinese have an example of how to grow a city against the odds. Forty years ago it was largely a refugee camp for people escaping the Communist revolution. Urban planners had shanty towns that needed to become liveable communities fast. Hong Kong rehoused as rapidly as it could, slum clearance occurred overnight and new estates and apartment buildings were thrown up fast. Though somewhat *ad hoc* in its creation, it is now a city with high population density but average levels of reasonable housing quality. There is workable public transport, sufficient office space and open parks and nature reserves as well.

Whether or not Hong Kong's population reaches the magic 10 million, the fact remains that it is one of Asia's key container ports and a center for commerce and finance, as well as being the gateway to southern China, one of the world's fastest-growing economic regions. Due to its history, Hong Kong has developed its own culture, social and corporate alike, which will continue to have an influence on the whole of the eastern hemisphere, both economically and culturally, despite any changes which may be brought in by the Beijing government.

Shanghai, Guangzhou, Beijing and Chongqing

Shanghai and Hong Kong have a great deal in common. Both were established by foreign colonial powers in China from previously undeveloped fishing communities, both are major seaports, and both are cultural and economic centers of key importance to the greater China region. The fact that Shanghai has set its sights on overtaking Hong Kong as the hub of Asian finance and commerce is indicative of how closely these two cities compete with each other.

Shanghai is favored by the fact that it is not as cut off as Hong Kong and has more land on which to expand. Confidence in the city has certainly risen, as testified by the former Japanese retail giant Yaohan's decision to move its Asian headquarters to Shanghai from Hong Kong. Although Yaohan folded, it has set a precedent.

Guangzhou has become a central hub for all the SEZs stationed around the Pearl River Delta and, as such, is the center for a region which is turning into a Pearl River megalopolis, similar in scope to the extended urban sprawl which surrounds Tokyo.

As the focal point of this region of high economic growth, Guangzhou is becoming a strong contender for the title of Asia's commercial capital, although interest in it is tempered by the way the boom town of Shenzhen is developing.

Both Shanghai and Guangzhou compete equally with Beijing, especially in political terms. Shanghai was the cradle of revolution in China and sees itself as the center of the industrial proletariat, so it does not take kindly to some of the decisions made by Beijing on its behalf. Likewise, Guangzhou perceives itself as the capital of southern China, a distinction which has more than geographical significance to the southern Chinese people who speak a Chinese dialect quite unlike the Mandarin of Beijing.

Beijing remains the country's political and cultural center. Without doubt a large degree of power resides in the city that is home to the Chinese government. The common Chinese language, *putonghua*, is based on Beijing dialect. Beijing has become the home to numerous multinational representative offices and embassies. The city is also next to Tianjin, China's major eastern seaport city, and is just a four-hour flight from Tokyo and close to Seoul too.

In one sense Chongqing is the world's biggest city. In 1997 the Chinese government declared Chongqing an autonomous municipality, meaning that the former city of 2.5 million became the world's most populous urban area overnight. In reality Chongqing is an industrial port on the Yangzi River with sprawling and run-down suburbs. With the completion of the Three Gorges Dam project, Chongqing is set to expand further in quantity if not in quality.

Mumbai, Calcutta and Delhi

Are the Indians really in with a shot in Asia? An awful lot of people think not, but then an awful lot of people in the west have not been paying attention to India lately. Many thought this might change in 1997 with the hype that surrounded the fiftieth anniversary of Indian independence. However, what westerners, and particularly the British, saw on their screens and read in their newspapers had very little to do with modern India. *The Raj*, *Gandhi* and *Jewel in the Crown* were shown again to remind those interested in the Empire what a fun time it was. Arundhati Roy, an Indian who writes in English, had a bestselling book in *The God of Small Things* and there were some firework displays.

The reality is that while the west has concentrated on the Merchant–Ivory view of India, Mumbai (Bombay) has increased its population by 400 percent since independence.

Little if any of the new Indian consciousness has filtered through to the west. The boom in entrepreneurship, technology and business in India has been missed. The fact that increasingly India is looking towards Asia, including China, as its sphere of influence has been glossed over. But the west sat up and began paying attention when, in May 1998, India began testing nuclear weapons. Now that it has got people's attention, it will perhaps begin to attract much more of the interest it deserves.

The future for Asia's cities

Without doubt Asia's cities are set to grow and urban populations will increase as greater numbers arrive from the countryside. This could make them increasingly difficult and stressful places to live. Traffic congestion has arrived and cities like Beijing are on the verge of encountering their first gridlocks. Public transport will ease this to an extent, but the growing Asian love affair with the car will not be ended easily.

On the other hand, despite the economic turmoil Asia's cities are increasingly home to the world's major corporations, most powerful governments and residues of talent and creativity. Traffic jams and overcrowding not withstanding, they still remain among the most vibrant in the world.

8

Infrastructure

Anyone traveling through Asia in the last decade would have found it easy to believe that the whole region should be designated a hard-hat area. The pace of clearance, construction and development was hectic and plain to see.

Take Kuala Lumpur, not the worst-served city in Asia in terms of infrastructure by any means. Its skyline is dominated by the symbol of new development for all Malaysia, the Petronas Twin Towers that reach up into the sky. On a September day in 1997, in the first weeks of the ringgit's crisis, the tips of the tower were hidden beneath the blanket of haze that covered the country. The haze itself could be seen as a symbol of the erratic development of the region and its growing interdependence. Generated largely by Indonesian landowners setting fire to thousands of acres of forest, it made breathing difficult. Children were kept indoors, the old and infirm confined to their homes and anyone who could stayed in and caught up on the latest news about the crisis on TV. Walking around the city became a dangerous activity and caused lethargy.

Yet still the numerous building sites kept on working. Malay and Bangladeshi workers kept on climbing the scaffolds and digging out the foundations for the new hotels, plazas and condos. The dump trucks kept on rolling through the choked KL streets, the dust from the building sites mixing with the million exhaust pipes of day-long traffic jams and merging with the haze. The building work went on 24 hours a day, seven days a week. Visitors to the city could look out of their hotel rooms at four in the morning and see sites lit by arclights with workers in bright yellow hard hats scurrying around.

A trillion dollars should do it ... for now

A recent report by the Asian Development Bank forecasted that by 2025 Asia will have 20 megacities with a combined population of 400 million people. The same report warned that a sustainable quality of life and productivity would be impossible without improvements in water supplies, waste management, pollution controls and public transport. In other words, without adequate infrastructure Asia's major urban areas are headed for trouble. Solving this problem will not be cheap. Some have estimated that the bill for infrastructural work between 1996 and 2000 will top US$1,000,000,000,000.

All commercial activity is built around the transfer of goods, from primary raw-material producers to manufacturers to distributors to retailers and finally to consumers. For this process to be achieved solid transportation infrastructure is essential. The infrastructure will determine the pace of development of a consumer society in the region, linking nations, cities and communities together. In post-turmoil Asia the pressure on politicians to stop funding infrastructure projects is immense. If they submit, all the bank restructuring in the world won't solve the problem.

Right now there are thousands of massive infrastructure projects underway to support the expanding consumer bases of the cities and their suburbs. These projects will gradually extend consumerism and consumer power to the rural and remote areas. The rural areas of southeast Asia and China are being brought into the orbit of modernization by the construction of air and sea ports, railways, road networks, electricity grids and treated water.

In the current economic climate some projects have been put on hold. So far, these have been the grandiose projects, the show-off jobs. Asia can afford to hold back on these. On other projects it cannot.

It has been estimated that every additional 1 percent growth in GDP in a given Asian nation requires at the very minimum a further 1.5 percent additional investment in the national infrastructure. The Manila government has stated that infrastructure spending in the Philippines must rise from 5 to 9 percent of total GDP if the country is to support its current growth rates.

The World Bank has estimated that Asia needs to spend roughly US$1.5 trillion on energy, transportation and communications projects between 1995 and 2004. The four nations of Indonesia, Thailand, the Philippines and Malaysia will need, according to the Bank, to spend US$440 billion between them. However, it is China, with a projected necessary spend of US$750 billion, that will be the major expansion point. It is clear that China's infrastructure will be the launch pad for extending the consumer market into the massive inland regions that have lain untapped for over five centuries. From the initial opening up of the economy until 1994 China sucked in US$12.1 billion in foreign investment alone to build 64 power projects. The Chinese coal industry swallowed as much as US$3.76 billion in foreign capital.

The Indonesian way

In his 1995 budget address former President Soeharto told the Indonesian Parliament: 'the great obstacle that now stands in our way is the limited infrastructure'. The country's growth and recovery from economic crisis may well be limited unless those words are heeded.

Public electricity generation capacity grew from a mere 500 megawatts in 1970 to the present 13,000 megawatts and this still falls short of consumer demand, which is growing daily.

In 1970, there were just 142,000 telephone lines. At present capacity is about three million lines, only 1.6 lines per 100 people, the lowest of the ASEAN countries and contrasting with 67 per 100 in Australia.

In 1970, there were only 20,000 km of paved roads. Now 100,000 km of paved roads spread over most of the country, though in many regions the road network is basic to say the least.

Indonesia's cities have grown rapidly without the development of effective rapid mass transit systems. The problem is particularly acute in Jakarta where car registrations grew by 65 percent from 1988 to 1993 and show no signs of slowing, unlike the traffic.

The public water supply system is inadequate and underdeveloped. Piped water is provided to less than 25 percent of urban households.

Despite Indonesia's infrastructural shortcomings, consumer expectations about living standards are rising as a large middle class and higher income groups emerge. To threaten these expectations is politically dangerous, as the upheavals in 1998 showed. This infrastructural shortage is compounded by demands for high-tech support such as mobile phone networks, pager systems, plane trips and cable TV. Indonesia's growing number of car owners are concentrated among these same consumer groups and they are as intolerant of congested roads and city-center traffic jams as they are of inadequate water and power supplies.

Similarly, a large percentage of Indonesia's population still have low incomes and poor living conditions. Hundreds of thousands of urban poor use communal toilets and washing facilities. In rural villages, millions of people have no electricity supply and have to rely on kerosene lighting and dry cells to power televisions and radios. Given the figures above, anyone can see that effectively 75 percent of the population are barred from owning a washing machine and a large percentage from owning a microwave oven, a TV or a stereo.

Poor infrastructure is also increasing company costs in Indonesia. For example, 50 percent of all power for industry is provided by captive generators, invariably high-cost diesel units necessary due to the inadequacy of the public grid. The sparse water supply has left businesses relying on expensive deep-water bores. When the World Bank surveyed Indonesian manufacturers it found that 64 percent had been forced to buy their own private electricity generators and 59 percent had bores for water. Indonesia's largest businesses invested as much as 18 percent of their total capital on private infrastructure, yet their generators were underused and operating at only about 50 percent of potential capacity.

Soeharto was right to claim that infrastructural limitations restrict growth. Lack of power, water and other utilities means that even a society with growing aspirations and incomes as well as access to goods cannot purchase them. The lack of infrastructural support prevents many people from taking the first step into consumerism. And Indonesia is not the only country that needs to upgrade its infrastructure.

In the beginning...

One only has to look at a map of Asia – the thousands of islands and areas of mountainous terrain – to see that transportation on a large scale faces many difficult topographical problems. Just try mapping out a power-supply network for the Indonesian archipelago or a national water-treatment system for the Philippines. It was the shape of the continent which kept it in relative isolation from western Europe for many centuries, making Asian produce difficult and dangerous for European merchants to thrive in, and consequently rare and expensive to buy back in Europe.

But with the coming of new trade routes, industries and demands, Asia and its constituent nations have had to open up, build themselves into modern nations and realize the need for extensive infrastructure.

The 'grand gesture'

Asia has been on a building spree in the last 20 years. The 'grand gesture' in construction has been in vogue, though of course it is not unique to Asia. Malaysia's Petronas Twin Towers, Hong Kong's skyscrapers, the oversized pagodas of Beijing and the giant hotels of Taiwan reflect national pride and achievement as much as do the cathedrals of England and France or the skyscrapers of New York and Chicago. Major international architects have accepted commissions in Asia, including IM Pei in Singapore and Cesar Pelli, the architect of the Twin Towers.

Across the region local architectural practices began to create internationally recognized buildings. These are inspired by Asian history, culture, religion and philosophy. The May Bank building in KL reflects Malaysia's Islamic-influenced culture, for example.

Perhaps the architect attracting most interest in the region is C.Y. Lee of C.Y. Lee & Partners, a Taiwanese architectural practice. Lee has perhaps done more than any other Asian architect to show that regional architecture can be stunning, functional and reflective of national characteristics. Taiwan's buildings have not attracted the worldwide press attention of some other Asian constructions, good and bad, but Taipei's skyline has been transformed by an array of modern buildings such as the 46-story Shin Kong Life Tower (buildings in Taipei are restricted to 60 meters in height by the proximity of Sung Shan domestic airport) and the highly traditional Chiang Kai-Shek Memorial Hall.

C.Y. Lee has been the main motor behind this transformation in design terms. His projects include the Grand 50 skyscraper, numerous condominiums and the 408-meter T&C Tower in Kaohsiung, Taiwan's second city. His first project was the Asia World Plaza, a 140,000 square meter mixed-use development with a hotel and department store. Lee, like many Asian architects, is American trained but has broken with US style. His Grand 50 building was perhaps the first authentically Chinese-style skyscraper. There are influences from New York's Chrysler Building but its pronounced cantilevered cornices lend it a uniquely Chinese feel as well as dispersing incipient wind vortices that can disrupt life at street level.

Lee's T&C Tower dominates Kaohsiung's skyline – 85 stories, a bipod structure with specially constructed towers to prevent the damage possible from typhoon wind loadings. Another innovative Lee building is Taipei's Hung Kuo office building, a 19-story, 60,000 square meter head-office development featuring battered granite-clad walls with deep recesses and a three-story marble lobby. Now Lee is set to take the mainland by storm. Designs for buildings such as Shanghai's Concord Plaza, Zhengou's Yuda World Trade Center and Tianjin's Post & Telecommunications Tower are all scheduled for completion in the twenty-first century.

Whatever these brash new buildings do for Asian self-esteem in a post-turmoil culture is fine, as well as originally being giant sinks for the new-found wealth of the region. However, it is the not so obvious projects that will make the long-term difference. The fiberoptic and satellite links, the mass rapid transit systems and the giant airport terminals will provide the impetus for lasting growth in the region when the immediate economic crisis recedes. Indeed, they must be built if growth is to be maintained.

The nascent automobile market will stagnate without an adequate series of national road networks that requires motorways, bridges and tunnels as well as traffic-control systems, lighting and drainage.

The market for electrical goods, including fridges, freezers, TVs and stereos, will not reach its full potential without widescale household connection to national electricity grids that can guarantee uninterrupted supply.

The market for washing machines, central heating and other electrical items requiring water will not flourish without adequate household connection rates to supplies of treated water.

Consumers cannot talk, teleshop, call the helpdesk or complain without a phone system. Countries need advanced telecommunications systems, including fiberoptic cable and satellite, to broadcast, communicate and provide the services that manufacturers and retailers will require.

The volume of airline traffic and passenger throughput is increasing year on year. China buys one out of every six aircraft that Boeing currently makes. New large-capacity airports are coming on stream throughout the region as each country expands its hub terminal and develops secondary city airports too.

The need for basic infrastructure to relay vehicles, power and information appear obvious. But infrastructure is complex and expensive. Cities expand, the rural areas change, infrastructure just keeps on needing to be extended, maintained, modernized and upgraded to meet new needs. Infrastructure can cause dislocation, disruption and upheaval before its benefits become obvious.

Roads

Terrestrial, or land, transport is the most ancient form of human movement. In Asia, trade routes built up along the most accessible passes, such as the Silk Route, which was that taken by Marco Polo to reach China in the tenth century.

Land transport is cheaper and more accessible to more people, even those without vehicular transport, and so roads became the main trading routes across continental Asia. The building of new roads has therefore been one of the main infrastructural spending targets. Governments have increasingly understood that factories (which produce the goods that can earn much-needed foreign exchange) must be reached easily by suppliers of the raw materials for production.

Road building has another effect. New and better roads mean that people can travel easily from town to town and between cities in search of work, making the population more mobile. With mobility comes exposure to new economic environments, new opportunities, new cultures, all of which can change people's outlook and their consumption patterns.

The roads debate, Vietnamese style

The Ford Motor Company has a production plant 50 miles outside Hanoi. For a company dedicated to the furtherance and sustenance of the automobile, Vietnam can look like heaven or hell depending on your point of view.

Hell for auto makers is Vietnam right now with its poorly built roads dominated by bicycles piled high with agricultural produce, cows pulling lopsided wooden trailers and decidedly unroadworthy Chinese- and Soviet-built trucks belching fumes over the paddy fields that line the autoroutes. Very few private citizens own cars and there is no significant domestic producer.

The heavenly view for automakers goes like this: poorly built roads dominated by bicycles piled high with agricultural produce, cows pulling lopsided wooden trailers and decidedly unroadworthy

Chinese- and Soviet-built trucks belching fumes over the paddy fields that line the autoroutes. Very few private citizens own cars and there is no significant domestic producer.

In other words, vehicle manufacturers can look at Vietnam and see a money pit or they can see a vast market opening before them.

It would appear that the latter view is more popular with global auto manufacturers. Ford's plant represented an investment of US$102 million. Mekong Motors makes four-wheel-drive vehicles assembled from South Korean parts. The Vietnam Motors Corporation (VMC) is a Filipino joint venture assembling and marketing the BMW 320i and 528i as well as South Korean Kia Pride cars that are becoming Vietnam's taxi. The trickle of auto manufacturers that braved Vietnamese conditions in the early 1990s is now a flood: Mitsubishi, Mercedes, Toyota, Daewoo, Daihatsu, Honda, Nissan, Peugeot, Suzuki and Isuzu are all resident now. Over 30 types of car, truck and bus are rolling off the production lines.

All this for a country with just 150,000 cars and with two-thirds of the auto market commercial. Motorbikes are common but then they don't need parking spaces and Vietnam has yet to see mass construction of multistory car parks. The pickings aren't rich at present given the level of investment required. Mercedes sold just 383 vehicles in 1996, Suzuki 128. VMC did best, selling just over 2000 vehicles. In all 34,000 new vehicles braved the potholes in Vietnamese roads in 1996.

And with the automobile comes a host of problems for a developing country. Seven years of traffic, however limited, on Vietnam's roads have meant 30,000 deaths and 100,000 injuries. Fatalities have increased 300 percent a year since 1991. Hanoi's vehicle density is amongst the lowest in the world, which is just as well considering the amount of oxen you have to share lanes with and the lack of pavements in many areas meaning that pedestrians mingle with traffic.

The Vietnamese government estimates that there are just 150,000 cars on the road, more than enough for a country without a give-way sign, where left-hand turns from the right lane are a regular occurrence, speed limits are non-existent and the right side of the road to drive on is open to debate, as is the correct way to go

ASIA'S GROWING CAR CULTURE – NEW CAR REGISTRATIONS

Country	1997 ('000s)	2005 ('000s)
China	450.0	1000.0
India	535.0	1350.0
Indonesia	49.0	212.0
Malaysia	310.0	400.0
Philippines	102.0	165.0
South Korea	1050.0	1500.0
Taiwan	390.0	425.0
Thailand	168.0	332.0
Vietnam	3.6	10.0

Source: Industry estimates

round a roundabout. There is no required driving test at present. The French government helped fund the installation of 35 traffic lights.

Despite all this and the fact that, according to the *Vietnam Investment Review*, the parking system meets 0.12 percent of the city's demand, it seems people still want to own cars. Without the necessary infrastructure of roads, regulations and parking, this will mean either thwarted aspirations or complete chaos. And Vietnam is not the only country with a burgeoning car-owning population and a road infrastructure lacking the ability to cope.

China takes to the road

Between 1990 and 1996 the Chinese car market grew from sales of 121,000 vehicles to 378,000. Competition in the automobile industry is hotting up as a growing number of manufacturers bid to woo potential Chinese car owners in a market growing by 23 percent a year. Western manufacturers have been eyeing up the Chinese market since the late 1970s. Detroit's AMC signed up for a joint venture in the 1980s and found itself facing incredible obstacles to vehicle production, as outlined in Jim Mann's book *Beijing Jeep* (Westview Press, 1997).

Shanghai VW instituted a series of price cuts in summer 1997, bringing down the price of the popular Santana 2000 Sedan by at least 5 percent. Meanwhile, the Beijing Jeep Corporation is expanding its product range and Volkswagen, in another German joint venture with First Automobile Works of Changchun in Jilin province, increased output of the Jetta range by over 100 percent in 1997. The Jetta has 9.1 percent of the market – the most popular car in China. German manufacturers have also done particularly well with the black-and-smoke-windowed Audi A6 now invariably chauffeuring Chinese party functionaries around Beijing.

Competition is continuing to hot up in the race to clog China's roads. Kia Motors Corporation of South Korea is shipping in 50,000 of its Pride cars every year. At the moment Kia and the two other major Korean manufacturers, Hyundai and Daewoo, are selling approximately 3000 cars a year each in the country, so clearly expansion is expected.

The car market in Asia has been a victim of the turmoil. Sales are down in many countries and manufacturers have scaled back estimates of sales for the next few years. In many countries this downturn is more likely to hit imports and foreign brands as local manufacturers stress the need to support local cars. Malaysia's Proton has seen sales increase in a market with declining overall sales. The casualties have been Mercedes and other foreign makes. Proton still expects to sell over 150,000 vehicles in 1998 with another 40–50,000 set for export. Indonesia's 'national' car, the Timor, is also protected through tax and tariff advantages not afforded to rival makes.

Countries such as Indonesia and Malaysia that heavily tax imported vehicles were talking of opening their markets, but this now seems unlikely in the near future. This is bad news for the Japanese manufacturers in particular who initially supplied the skills needed to set up southeast Asian production. It was Mitsubishi that nurtured Proton while Indonesia's Timor manufacturer is dependent on Korea's Kia technology and Korea's Samsung itself relies on Nissan's knowhow.

Railways

The railway is an even more effective method for moving people and goods. Whereas in Europe and North America rail networks have remained static, or in some cases shrunk, in Asia new networks and lines are being built at a rapid pace. These new rail systems amplify the ability of people to move around a country, and from country to country in some cases.

China is a prime example at the moment. With an extensive existing railway network, it has been very easy for workers, who lack economic opportunity in many hinterland regions, to migrate towards the developing city centers in order to find more profitable work and more opportunities to better their lifestyles.

This greater communication between regions works both ways, enabling both the migration of workers towards cities and for a greater volume and variety of goods to be supplied to outlying regions. This mixing of influences, enabled by mass transportation, has altered people's perceptions of their own regions within a larger context. Whereas previously a small village in Sichuan province may only have been influenced by the economy of its nearest market towns, now it can be directly affected by demand for its product in Shanghai, because companies in the city have found a market for that product in a country on the other side of the world.

Those countries in Asia with established rail networks are working hard to upgrade them at the moment. Vietnam's two major urban conurbations of Ho Chi Minh City and Hanoi have long been linked by rail, but the journey currently takes 36 hours. The government is investing US$350 million to cut the journey time down to 24 hours in a bid to regain passengers and freight lost to the growing number of local airlines.

Power to the people!

The growth of housing in Asia combined with greater ownership of washing machines, fridges, freezers, electric cookers, coffee makers, TV and all things electronic has boosted demand for power and regular supplies of it. Countries like Malaysia and the Philippines have historically been dogged by blackouts and insufficient power generation. As soon as supplies got low they were diverted to hospitals and factories, leaving consumers sitting in the dark cursing. The growth in demand is staggering. In Malaysia demand for power is surging by 13 percent a year due to rapid residential and commercial development. Following the infamous August 1996 Malaysia-wide blackout, massive investment was thrown into the country's power system resulting in a 32 percent reduction in blackouts by 1997, according to the Malaysian power conglomerate Tenaga Nasional Bhd.

The deteriorating power supply and the growing frequency of power cuts across India has forced the New Delhi government to announce a 'common minimum program' for reform of the power-generation sector. However, the country's power-generation capacity has declined in the 1990s under excessive bureaucracy and limits on foreign investment. Targeted additional capacity according to the Eighth Plan (1992–97) was 30,538 megawatts, but only 14,799 megawatts were added over the period. India now desperately needs an additional 57,000 megawatts of capacity and investment of approximately US$100 billion under the Ninth Plan (1997–2002) to begin to tackle the power deficit.

In the rush to provide infrastructure to Asia a new species of developer has appeared, such as Sam Leung whose Hong Kong-based Powerhouse Electric builds mini power plants in about 15 months for a cost of US$2.8 million a time. These plants cater to small towns and clusters of villages throughout China, providing them with a guaranteed, low-cost power supply. While a Chinese national grid would take generations to complete, Sam Leung can connect up relatively large areas rapidly, allowing them to move into a new swathe of consumer markets.

Water

As with power, water has also been a perennial problem for Asia. That is to say, water that is fit to drink. Massive investment has been plowed into water plants to keep the region drinking safely.

In Malaysia's Malacca province, the State Water Corporation has invested US$27 million in water treatment that provides 300 million liters daily.

In China, Cheung Kong Infrastructure is investing US$24 million in three water-treatment plants in Liaoning province with a combined capacity of 370,000 tonnes a day.

Again in China, a new drinking water plant at Lianjiang in Guangzhou province is being built and operated by a joint venture between Suez Lyonnaise des Eaux and New World of Hong Kong.

In February 1998, despite the continuing turmoil, Thames Water of the UK and Suez Lyonnaise des Eaux of France won the contract to manage the water utility covering Jakarta and now have the task of upgrading the city's water pipes and ensuring drinkability. Thames is committed to lay 1100 km of pipe in five years, a rate that will greatly increase access and reduce reliance on wells.

Malaysia's international trade and industry minister Rafidah Aziz recognized the problem of inadequate water supply when he admitted in 1997 that water disruption and pollution 'may have caused lost industrial production running into millions of ringgit'. The minister's comment followed a diesel spillage at Sungai Langat, which supplies about 463.5 million liters a day to consumers in the heavily populated Klang Valley. The spill resulted in a 27-hour shutdown of two water-treatment plants. This disruption followed regular water cuts of between 3 and 15 hours daily.

Water treatment is important to Asian governments, because the tropical or subtropical climates mean that many water systems are perfect breeding grounds for all kinds of disease. Malaria is still a problem in some areas, despite a long-term and concerted effort to eradicate it throughout the second half of the twentieth century. Hepatitis is also a major concern in many Asian countries, with levels rising when infected ice is used in catering establishments.

Perhaps nowhere understands the importance of water better than India. Five hundred million people live in the basin of the Ganges and its tributaries. From Nepal through India and Bangladesh, 114 cities dump their sewage directly into the river and it all arrives in the Bay of Bengal. The result has been that

India's holiest river is a mosaic of waterborne illnesses killing an estimated two million children annually. The issue of access to clean water is not simply one of health but a probable cause of war as nations battle for access. Plans are now underway to clean up the Ganges, a mammoth task but an essential one for India's future health and development.

Down the wire

The road and rail transportation of people and goods is not the only infrastructural element which can change lives. Telecommunications, and their ability to transmit new ideas and concepts to people in even the most remote regions, are another possibly more significant influence on people's perceptions of themselves.

That a villager on a remote island in Indonesia or a farmer on the plains of western China can both watch events which happen in New York or London the moment they happen, or adverts for refrigerators, watches, even cars, has had a profound effect on the aspirations of such people. An example of this would be a herder from Inner Mongolia saving up to buy a Jeep 4×4, thinking that this will enable him to round up his herd of cattle more easily, and in more comfort, than by horseback – a method which has lasted for several thousand years. Of course, the Jeep is also pretty cool.

The other main new use for communications technology is the Internet delivered over cable, land lines or ISDN. The Internet is catching on in a big way in Asia now that the initial problems of non-native-language software are being overcome. Internet service providers (ISPs) are springing up almost daily across the region. However, this is an example of where consumer desire and infrastructural development collide. In the Philippines, for example, the Internet has become incredibly popular and is thriving in the country's relatively liberal, deregulated air. However, the main obstacle to the future growth of usage there is the lack of standard telephone connections. At present the country has only 2.8 telephone lines for every 100 people.

From the heavens

Every Asian country, including Vietnam, has satellites creating a vital extraterrestrial link in their national infrastructures. Thailand alone has three satellites and China is planning a rolling series of launches up until the year 2000. Thailand's Thaicom 3 is equipped with 39 C and Ku-band transponders and joined Thaicom 1 and 2 in their quest to upgrade the country's national telecommunications system. And there is collaboration between countries: China's Long March 3B rocket propelled the Philippines' Agila satellite into orbit.

These satellites are having profound effects on people's lives, from predicting weather to running telephone systems to beaming infomercials around the region's living rooms.

Aircraft

Asia's skies are becoming increasingly crowded. It seems that every airline wants to fly there and if they can't get the slots then they get a partner, as Virgin Atlantic did by teaming up with Malaysian Air to fly into Kuala Lumpur.

There were some 200 new airports being built in east Asia in the mid-1990s, a figure set to more than double over the next few years. Travel through the region's airports and you spend a lot of time looking at the new airport being built close by. Fly into Hong Kong's Kai Tak, for example, and pilots point out the new Chek Lap Kok awaiting arrivals below; the bus route from terminal to plane at Beijing's international airport runs alongside the new terminal building under construction; and visitors to Kuala Lumpur's airport sit crowded tantalizingly close to the gleaming terminal building which is nearing completion.

Of the world's 25 busiest airports, four are in Asia-Pacific and they handled over 45 million passengers in 1997. However, until recently the lack of infrastructural development has stunted growth. The International Air Transport Association (IATA) estimates that 50 percent of Asia's airports will be turning away flights by 1999 unless serious upgrading is undertaken. In light of this stark warning, it seems that the airport authorities are acting to improve and enlarge as quickly as possible. In the aftermath of the economic crisis passenger numbers have dipped, but as the region recovers and exports grow the need for air transportation, both passenger and cargo, should resume. The skies are now home to a growing number of cargo planes as courier companies such as TNT and DHL have added additional inter-Asian routes for parcel deliveries.

Hong Kong is continuing to expand its hub capacity to a projected 38 million passengers by mid-1998. The Legislative Council has approved funds for a 34 km rail line linking Lantau to the new airport at Chek Lap Kok.

Malaysia is expanding Kuala Lumpur airport in the hope of becoming the major Asian hub destination of the twenty-first century. The new, improved KL International needs to handle 25 million passengers annually by September 1998 (when Malaysia hosts the Commonwealth Games) and 45 million by 2012.

The Philippines government has announced its intention to spend US$20 million on construction of an international airport in Laguindingan on the southern island of Mindanao to be completed by 1999.

Seoul airport in South Korea is being expanded to handle 40 million passengers a year by 1998 at a cost of US$8.6 billion.

Thailand is expanding Bangkok airport at a cost of US$4.9 billion to cope with 40 million passengers by 2010.

Vietnam's domestic airports are currently undergoing renovation in the expectation of increased arrivals. Noi Bai airport is building a terminal that can cater for 2.5 million passengers annually and Ho Chi Minh City's Tan Son Nhat airport is aiming for 8–10 million passengers a year.

Within China's current five-year plan, the CAAC has prioritized its airport-building program under the 1-8-6-6 scheme. These figures represent the one key project (the expansion of the Beijing International Terminal); eight airport expansions planned in Nanjing, Yinchuan, Zhengzhou, Fuzhou, Guiyang, Nanning, Hohhot and Hefei; six continuing projects at Haikou, Harbin, Nanchang,

PREPARE FOR LANDING

Country	Major airport	Passenger throughput ('000)	Total aircraft throughput ('000)
Hong Kong	Kai Tak	27,424	67
Indonesia	Jakarta	13,222	46
Malaysia	Kuala Lumpur	16,444	43
Philippines	Manila	11,389	44
Singapore	Changi	21,743	134
South Korea	Seoul	30,687	45
Taiwan	Taipei	9,422	13
Thailand	Bangkok	20,943	110
Vietnam	Hanoi	6,771	19

Source: IATA

Xiamen, Urumqi and renovation of flight paths throughout China; six projects to be started including a new airport at Shanghai Pudong, expansions of Chengdu, Lanzhou and Kunming airports and setting up of the Tianjin–Beijing fuel supply project and the Beijing area Control Center.

Air travel is in some ways the obvious way to overcome the transportation problems which have held back development of much of the Asian continent, the main obstacle being the physical shape of the land. High mountains and deep rivers have not helped the building of roads and railways, but all these can be surmounted given an ample supply of air transport.

Stuck on the runway

India's airports are a major obstacle to business in the country. They are too small, too crowded and underdeveloped. While individual states have been pumping cash into airport upgrading and construction, India has not kept pace with southeast Asia in this respect. Its five major airports – Calcutta, Chennai (Madras), Delhi, Mumbai and Thiruvananthapuram – are the main entry points, with Delhi and Mumbai accounting for two-thirds of all passenger throughput.

Unlike in many southeast Asian nations, airports in India have not accompanied the expansion of new regional centers. Bangalore has grown into a center of technological and business excellence but all the genius pouring into the city still has to stand in very long lines at the airport. At first the laws on inward investment were a hindrance, but following their relaxation a US$92 million upgrade is underway with international companies like Raytheon involved. Meanwhile the Airports Authority of India is working on creating 12 'model airports' to ease congestion at the traditional hubs. But until the upgrade is finished the Bangalore-based business community will have to get to other airports such as Mumbai, Madras or Delhi to catch international flights, and Bangalore-based exporters will incur additional costs through not having a decent local cargo terminal.

China's soon-to-be-crowded skies

Now that China and Hong Kong are reunited, China becomes the second most important country in Asia for air transport after Japan, and by 2010 will be by far the biggest market in the region, if not the world. This will have been a remarkable recovery for a country that until 1995 had the worst airport infrastructure in the region and an appalling safety record.

By 2005, 20 new international airports will be functioning in China and 40 existing airports will have been upgraded to international standards. The Chinese have already handed out US$80 billion worth of contracts to overseas firms alone. China is perhaps unique in Asia in that while it is expecting additional foreign aircraft arrivals it is the domestic market that will attract greatest interest. Huadu airport near Guangzhou is preparing for 30 million passengers per annum, the vast majority domestic. Shanghai Airport is forecasting 100 million passengers by 2002; Shenzhen is

> **GUANGDONG'S NEW AIRPORT**
>
> **1998 will see ground broken on Guangzhou's new international airport. It is being financed by the Civil Aviation Administration of China (CAAC), Guangdong province and the city of Guangzhou. 20,000 people have been relocated from the earmarked site which covers over one million square meters. The project is scheduled to be completed by 2001 in time for Guangzhou to host the ninth Chinese National Games. The entire project is budgeted at US$2.4 billion and the backers' aim is to attract foreign government loans to ensure completion. The airport will also become the base for Southern China Airlines, handling 80 million passengers and 2.5 million tonnes of cargo annually. The two-runway airport is 28 km from Guangdong and includes the ubiquitous hotel, rail link and retailing facilities.**

predicting 80 million and installing a 100-gate terminal to accommodate them all. However, figures being thrown around in China at the moment sound exciting but could also be an indication that airport building may go the way of Thai condos or Shanghai office property and end up in oversupply.

Chicken and egg

Sometimes consumers can only consume a product once the infrastructure is in place – there is no point in owning a satellite phone if there's no satellite to relay your message, no beeper without a beeper network. But sometimes the equation is more complicated.

What comes first:

- the out-of-town shopping mall or the road going to it?
- the tourist destination or the airport serving it?
- the suburban housing development or the water, drainage and power lines running to it?

These are issues affecting every developing Asian country right now and yet, as often seen already, the Asians have several advantages over the west.

There is in the main a decent supply of money and governments willing and able to make the investment. Contrary to popular belief, while the Asian tigers have embraced the free market in some respects, governments retain a large degree of control over state planning, whether it be in capitalist Singapore or communist China. Just look at the Chinese efforts to win the Olympics or Singapore's determination to be 'wired' and the commitment to public housing in both countries. This advantage has been eroded by the turmoil of 1997/8, but generally Asian governments are more favorable than western ones to public investment in infrastructure.

The infrastructural 'jump' factor has a part to play. Less developed countries like Vietnam need an efficient phone system if they are going to make the leap successfully from their present embryonic economic level to fully fledged long-term growth and consumer societies. However, Vietnam does not need to lay land lines into every house in Hanoi or village in the Mekong. Vietsat solved the problem by launching a satellite into orbit and providing an instant cellular service. Nevertheless, in Indonesia the explosion of cellular phones has not been without its downside for the operators hungry to tap this potentially massive market. Operators are now owed billions of rupiah in unpaid bills. The rush to connect those able to pay meant that credit checks were lax and competition between rival operating systems concentrated on signups rather than security. Users are now classified into three categories: white, grey and blacklisted.

Finding the labor for infrastructural development can be a problem. Unions exist and many countries have had to import workers from Indonesia, the Philippines or further afield, much like the Gulf States had to when following the oil wealth they created modern cities and infrastructures. Over one million Asians currently work in other Asian nations helping their competitors win the race to finish their infrastructures. Kuala Lumpur's impressive Petronas Twin Towers were built largely by Indonesian and Bangladeshi laborers. The meltdown has affected this – Malaysia has started to repatriate foreign workers and is now patroling its borders and coasts against an influx of economic migrants from Indonesia. Also, many Filipina housemaids in Hong Kong have proved an expendable luxury and have been sent back to Manila.

However, China has seen massive migration from the rural hinterland and much of this has been absorbed in the flourishing number of private and civic construction works. A similar pattern is reflected in Vietnam and Indonesia as well as Thailand. And while in countries like South Korea and Taiwan wages, benefits and job security have become as much of an issue as they are in Europe or North America, throughout much of Asia labor relations better reflect the Industrial Revolution than the Bolshevik version.

The 1998 Chinese Communist Party Conference in Beijing saw Prime Minister Zhu Rongji tackle the question of overstaffing and unemployment head on. His economic plan means that 'downsizing' has become a Chinese word, not just something that happens to American bank workers. Zhu Rongji appears to be advocating a form of Roosevelt New Deal solution with enforced layoffs in unproductive state enterprises being absorbed in a new round of infrastructural projects.

Infrastructural development can also promote business as it progresses. A survey conducted by Singapore's Mass Rapid Transit (MRT) authority found that retailers were setting up shop along the lines as they extended. The 48 MRT stations had become home to 122 stores, 60 percent of which were service providers, including banks, pharmacies and photo shops. Singapore's retail infrastructure is growing in tandem with the extension of the nation's transit infrastructure.

International involvement

Companies from virtually every western nation are hard at work in Asia bidding for infrastructure contracts. With the current political tide in Europe and the US firmly against additional spending on public works, companies such as Siemens, ABB and others are coming increasingly to rely on Asia for new contracts. When it was announced that the Manila Water & Sewerage System (MWSS) was to be split into two concessions and privatized, there was a rush of interest from countries including several French and British water companies. Across the region contracting, joint ventures and tendering are common activities, with most major western construction companies having established a network of representative offices.

Despite Asian countries often trying to limit international control – for instance the Philippines limits direct stakes in infrastructure ventures to 40 percent – increasingly they are looking for western expertise and capital to complete their infrastructural programs. And considering that the Asian Development Bank estimates that the Philippines alone has to spend US$50 billion in the next 10 years on infrastructure just to keep pace with development, Asia is going to continue to be the most exciting region for the world's construction, engineering and IT providers even in an environment of slower growth than previously.

ABB derives nearly 20 percent of its sales from the region, GEC 24 percent, Caterpillar 16 percent and Siemens 11 percent. Most of these companies are outwardly bullish about prospects in Asia. GE's Jack Welch has described the new Asian environment as an opportunity and ABB's Goran Lindahl sees the problem as only lasting two to three years at most. There is no doubt that deferred projects and non-completions will adversely affect the major players. However, they are well placed to understand the disparities in the region. They have taken hits in Indonesia, Thailand and Malaysia and to an extent Korea, but in China orders have continued to increase with contracts for the Three Gorges project awarded in August 1997. Companies such as ABB have also continued to increase their level of sales to Taiwan and the Philippines.

Good moves

There are numerous examples of major infrastructure and construction projects that have been successful and hugely beneficial to the peoples and nations of Asia. These include the following:

- The Malaysian cabinet's approval in early 1997 of the building of a bridge to replace the 74-year-old Causeway linking Malaysia and Singapore. Further infrastructural improvements are making it easier for commuters to travel from one place to another on new modes of transport such as the Light Rail Transit and the KTM Commuter linking residential, business and retail areas of the country.
- Indocement Tunggal Prakarsa, Indonesia's largest cement producer, thrived in the infrastructure and construction boom. The company doubled its annual production to 11.3 million tonnes, accounting for 50 percent of the country's needs. Meanwhile another cement manufacturer, BKPM, had to build three new factories to cope with demand.
- The planned Indonesia–Malaysia bridge between Malacca and Dumai will cost approximately US$1.6 billion and at 95 km long will be the world's longest bridge.
- Hong Kong is planning a number of new developments and towns to be built on Lantau Island. Several sites on the north Lantau coast are marked for development potential after the 12.5 km North Lantau three-lane expressway opened in 1997 connecting the Lantau link with Tung Chung and the new airport at Chek Lap Kok. This is an example of infrastructural development allowing greater house building in the overcrowded administrative region. The new towns are expected to house about 260,000 people and include a hotel, commercial and industrial areas.
- Vietnam has worked with telecommunications companies such as Canada's Nortel and Australia's Telstra to provide an optical fiber loop system that increases capacity 63 times and allows high-speed communication technology in the remote highland regions for the first time. A fixed wireless system has also been installed in Ho Chi Minh City that will allow outlying areas access to communications without the need for laying cable. The country is expanding its telecoms network at the rate of 70,000 new lines a year, tackling the problem of the current ratio of one phone per hundred Vietnamese.

The inevitable mistakes

With development as rapid as has been seen in east Asia over the past decade, there are bound to be mistakes. Cutting corners, especially in countries where corruption is an ever-present curse, can often lead to the use of low-grade materials, bad plans, incompetent engineers and corrupt officials drawing off some of the budget for such projects into their own bank accounts.

Sometimes things work out satisfactorily, usually because the work involved in a project was overquoted in the first place to allow for a certain amount of leeway. But often disasters are waiting to happen.

The sheer number of new buildings constructed in Asia over the last decade has raised questions about just how sound some of them are. In South Korea in 1995 the Sampoong department store in Seoul collapsed with the loss of 300 lives and a further 900 injured, resulting in a debate about poor building standards and the need to tighten them. And in Mumbai in September 1997 the top three floors of an office building crumbled after the structure began shaking violently.

In January 1997 Bangkok City Council ordered the demolition of seven illegally expanded department stores. Allegedly 52 buildings were found to have encroached on public land, while 77 others had not been built in line with construction designs approved by the authorities.

The rapid demand for entertainment from affluent young Filipinos combined with the new political freedoms has driven the growth of nightclubs in Manila. However, many of these have been hastily opened and a fire, caused by poor electrical wiring, that led to the deaths of 50 party goers in 1996 has sadly not been an isolated incident.

The rise in air traffic across the region has heightened the need for improved air traffic control. The number of accidents is still too high and without improvements will continue to worsen as more planes take to the sky.

A further example of a bad move would be the factories which have sprung up in China's Special Economic Zones, most famously in Shenzhen. In 1995, a toy factory in Shenzhen caught fire. Because factory management wanted to cut staff breaks in order to squeeze out more profit, emergency exits were locked and windows barred. The result was a catastrophe. What made this worse was that the factory was too close to an area used for storage of flammable chemicals, which also caught fire and exploded. The explosion was heard in Hong Kong, over 50 miles away. The government rightly came down heavily on the culprits and has also begun to fine infringers of work safety laws, when they are reported. But since most workers in these factories rely on their income from these jobs to support their families and don't wish to be blacklisted as difficult employees, the incidence of reporting is low. Most factory workers come from the countryside and have little idea of what their rights are or about safety regulations.

Malice is not the only reason for building failure. In Taiwan, it was poor communication between contracting firms from different parts of Europe and Asia which led to the incompetence seen in the building of Taipei's monorail and underground system. Tendering out of too many small parcels of work to too many disparate companies led to planning problems and the monorail system, which was set over the top of the underground rail in the middle of some of the city's main thoroughfares, collapsed into the underground. It was also not good planning to build the monorail so that the corners which the trains had to negotiate were too sharp, causing test trains to fly off the rails.

Ecological effects of infrastructural growth

Infrastructure projects often involve massive displacement and movement of people. People naturally want electricity and clean water and all the benefits that infrastructural development can bring, but the price is often high, not just in financial terms. Below are three examples, but similar ones can be found across the region.

In early November 1997, the first real step towards damming the mighty Yangzi was taken, when the river was diverted into the parallel shipping channel which will allow the building of the

Three Gorges Dam. This was an event watched over by China's leader Jiang Zemin, whose government insists that the project will be completed, despite costs likely to run into billions of dollars, causing the relocation of over a million inhabitants of the river valley and the drowning of whole cities, historical sites and important natural habitats. This also sealed the fate of the famous Yangzi gorges, some of China's most famous geological sites and areas of great natural beauty.

All this is a price worth paying, says the Chinese government, to gain much-needed hydroelectric power to supply growing industries and provide a clear shipping route to the center of the country. Critics claim that the silt carried by this vast river (the world's third longest), which created the fertile plains around down-river cities like Nanjing and Shanghai, will all too soon clog up the waterways. They also claim that the untreated sewage from the many millions of people living in Sichuan province above the dam, and the heavy industries along the banks of the river, will quickly turn it into a heavily polluted waterway.

However, the project goes on despite the protests, which don't only originate from outside China. Certainly, for China to build what will be the world's biggest dam by itself will no doubt be held up as proof of its industrial, political and economic might. In some ways, the dam will be seen by the Chinese authorities as proof of their ability to carry out huge social and infrastructural programs successfully, unlike the disasters of the Great Leap Forward and the Cultural Revolution.

Yet if the critics are proven right and the dam, rather than fulfilling the power and inland shipping needs of the Chinese interior, ends up as a huge, polluted, silted-up liability, then what? If this project does go wrong, it could be a failure which the Chinese authorities cannot shake off through internal reorganization and vilification of retired leaders. By then, the Chinese people will no longer be a pliable mass of proletariat workers and peasants, but a sophisticated, modern group of consumers, increasingly middle class and well able to make judgments without resorting to political dogma.

At the beginning of May 1997 work began on the San Roque multi-purpose dam at San Manuel in the Pangasinan region of the

Philippines. The US$746 million project is scheduled for completion in 2005 and should provide an additional 345 MW of hydroelectric capacity and the irrigation of 87,000 hectares of agricultural land across three provinces, while also hoping to reduce the danger from the periodic flooding to which the region is prone. The scheme has been earmarked as a flagship project by the regional administration and described as a disaster by the local communities of the Agno river who are due to be displaced to make way for an 850 cubic meter reservoir. Here, as across the region, the need for infrastructural development collides head on with the desire of people to continue living where generations of their family have always lived.

The great haze of September 1997 was a little like the currency crisis. Events in one country affected another and then another. It brought home the region's interdependency in a shared environment. The burning of forests in Indonesia by Malaysian, Singaporean, Indonesian and other land-owning companies led to a blanket of smog covering the region with even the twin tips of the Petronas Towers invisible. Children were kept home from school in Sarawak and Borneo while Singapore had to improvise emergency care for the elderly. People across the region saw their quality of life drop considerably and the health of many may be affected for years to come. The Borneo forests were devastated and plane schedules reduced to chaos. This is perhaps the best – or the worst – example of the damage that can be caused by rapid development.

Not lagging behind

As the nations and peoples of Asia become more conscious of environmental issues, there is growing recognition that resources such as trees for paper, building materials and fuel for transportation are all finite. Reducing consumption of these raw materials is recognized as being a way of preserving natural resources, including such concepts as biodiversity, helping to reduce pollution and, most importantly for the short term, saving money. Certainly Asian nations are environmentally aware. Beijing residents are encouraged to recycle, car use is limited and heavily taxed in Singapore and the Asian market for environmental technology and expertise is growing rapidly.

It is a fact that many of these Asian countries have done most of their economic development since the Second World War. They are perhaps more able to adapt to new technological advances and better equipped to incorporate them into their day-to-day cultures than are the so-called advanced nations. And while Asia may lag behind the west in infrastructural development, in the realm of technology it's a whole other story, as we shall see in the next chapter.

9
Wired Asia

Ride Singapore's Mass Rapid Transit system trains from City Hall station with its on-platform TV sets out to the Tampines residential development in the suburbs near Changi Airport. The whole journey is characterized by the most distinctive and all-pervasive sound in Asia – a sharp trilling. Again and again you hear this noise, often a chorus of electronic sounds in the same carriage.

As soon as the sound starts everyone begins rummaging. School kids in neat green or brown uniforms rip open their backpacks, businesspeople click open their briefcases, even little old ladies dive into their shopping. Most faces reappear looking a little sorry, but one person will start talking. The others needn't worry – it won't be long before the ringing starts again. This is the mobile phone revolution in action. Everyone has one, and the few that don't have pagers attached to their belts by little gold clip chains. And it isn't just on the MRT...

Walk through the malls of Orchard Road and the trilling never stops, through the Central Business District and it sounds like a thousand tropical birds all talking to each other. In Chinatown and Little India, up in the Arab Quarter, out on Sentosa where you're supposed to get away from it all, on the steps of the Funan Technology Center on North Bridge Road where you're supposed to get into it all and in the restaurants of Bugis Junction – that same electronic beeping.

In other Asian cities the sound is slightly different depending on who the main service provider is: SingTel, Hong Kong Telecom, Telekom Malaysia. You can hear it waiting for the ferry at Tsimshatsui in Hong Kong, throughout Kuala Lumpur's Golden Triangle and even standing in the middle of the vastness that is Beijing's Tiananmen Square. It's all the same sound really – Asia talking to Asia by the million.

Asia wires up

Asia is wiring up – from cybercafés in Bangalore through mobile phones in Shenzhen to cable TV in the Philippines. Why is technology so important to consumers?

- It is producing the communications revolution that is opening up Asia.
- It is just the latest form of networking in a network-crazy region.
- It is unleashing the dynamism that characterizes the region both in the boom years and now, post-turmoil, with all to play for.
- Whether it is phones, TV or the Internet, it allows Asians to be where they so eagerly want to be, ahead of the game, modern and at the cutting edge.

Perhaps nowhere symbolizes this phenomenon better than Malaysia's Multimedia Super Corridor (MSC). The MSC is a unique zone aimed at housing a host of twenty-first-century technology companies featuring smart cards, smart schools, remote manufacturing, telemedicine, borderless banking and the wholly wired city of Cyberjaya. All of this is being largely funded by the Malaysian government itself in an exercise of commitment to technology unimaginable in the west where market forces reign supreme. The government has moved its administrative headquarters to the so-called paperless city of Putrajaya in the heart of the MSC. We will come back to the importance of Cyberjaya later – first, just how wired is Asia right now?

COMPUTER SALES IN ASIA

Country	Units	Annual growth (%)
Korea	1,900,000	28
China	1,700,000	53
Taiwan	500,000	15
Indonesia	425,000	33
Malaysia	335,000	27
Hong Kong	335,000	24
Thailand	330,000	26
Singapore	300,000	34
Rest of Asia*	1,425,000	36

*=not including Japan and India

Source: Manufacturers' estimates

- ✦ In 1996 Asia accounted for 25 percent of world IT sales.
- ✦ Since 1990 the number of telephone lines in Asia as a whole has grown by 11 percent annually, in the Philippines by 25 percent and in China by 30 percent, according to the International Telecommunications Union.
- ✦ By 2000 China will have laid 300,000 km of fiberoptic cable.
- ✦ By 2000 over 30 million Asian households will be online to the Internet.
- ✦ Microsoft's Indian subsidiary is confidently expecting to surpass US$100 million in sales by 2000.

The healthy cash balances which the tiger economies amassed over the last 10 years are funding the wiring of Asia in conjunction with foreign investment and international aid. US$1000 million of government money for Malaysia's MSC and US$325 million for Singapore's Cluster Development Fund established by the country's National Computer Board are typical of the sums floating around at present. Naturally, the economic crisis has placed strains on this expenditure, but while project deadlines have been extended they have by no means been indefinitely postponed. Both Singapore and Malaysia are investing for the future, not just to promote the industries of the next century, not just to catch up with – and surpass – the west, but also to capture a domestic market that is eager for technology and hungry to buy. The computers built by regional technology companies such as Taiwan's Acer have found domestic as well as international markets.

Asians are going digital with remarkable speed. China's PC market exploded by 53 percent in 1996 and, despite widespread poverty, is Asia's third largest behind Japan and South Korea. The Asian PC market is growing by up to 40 percent a year, selling over seven million computers annually and spending US$14 billion on hardware, software and gadgetry.

In China, it is estimated that there are now between four and five million home computers in use, yet this represents only some 1.5 percent of the total potential market of 300 million households. Computers are the new consumption fad for Chinese middle-class families, many of whom have already purchased their TV, video, refrigerator and washing machine. Where the small, middle-class minority leads, the lower-income groups desire to follow, especially as many Chinese view the education of their – now often single – child as their most important sphere of investment. Ability with computers has come to be seen as a key need for their children's future success in the increasingly tough Asian labor market.

Thousands of schools across the region have been wiring up and the instant success and popularity of the Internet throughout Asia is witnessed by the sheer volume of Web pages the region is generating.

India has become a major producer of technology, computer software in particular. However, widespread implementation of technology throughout the country is being held back by lack of resources, political will and bureaucracy.

The 'jump' factor

One of Asia's historic deficits has become its current asset in the race to wire up the region. Traditionally it was not considered to be a technology region – that was the preserve of California and a few other high-tech areas in the west. The Japanese were world leaders in production (though introduction of computers into Japanese offices and business has been pathetically low) but across the rest of the region the main economic asset was low pay, plentiful labor and low startup costs. The Koreans produced steel, the Malaysians assembled components, the Chinese entered the international garment trade – all so-called twilight industries in the west.

The Asian tiger economies achieved growth and wealth through this approach. They realized the need for technology and that they had to acquire it quickly if their position was to be secured in the world's trade network. They could not rely on assembly and production forever. They had to break free of what in the west were being called the 'heavy' or 'sunset' industries or they would begin to acquire rust belts of their own before making the next leap.

And Asia has one major asset in making the leap from traditional industries to the technology age, an asset that was all too often lacking in Europe and North America – the willingness of the people to embrace any and all technological innovation. This willingness and fascination with all things technical have been Asia's hidden assets in its emergence as a global technology center rivaling the silicon valleys, glens and plateaux of the west.

While many groups of workers in the west have resisted technological change in manufacturing processes, it has been embraced and accepted in Asia as the way to do things. This acceptance has largely been because pre-turmoil its implementation did not result in mass layoffs or downsizing. Ordinary Asians also jumped feet first into technology without the stubborn resistance shown by many westerners. Technology has been used to bring them up to speed:

- Why bother installing mile on mile of landline when you can put up a satellite and jump to a cellphone network in a matter of months?
- Why develop a fully fledged postal system when you can jump straight to e-mail and FTP?

- Why limit yourself to a few TV networks when you can jump to cable, satellite, pay-per-view and digital for people buying their first set?
- Why go to the expense of establishing a nationwide bank branch network when you can jump straight to remote and telebanking?

How do you see the world if your first phone is a GSM, your first camera a digicam and your first computer a laptop with Internet access? You perceive a wired world where technology is not only essential to everyday life, both in terms of business and pleasure, but also natural. Surfing the Internet or using a mobile phone become as much acts of everyday life as microwaving your morning coffee or getting cash from an ATM on your lunch break. Singapore newspaper the *Straits Times* lists on its Web page all its e-mail addresses and what it calls its 'snail-mail' postal address. And the speed with which Asians are adapting to the new technology on offer is dizzying. Ten years ago Vietnam had a grand total of nine phone lines to the outside world, now mobile phones, at US$600 a time, are selling fast and the subscriber base was 105,000 at the end of 1997.

However, Asian countries do not appear content just to let people wire themselves. Across the region, from smart schools in Singapore to information ports in China, national governments and local administrations are putting in place measures that will ensure it remains wired. Malaysia's Cyberjaya, Singapore One and China's burgeoning high-tech zones are just three examples of how the region is capitalizing on technological gains.

Welcome to Cyberjaya

Cyberjaya is the heart of Malaysia's Multimedia Super Corridor. The MSC covers 750 sq. km near Kuala Lumpur. It is Malaysia's answer to Singapore's success in attracting high-tech inward investment. The determination to build the MSC comes at a cost:

- Kuala Lumpur International Airport – the main entry point to the MSC, capable of handling 25 million passengers and costing US$3.2 billion.
- Telecommunications infrastructure – the MSC must be wired with a fiberoptic backbone capable of handling the expected traffic, at a cost of US$1.4 billion.
- Petronas Twin Towers – the architectural symbol of the MSC, the tallest building in the world and costing US$700 million.
- Putrajaya – a technology park and federal government administrative center covering 4600 acres and planned to be completed in a decade at a cost of US$7 billion.
- Cyberjaya – a fully wired city of 250,000 high-tech inhabitants with a 'multimedia university' to train the next generation of wired Malaysians, costing US$3.5 billion.

Right now Cyberjaya is forest, palm-oil plantations and countryside, but its transformation is the bet the Malaysian government has placed to transform the country from one based on manufacturing to one reliant on high-tech industry. Cyberjaya hopes to house the IT companies at the heart of this endeavor. The inducements to settle there are pretty good: an investment tax allowance for 10 years, no import duties on multimedia equipment, unrestricted employment of foreign 'knowledge' workers and the freedom to source capital globally. Of course there are other planned attractions – supposedly Cyberjaya will be traffic-jam free, pollution free (how exactly it would have escaped the 1997 haze is not clear, however) and no high-rise buildings.

Putrajaya is a little further down the line, with the first government offices relocating in 1998 and the population expected to rise to 70,000 by 1999. But just how the MSC will eventually turn out is a big question: the plans feature lots of trees, clean houses and no traffic, but they are just drawings. What is clear is that the Malaysian government has already dedicated substantial capital to the project, as have the main private-sector partners in the project. This is investment in technology on a grand scale. The economic turmoil of 1997 put development of the MSC back somewhat, but Malaysian prime minister Dr Mahathir has stated that it 'is essential to the country's intended transformation from assembly manufacturing to information technology'.

Singapore One

Singapore One is a national broadband multimedia network which is intended to provide the core of the national government's Information Technology 2000 strategy. The ultimate aim of this strategy is to turn Singapore into an 'intelligent island' by the turn of the century. The project is co-sponsored by the Telecommunication Authority of Singapore and is effectively a super Internet for the country, building on technologies used by the National Computer Board, the Economic Development Board and the Singapore Broadcasting Authority.

Singapore One is envisaged to include intelligent multimedia kiosks, access to school curriculum materials from the home, a digital library, government services and commercial space. The projected cost is US$22 million. Entertainment services include karaoke on demand, video on demand, news, online games, electronic retailing and videoconferencing. The government has brought Singapore's major corporations on board to provide an additional US$65 million of funding for the project. As with Malaysia's MSC, the aim is to extend technology throughout the country and to make it an integral part of national life and culture.

China's high-tech zones

China now has 52 high-technology development zones aiming to attract investment from overseas technology companies and provide a backbone to the country's wired future. Technology may be more apparent in thought than in fact in many of the zones, but they are a start. At the moment many are home to low-wage factories with poor supporting infrastructure, but they prove that the country, while fueling growth in low-wage assembly, has grander plans for the future.

Other Chinese high-tech zones are clustered around universities and allow for the sharing of often scarce resources. Many of these were the result of a government program called Torch that aimed to develop high-tech zones in a similar manner to the development of the Special Economic Zones (SEZs), with significant autonomy and regulations more attractive to foreign investors.

While countries such as Malaysia may have been more successful at attracting investment from technology companies in the electronics sector, China has gained investment from high-tech pharmaceutical and biotech companies. Medtronic, Roche, Nycomed and other cutting-edge drug developers have established joint ventures near Zhangjiang, the region now being called China's Pharmaceutical Valley.

The success of Zhangjiang is attracting a wider range of technology companies to the area, allowing development of a software park that has helped pull in companies such as Motorola which makes pagers there and Shanghai Valeo, a Sino-French joint venture and a manufacturer of electronically powered automobile engines. Also in place is Matsushita which is manufacturing microwave ovens in the area.

Other Asian countries have also developed high-tech centers. The southern Indian city of Bangalore is claiming the title of the subcontinent's Silicon Valley. A network of software technology parks earns the country US$2 billion in exports annually. The software industry has also proved resilient to wider economic woes, with exports up by 65 percent in 1997 over 1996. Historically, domestic implementation of technology has been hampered by India's notorious bureaucracy, but now officials claim that the red tape has been replaced by the red carpet.

www.asia

The Internet has arrived in Asia with a vengeance and proved to be just the thing for wired Asians. Asian leaders are talking volumes about the Internet. Some are saying it's the worst thing that could

ASIA LOGS ON

Country	Internet users ('000)	Domains	ISPs
Hong Kong	185	4500	67
Singapore	180	3000	4
South Korea	180	2750	13
Taiwan	175	3000	57
China	125	900	5
Malaysia	90	1000	3
Thailand	65	530	5
Indonesia	43	500	5
India	35	225	4
Philippines	23	210	85

Source: Authors' research

happen, while others are embracing the technology as a means to build regional unity and cross-border alliances and understanding. Whichever is the case, Internet entrepreneurs both regional and international are taking Asia seriously.

Leading Web developers such as Yahoo! have recognized the ease with which Asians have embraced the Internet and now provide Chinese- and Japanese-language versions of their software, helping Asians to surf in their native tongues.

Hong Kong-based China Internet Corporation has established PointCast Asia, an Asian version of the phenomenally successful, advertising-revenue-driven narrow-cast service that has swept computer screens in Europe and the US. The service is available in both Chinese and English with content providers as high profile as Reuters, Bloomberg, Nikkei, Dun & Bradstreet and the Financial Times. A South Korean service is also planned.

Traditional Asian publishers have been quick to get on the Web. The English-language *South China Morning Post* has its own specially designed Web pages, as do a host of other Asian newspapers and magazines including the *Korea Herald* and the *Bangkok Post* (a fuller list of Web sites is provided in the Appendix).

In 1995 13 percent of Korean households owned a computer, translating into 1.2 million hookups. Only 6 percent of PC-owning households were online, roughly where the US was in 1990. However, this is largely because the Korean language is a barrier requiring specialist software. At present South Korea has the greatest Internet penetration in Asia. The number of ISPs has grown rapidly in anticipation of future growth and the majority of Internet users appear to be Korean university students.

With the developed consumer economy in Hong Kong and a proven demand for technology, it appears that a large slice of the household market is ripe for potential business for the PC manufacturers. Online interest is already quite high, with free subscriptions to online services boosting household penetration throughout the SAR. Hong Kong has over 60 ISPs at present, with the number seemingly growing weekly.

Taiwan is a relatively small country but is highly advanced as far as information technology is concerned. The country is one of the leading producers of high-tech commodity items and has an advanced telecommunications system with over 7.8 million telephones in operation. Due to the combination of cheap computers and a superior telecommunications system, it is no surprise to discover that the Internet has proved to be popular. Consumers have embraced it as a source of information and entertainment.

Singapore, like Hong Kong and Taiwan, has an advanced telecommunications infrastructure and has experimented with advanced telecommunications systems such as asynchronous transfer mode (ATM). There are over 1.1 million telephone lines in use in the country (averaging out to at least one per household) with 46 percent of households owning a PC and 230,000 subscribers with Internet access. As such, it is not surprising that the country is well provided with ISPs. Cybercafés are also becoming popular. The first was opened in August 1995 allowing Singapore's netheads to surf away while sipping a double mocha latte.

Intranets have also boosted the numbers of Singaporeans surfing the Net. Most major companies have them and quantifying the number of users is difficult, but it could be as many as another 100,000. Along with this development has come the necessity of adding your e-mail and URL numbers to your business card. Private users are coming online fast. Local ISP SingNet predicts 500,000 subscribers by 2000 and a growth rate of 100 percent for just itself.

Malaysia has seen massive growth in demand for Internet access over the past two years. The leading ISP, Jaring, now has over 20,000 users and it has had to revamp its equipment to cope with demand. Indeed, many Malaysian Web surfers have dialed into Singapore-based services. In line with development of the MSC schools have been hooked up bringing a whole generation of Malaysians into cyberspace.

The Philippines is one of southeast Asia's leading advocates of the Internet, with over 80 ISPs. The popularity is largely being driven by Filipino computer science engineers, considered to be among the best in the region. However, eagerness for the Internet is currently dampened by the lack of regular phone connections.

The Vietnamese government has established an Internet Committee to consider the ramifications of this new technology for national wellbeing. A directive from the committee warned that 'some may use the Internet to transmit false reports, propaganda, and stolen national security information' and to propagate 'unhealthy lifestyles and cultural values'. At present, full access to the Internet is still not available to the general public. However, various organizations have penetrated cyberspace and offer limited online services in intranet form with access to e-mail. The market is small at the moment with an estimated 10,000 potential users.

The Indian government has targeted the Internet as an area for growth, with plans to get a million people online by the year 2000.

My Web page or yours?

The World Wide Web has become a place that Asians populate as commonly as anyone else. However, some governments are worried. In Vietnam access is restricted by the sole state-owned gateway provider. The Vietnamese got nervous about the Web around the same time as they were becoming edgy about satellite broadcasting and foreign advertising. In many countries the Net is seen as a transmitter of western values.

Singapore has sought to control the sort of Web pages people have access to. Pornography is not popular with the government. Likewise in China, where pro-capitalist and US pages are not well liked and are often banned.

Asian Web pages and chat groups cover every subject from teenage angst in Singapore, Cantopop trivia and student politics in South Korea through to Islamic education services in Malaysia and lonely hearts in Vietnam.

But who exactly is on the Net in Asia? Unsurprisingly, patterns of usage have followed those of Europe and North America. Net users tend to be from the upper- and middle-income groups and typically male, but this is changing. Already in Thailand children are more likely to be surfing than adults and the number of women users is increasing rapidly.

The great leap forward in China Tech

China, with a population of over 1.2 billion, is a greatly underdeveloped consumer technology market. While the government may be a little perplexed by the Internet, a growing segment of the population is not. Beijing has cybercafés where the digerati log on and communicate with e-mail friends around the world. And it seems that the very highest organizations in the country are now getting involved. Beijing's Spark Ice café, selling coffee and Internet time, is partly run by Unicom which is owned by the People's Liberation Army. The cafés are potentially big business if they are able to expand their outlets from the six presently open. They could be serving the thousands, perhaps hundreds of thousands, of young cyberaware Chinese unable to afford a computer but eager to get on the Net.

Domestically manufactured machines are competing with imports and the northern port city of Tianjin has been earmarked as an 'information port'. In 1996 Tianjin began a policy of using computers to promote the sharing of information across the city.

Fears on the part of the government about what unlimited access to the Internet could do to the country's social stability have meant that Internet access in China has been kept down to a chosen few. The few are those whom the government can trust not to go downloading radical political material or, more basically, the likes of the Cindy Crawford Web site. This well-grounded fear led to the government's forcing all those with access to register with the Public Security Police as of early 1996. This has restricted Internet access in China to some 100,000 individual computers, the users of which have all been made very aware of the strict penalties they would face if they are tempted to abuse their favored position, especially if caught downloading anything which might be construed to be harmful to national security or anything pornographic.

The fact that for every connected computer there are probably five people with access to it means that there are probably some half a million Chinese with access to all that the Internet has to offer. But they all know that what they look at or download is monitored and that they have to be very careful, especially when the definitions of what is subversive or pornographic are vague.

Getting wired is also expensive in China, another means the government has of restricting who can use the services. China Internet is controlled by Guangdong Provincial Data Communications Bureau, itself a division of the Provincial Post and Telecommunications Bureau. It offers users dialup speeds of up to 9.6 kbps at a cost of about US$73 for the first 40 hours each month, with additional hours charged at US$2. This is a fairly large sum when it is considered that the average office worker earns approximately US$250 a month.

What has become known as the Great Firewall of China is the government's response to the realization that it cannot avoid the benefits that access to the Internet can bring to internal communications, and that trying to ban it would only make its underground use more attractive. The solution has been the development of a nationwide intranet, which mirrors a slice of the Internet.

What makes this intranet possible is that, unlike the Internet, it is based in the Chinese language and therefore is much more accessible to the masses of Chinese who have little or no knowledge of English. While this may not please everyone, it will allow citizens to connect to a Chinese language-based service. China Internet Corporation launched the China Wide Web in October 1996 providing news and economic information gleaned from Xinhua, the official Chinese news agency, Reuters and Bloomberg. The initial fear that no foreign content would be permitted appears to have been dissipated with the announcement that Rupert Murdoch will launch a China Internet service in association with the *People's Daily* with western news translated into Chinese.

China's golden bridge

Technology is being touted as a potential 'golden bridge' to the future in China, tools with which it can leap forward to national networks of financial services, retailing and communications without undergoing the costly developments undertaken by the western nations who had to lay millions of miles of cable.

This is best exemplified by the development of mobile phone systems. Due to China's huge size and difficult terrain, laying telephone cables was always going to be a problematic task. Add to this the considerable rise in demand for telephone lines in China in the past few years and this task became even more mammoth.

The answer lies in the development of mobile phone networks, which now, thanks to companies like Nokia and Ericsson, span most of China. The Chinese are moving straight into the mobile communications world, faster than is being witnessed in the west. Many Chinese now have a pager or mobile phone without having a terrestrial line telephone.

Terrestrial lines are nevertheless in demand and demand still outstrips supply. One of the most recent developments is the growth of home computer ownership, with an estimated 1 percent of urban households owning a computer by the end of 1996. New computer sales are often for units containing built-in modems, hence the need for a link to the telephone system. The greater use of modems is likely to see many Chinese companies in the future bypassing conventional fax technology and going straight for fax modems.

Another important concern in terms of consumer practices is that home shopping in China, though still in an early stage of development and largely carried out over the telephone or through TV advertising, could very soon become predominantly an online affair, allowing retailers to penetrate the hinterland.

Vietnam calling

Most Vietnamese villages used to have a phone – just the one that the lucky owner could rent out for a few hundred dong to other villagers needing to make a call. Now in many of those villages every resident has a phone. The Communist Party's goal enshrined in the 1996 Congress was that by 2000, six out of every 100 people would have their very own phone, actually a tripling of usage in five years.

The 80 million largely phoneless population made the international telecoms giants sit up and listen and Bosch, NC, Alcatel, Motorola all dived into Vietnam. The four lucky companies that got major contracts for line installation were France Telecom, Nippon Telegraph and Telephone (NTT), Cable & Wireless and Australian Telstra. These giants are looking to do a US$194 million upgrade of Hanoi's north and east quarters for 250,000 new lines, US$300 million in lines for Ho Chi Minh City and another 500,000 lines throughout the countryside.

A fully wired future for Asia

Computers, faxes, modems, pagers and mobile phones are all now widely used in Asia and in some countries there is greater use per capita than in the US or Europe. Hong Kong, for example, has more mobile phones per head of population than any other place in the world. Asian Internet connections are higher than those of many European countries.

The market is being propelled by the breaking down of the old national telecoms utilities and the globalization of technology. Until 1996 the state telecommunications company in South Korea controlled 90 percent of the cellular phone market. Then in 1997 three licenses were granted to new entrants, including LG and Hansol. Battle commenced and previous taboos such as discounts and free airtime appeared. It seems that the winners are consumers and in Korea's booming market (until new competition only 9 percent of Koreans had mobiles compared with 16 percent of Singaporeans and 20 percent of Hong Kong residents) it is expected that 10 million Koreans will be using mobile phones by 2000, creating an estimated US$11 billion market.

Business across the region is investing in IT, intranets, communications systems and all manner of peripheral technology. Take the example of Indonesian retailer Matahari. In a bid to improve margins the company has invested in its own communications system linking all its outlets and warehouses by satellite. It has centralized administrative operations at a new 18-story office complex constructed on a greenfield site in Tanggerang complete with a local area network (LAN) for its computer operations. Companies across the region are finding that investment in technology is streamlining their businesses and cutting costs in the long run.

Technology hungry as the Asians are, they have not been mere consumers of western electronics but have in some fields become major producers, adapting and refining western technology to make better and cheaper versions of their own. The fact that most people in the west have a Japanese hi-fi or a Chinese clock radio is tribute to this.

It is not just copies of western goods which attract sales in Asia. Demand is high for consumer electronics and electrical goods designed for Asian consumers' needs. Pagers which can deal with the complexities of Chinese and Japanese scripts take up much more system memory than those designed for Latin characters, but designing efficient technology has taken only a matter of months from perception of the demand.

Asians are more open to the new technology now available since they have not had a real chance to get used to, and sentimental about, previous technological stages of development. Buying vinyl records in Asia is almost impossible and even cassettes are being largely pushed out by compact discs. This not only means that present-day Asians are more technology hungry than most people in the west, but they are also more in tune to the application possibilities offered by such technology.

In some ways, this technophile attitude is helping Asians to become better equipped to face the future. Technology is not seen to be the realm of academics, scientists, businesspeople and nerds, as it is in the west. Asians are already building up virtual libraries for use by schools and information networks for the promotion of leisure activities, so technology is being applied to the lives of children and retired people as well as to universities and business.

Software allowing people to type in Chinese, Japanese, Thai, even Tibetan is readily available. It comes with a wide range of creative fonts, DTP and design capabilities and the like. These systems are user friendly and easy to learn and work just as well with standard PC software packages and keyboards developed for the Roman alphabet. This also applies to other types of information technology, such as pagers, faxes and cash machines.

Singapore has one of the most forward-thinking policies regarding information technology and is building a network of online libraries for education, governmental home pages, systems for paying telephone bills online and so on. Malaysia is following suit and other Asian countries are not far behind.

The fact is that many governments in Asia have seen how building information technology will work out cheaper, in the long run, than building physical information organizations, such as new library buildings. The attitude seems to be that the faster things can get done the better, and technology helps to make things faster.

10
The Media

The media combine to form one of the single most influential shapers of consumer trends in the modern world. As Asia has developed very rapidly over the past few years, so the media environment has kept pace with the resulting social transformations. The opening up of many Asian nations' skies to satellite TV, the lifting of numerous press taboos, the proliferation of media thanks to technology and the growth of an advertising culture all go hand in hand with a new consumer market.

The media rush

Whether in print, radio, TV or any other medium, the rush is on to cash in throughout Asia. There's a simple reason for this – estimated advertising expenditure of over US$100 billion by the turn of the century. This very large pie is attractive enough to make all the international media players and ad agencies rush to the region and also to be the cause of numerous media startups by local content providers. Hardly a major media conglomerate or operation is proving too shy to join in:

- Reader's Digest launched a Thai version called *San Sara* in 1996 backed by sweepstakes and mystery gifts for new subscribers – 300,000 Thais decided to start reading.

- Walt Disney has started airing a 30-minute branded radio show on China National Radio with the US's Northwest Airlines as the primary sponsor. The show backs up the output of over 100 Chinese companies licensed to distribute Disney merchandise across China.
- Shanghai Television initiated a buying frenzy and needed to draft in 20 extra telesales staff in 1997 after airing a 28-minute infomercial for an exercise machine called the Power Rider.
- Reuters recently bought a 49 percent stake in Bisnews Information Services, a Thai supplier of news and data prices to the country's burgeoning financial community. Reuters is now the leading supplier of business information in Thailand after beating out rival Knight Ridder.
- The potential size of Asia's audience was brought home in 1997 by the Chinese blockbuster TV series on the life of Deng Xiaoping – over 220 million Chinese tuned in, but that's just 28 percent of the viewing population.

Another reason for the media rush has been the loosening of regulations around the region. Malaysia repealed its ban on satellite TV in 1996 giving its people an additional 20 channels of entertainment. It and other countries had initially held back for various reasons, political control, national security and fear of increased programming containing sex and violence. But programming is still censored and filtered through the government-controlled Measat-1 satellite: the V-chip writ large.

Likewise, the Chinese government has been eager to remain in control of the media entering the country. This has meant barring foreign satellite operators and confiscating the thousands of satellite dishes bought by many Chinese TV addicts.

No walkover for the media barons

For a while it looked as if the media rush in Asia might have been a party gatecrashed by foreign guests. Rupert Murdoch's News International, Ted Turner's CNN and Turner Entertainment, HBO,

ESPN and all the other giants of the international media were tipped to have the Asian airwaves as their playground. All they had to do was circumvent the local regulations, provide suitable programming and find the right local partners. But the locals have fought back:

- Malaysia will soon have two satellites. Measat-2 will broadcast tailored programming for an Asian audience to Malaysia, India, the Philippines and Taiwan.
- *Baywatch* may be unbeatable in western TV ratings but in Indonesia it's a poor loser to *Si Doel Anak Sekolahan* (Doel the Student), a locally produced drama series.
- In India, 99 percent of TV ad spend still goes to local stations.

The international media haven't been thrown out, just marginalized. But they still can't complain too loudly. Essentially, they have adapted to local conditions. It is no good riding in roughshod with programming that worked in Milwaukee and expecting it to succeed in Sarawak. So the media barons have opened local broadcast facilities and contracted local program makers. The strength and importance of the Chinese market was further evidenced in 1998 by the desire of the leading players to stay in the game. No one was overly surprised when it was suggested that Rupert Murdoch had ordered former Hong Kong Governor Chris Patten's book to be canceled in case it interfered in his Chinese media ambitions.

While local programming is being strengthened, the favorites of the west often translate too. Shanghai Television airs Chinese-language versions of *Sesame Street* under its Chinese name *Zhima Jie*. The series reaches 100 million viewers. Asian versions of western shows such as *ER* and *Chicago Hope* are also increasingly popular. Hong Kong's TVB is producing a medical drama in part to ride the wave of the popularity of this kind of show and also to raise the standing and reputation of the Hong Kong Hospital Authority.

On the newsstand

The Asian newspaper business isn't going to let TV take all of the US$100 billion ad spend pie without a fight. Generally, Asians like a good read. In Singapore 80 percent of the population reads a daily, over 70 percent in Hong Kong and Taiwan. Hong Kong is the most crowded print media marketplace – 76 dailies and 663 periodicals with competition between local product such as the *South China Morning Post* and *Apple Daily* alongside local editions of the *Financial Times* and the *Wall Street Journal*.

In Thailand the newspaper business has been hit by the property slump, realty companies being the largest buyer of classified ad space, but a 92 percent literacy rate and a growing middle class mean that 60 percent of the Bangkok population over 15 reads one of the 48 national papers daily.

Wattachak is a multimedia giant in Thailand, yet its most recent title, *Thailand Times*, crashed in sales terms and found itself unable to gain share in a crowded English-language daily market. This lesson didn't stop Singapore Press Holdings launching a fourth English-language daily, *Business Day*, aiming to end the dominance of the Dow-Jones-owned *Asian Wall Street Journal*. Bangkok now has as many English language dailies as New York.

English-language dailies may only have a total market of 3–4000 native English-speaking readers, but they are generally high-income consumers and the English-as-a-second-language community tends to be professional and wealthy. Indeed, it's not even really a question of selling papers – often they are given away – more of getting copies into the right hands.

Many look enviously at Singapore Press Holdings (SPH) whose three main titles (*Sunday Times*, *Straits Times* and *Lian He Zao Bao*) have a combined circulation of approximately 980,000. Naturally, SPH has the highest rate card and captures 50 percent of total ad spend in Singapore. Low-level competition means big rewards in Asian media, as Anthony Young, Saatchi & Saatchi's regional media director, told *Campaign* in 1996: 'The media options in Singapore are quite straightforward.' Basically, it's SPH.

ASIAN NEWSPAPER CIRCULATION – THE BIG TITLES

Country	Title	Circulation per day ('000)
China	*People's Daily*	4500
	Reference News	4000
	China TV News	2800
	Worker's Daily	1730
	China Youth News	1420
Hong Kong	*Oriental News*	650
	Apple Daily	290
Malaysia	*Berita Harian*	1803
	Utusan Melayu	1419
Thailand	*Thai Rath*	750

Source: Publisher information

As the battle for readers has intensified so new forms of journalism have been introduced. Many Asian newspapers now copy the multisegment issues common in the US and Europe, targeting children, women, sports fans and businesspeople. Even in heavily regulated China, tabloids have appeared. The *New People's Evening News* in Shanghai is an example of this genre with a mix of standard news and human-interest stories. A typical issue would cover Jiang Zemin's latest speech, quack doctors, the poor state of Chinese public toilets and gossip. When a publication as staunch as the *Chinese People's Daily* has features on stock tips and the preponderance of mini skirts in Beijing, things are changing.

The art of niche publishing

Asia's magazine racks are filling up weekly with new titles from both international and local publishers, all targeting different groups. International publishers have been keen to enter into local alliances. For instance, in 1997 Condé Nast's title *Glamour* hit South Korean newsstands, published in Korean by Doosan Dona-A which also publishes *Vogue* and *Reader's Digest* in Korea. *Glamour* has 340 pages an issue with an ad-to-editorial ratio of 60:40.

It seems that most publishers are looking for local versions of their bestselling international titles. Hong Kong has a Chinese-language version of *Cosmopolitan* and Time Asia is producing local-language editions of its bestsellers, including *People* and *Time*.

Local publishers are not just sitting back and letting the international conglomerates tell them how to do it, however. Singapore's Asiamedia publishing house has recently launched a new twice-yearly title aimed at well-to-do new homeowners. *Home & Design* focuses on residential property and sells for S$6 (US$4.50).

Taking China

The possibilities in the new Chinese media-friendly society (at least in comparison to previous years) are vast. Take the success of Boston based International Data Group (IDG). IDG is run by Pat McGovern, a man who has not been slow to see the possibilities of China. He currently oversees an international media empire encompassing 285 computer magazines in over 80 countries generating annual turnover in excess of US$2 billion. Fifteen of those titles are for the Chinese market and have earned IDG something like US$80 million already, making the country IDG's third largest market after the US and Germany.

The problems that IDG and McGovern have faced in China are ones many publishers would envy. Shortage of resources meant that its *China Computerworld* title was limited to 240 pages a week and staff were turning away advertisers. McGovern had the answer to that problem – raise ad rates by 50 percent. Now *China Computerworld* runs to 288 pages with a substantial 70 percent dedicated to advertising, 150,000 subscribers and 2 million readers. China only has an estimated 2.1 million PCs in action, indicating that demand for knowledge about computers is currently outrunning ownership.

Playing it local

In the media it's not enough to break Asia down by nation: 99 percent of media ad spend is at a local level rather than pan-regional. Newspapers and TV stations must reflect the multiethnic composition of the region, whether across multicultural countries such as India and Malaysia or those with immense internal disparities such as China where people in the countryside do not necessarily want to watch what Beijing does, let alone Hong Kong. A viewer only has to see the difference in programming between Beijing and Hunan TV to perceive the different tastes.

Audiences are also incredibly diverse and need programming reflecting different sensibilities, different dialects and different interests. Singapore Cable Vision has introduced more Cantonese programming for the dialect-speaking audience; previously Cantonese speakers had to rely on specialist video stores for films in their language, Mandarin being the dialect encouraged in Singapore. The same station has also started to introduce programming in Hokkien and other regional Chinese dialects. In Indonesia, Bahasa programming is growing, in India regional dialects are finding air time too.

Companies such as MTV have responded to this regionalization and broken down their programming accordingly. MTV Asia produces shows in English, Mandarin and Cantonese. MTV India now does 90 percent of programming in Hindi as well as mixing in additional Hindi videos with the station's usual playlist. MTV is continuing to break down the region with new programming specifically oriented towards Indonesian music and other national genres.

TV in Asia

The media rush in Asia has led to an explosion of channels, content providers and program makers. This is not just in terrestrial TV but cable and satellite as the skies get crowded with in excess of 60 satellites beaming down programming to the continent. Only belatedly are governments trying to ensure that what goes out over the airwaves is what they would like their populations to see. Typical of the sort of legislation winding its way through national parliaments is the 1997 executive order issued by then President Fidel Ramos of the Philippines on the operation of cable television. Executive order No. 436 proclaims: 'Filipinos must be given wider access to more sources of news, information, education, sports events and entertainment programs than those provided for by mass-media and regular television programs to attain a well-informed, well-versed and culturally refined citizenry and enhance their socioeconomic growth.' Laudable but complicated – does *Power Rangers* make the grade or not? How about *The Simpsons*?

The reams of legislation, comment and opinion that the explosion of television services has generated have echoed the sort of debate about media seen elsewhere in the world. Is it a force for good or evil, will it damage children with negative images or not? Ultimately what the concerns reflect is the power of television to reach people. Politicians, legislators and commentators are only obsessed with TV for the same reasons as advertisers, manufacturers and retailers, namely that everyone is watching.

Channel-surfing Asia

China has over 600 TV stations and a TV advertising market thought to be in excess of US$2 billion a year. Add the proliferation of cable and satellite services and an 84 percent TV penetration rate in urban households and the country is becoming a major television market. As the TV industry has boomed so niche programming has already arrived to target advertising and shows at those groups of consumers that advertisers like so much. Guangdong Economic Television Station (GETS) specializes in business programming. However, the status of GETS is questionable – it is funded by a private company called Zhongjia Group, yet private TV stations are still not recognized in law.

MAJOR URBAN CABLE TV OPERATORS

Operator	Market	No. of subscribers
Beijing Cable TV	Beijing	1,200,000
Rebar Telecommunications	Taipei	1,200,000
Wharf Cable	Hong Kong	260,000
Lopez	Manila	180,000
International Broadcasting Co.	Bangkok	120,000
In-Cable Net	New Delhi	65,000
Mega TV	Kuala Lumpur	40,000
Singapore Cable Vision	Singapore	30,000

Source: Company information

There were around 1200 cable TV stations covering 40 million subscribers (estimated actual viewers 200 million) across 29 provinces operating under government license in 1996 (and perhaps a similar number operating illegally). The largest provider is Shanghai Cable TV with 1.82 million subscribers. Cable takes a 9 percent viewing share in the big cities and some shows capture a third of the viewing audience. Similarly, satellite dishes have been officially banned since 1993 but continue to pop up on buildings in the big cities. Media analysts have estimated that 1 percent of TV households in China could pick up satellite programming from Hong Kong and Australia.

In South Korea 100 percent of households own a TV set and 87 percent a VCR, but until 1995 all programming was government controlled. Since then regional channels for Pusan, Taegu, Taejan and Kwangju have been established but not a lot else. Historically TV has been a public service tool in South Korea with limited advertising opportunities and restricted viewing hours. Into the gap stepped the satellite companies with Koreasat 1 and 2 launched in 1995, still controlled by the government, but attracting 500,000 households to buy a dish purely out of interest in watching something. Now the government is promoting cable TV, which is easier to control, after suspicions that Koreans were watching more than Koreasat as their dishes could pick up all sorts of programming bouncing around the skies.

The media rush is building in India and with the government's planned privatizations and the number of domestic and foreign media companies eager to get into Indian homes, the current rolling wave will soon become a tsunami. First of all, the set manufacturers have a job to do – there are 900 million people and only 55 million households, about a third, with TVs. Certainly advertisers get excited when they see the Indian population's addiction to the serials and films, invariably based around Indian myth and legend, that attract in excess of 100 million viewers. State-controlled TV has begun to vary its programming in the last few years thanks in part to competition from channels such as Star/Zee TV. However, Doordarshan (DD), the public TV channel, still dominates the schedules and the advertising revenues (estimated at in excess of US$350 million), with a growing number of programs being sponsored by international FMCG corporations.

In India as in many other Asian countries, the 1991 Gulf War boosted satellite dish sales and stations such as Zee and CNN found sizeable audiences as 15 million households subscribed to cable TV over the following few years. Stations have popped up all over the country serving the Hindi market, the news market, the English-speaking market and many others. CNN has not been the only successful US channel to adapt to India. ESPN, the US broadcaster of basketball and other all-American sports, has built audience share with ESPN Asia covering the national game of cricket.

In Vietnam, one of the most restricted TV markets in Asia, 70 percent of the population now has access to local and national programming. The government is actually keen for everyone to watch TV, so keen that it provided 6918 free sets to communes across the country.

Cable TV has started to attract major advertisers. CNN, a global news network with broadcasts throughout Asia, was chosen as the medium for Japanese cosmetics giant Shiseido to launch the campaign celebrating its centenary.

Cable TV in Taiwan

Taiwan's cable TV business is a prime example of the chaos that can characterize Asian television. In 1993, on introduction, it was an exciting market with potentially big ad revenues (estimated in 1997 to be well over US$1.5 billion), well-heeled consumers and good infrastructure. But now the country has a growing number of disgruntled cable customers and a plethora of TV companies losing money. Not that this is stopping investment – Sony bought 25 percent of Super TV, the second largest cable channel, in September 1997, with announcements of increased local content for Chinese-language markets and a pan-Asian action-adventure channel called AXN to be launched. And 1998 saw the introduction of direct-to-home TV services.

Currently 75 percent of Taiwanese households are cabled up, totaling about four million homes. However, illegal 'tapping' of cable TV means that only about three million actually pay for cable. In 1993 there were 600 operators, now down to approximately 100, still extremely high by international standards. Complicated rules and fees have meant that Taiwanese households have to scan their TV guides to see which channel their favorite soap is on this week, indeed what channels are actually on air that week.

Creating local content

Television exemplifies the trend towards demanding local taste and influence mixed with what is regarded as good from the west. The successful Channel V music station had no problem inviting the British Spice Girls to perform at its annual awards in New Delhi in 1997, a program that regularly attracts 20 million viewers regionwide.

Formats change little around the world – game shows, talk shows, soap operas. The families may look different but the characters and plot lines from popular Asian soaps, such as China's *Western Cop* or *Wu Zetian*, are not that different from US soaps like *As The World Turns* or *Sons & Daughters*. On the whole Asian soaps tend to be either historical or fast moving rather than kitchen-sink-type social commentaries. Asia has its versions of *Oprah* and the other talk shows. However, there is a subtle spin in that the Asian versions tend to highlight the model citizens and achievers rather than the array of misfits and freaks paraded across the stage in the US versions – more the successful marriage of 30 years and why it worked than the 'My Husband Slept with my Sister and then Eloped with my Brother' variety.

The sheer number of channels and stations now available and the many more planned are making it impossible for local program makers to produce all those hours of content. Many TV companies are looking to commission content from the west. Televisi Pendidikan Indonesia (TPI) commissioned Australia's Grundy Television (the Pearson-owned makers of the hit soap *Neighbours*) to produce versions of the two famous game shows *Sale of the Century* and *Take Your Pick* in the Bahasa Indonesian language.

Local content doesn't necessarily need to be confined to one country. Japanese TV companies produce shows like *Asia Bagus!* (Malay for excellent) which tapes in Singapore and features amateur acts from Indonesia, Japan, Malaysia and Singapore. When it airs in Malaysia on Saturday night primetime it gets 50 percent of the viewership. Mandarin-dubbed Japanese shows have done well in Taiwan and Hong Kong. Japanese soap operas tend to be centered around big-city yuppies and one of the reasons they are so popular in other Asian countries is that they portray the lifestyle to which so many of the viewers are aspiring.

With the massive ethnic Chinese population throughout Asia, it is perhaps not surprising that programming emitting from the mainland should find ready audiences. The highly acclaimed Chinese-made series on the life of Deng Xiaoping was sold to 20 countries and earned US$450,000. In total, sales of Chinese-made programming overseas earned the country US$6 million. Serializations of Chinese classics such as *The Romance of the Three Kingdoms* and *A Dream of Red Mansions* attracted high viewership in Thailand and Hong Kong, while a 41-part series, *Outlaws of the Marsh*, was ordered by 10 countries including South Korea and Singapore.

In March 1998 Chinese television started screening a 19-part series called *An Opening*. This is a new form of programming for China and shows just how closely TV is used to reflect and influence social life. The story takes place in a Beijing courtyard and portrays the struggles of recently laid-off workers trying to survive in the city. It would be hard to get more current on Beijing TV right now.

However, before Asia can start creating content on a scale capable of satisfying the proliferating number of channels and stations it needs facilities:

- India has a head start thanks to the success of its indigenous film studios, known colloquially as Bollywood, which have moved into the business of TV serials and miniseries.
- Malaysia is in the process of setting up Film City, an Asian Hollywood in Pahang. This is Malaysia's attempt to become Asia's center of movie making and cash in on the growing market for movies, videos and TV. As the number of cinemas and TV stations increases so the demand for local content grows.
- Indonesian company PT Yasawirya Tama Cipta (YTC) is building a US$25 million multimedia centre that, while expensive, may save the country US$40 million a year otherwise spent abroad for commercial advertising production. The center is a 16-story building outside Jakarta that incorporates live broadcast studios, a Kodak film-processing lab and all the latest technology in four international-standard studios.

Radio Asia

It's also worth a quick mention of the explosion in radio stations across Asia in the last decade. Radio penetration is almost total, even in countries with lower than average TV ownership. Again, governments have rolled back restrictive legislation and doled out the licenses, creating a rush. Taiwan alone passed out frequencies to 158 stations on both FM and AM between 1993 and 1995, partly as a response to pirate radio. Beijing cab drivers now assault your ears with one of the many 'lite' FM stations that sound virtually identical (both in terms of playlist and advertising) to anything heard in the west.

Radio has fought back against TV with 24-hour programming and severe competition between stations. In Singapore, the five major English language music stations send their DJs on non-stop promotional tours. The country's music airwaves are dictated by computer-generated playlists, hence the musical format is identical. Capturing listeners comes down to DJs' personalities.

Madison Avenue goes east

There is now hardly a western advertising agency of any size without an Asian presence. The prize they are all seeking is the rash of new accounts opening up as Asia becomes a consumer market of enormous size. Consider these benefits: DMB&B Hong Kong landed the Vietnam Airlines account for US$5 million; Bozell Philippines took the Swift foods account for US$1 million as well as the Visa and Mastercard accounts for US$700,000. The penetration has been so great that in Taiwan six of the top ten agencies in revenue terms are US owned. But this is hardly surprising. The ad industry places great reliance on statistics – *X* percent liked this ad, *Y* percent hated this brand name – so show an advertising person a statistic such as that Taiwan's monthly disposable household income in 1995 was US$31,522, almost a 30 percent increase since 1991, and they just can't walk away.

Ad spend in the 1990s grew across the region, by as much as 62 percent a year in Vietnam and 23 and 25 percent in South Korea and India respectively.

The reason for this eastern expansion is the same as for the explosion in newspapers and magazines and the growth of electronic media. The ad spend pie that is creating the media rush requires more and more ad agencies. In a market where reputation is everything, the international agencies with their international clients have a head start. When food giant Heinz decided to launch its tomato ketchup in India, local subsidiary Heinz India chose

Chaitra Leo Burnett. Additionally, the wealthy international agencies are simply buying up the local competition. Bates Worldwide recently moved to buy one of India's largest agencies, Clarion, picking up US$18 million worth of accounts with companies such as Indian Airlines, Siemens and Unilever India.

As competition in Asia's consumer markets continues to hot up so advertising is becoming more and more aggressive, with consumer products leading the way. In Indonesia major brands like Sunsilk shampoo, Pepsodent toothpaste and Marlboro cigarettes spent more than 34 billion rupiah on advertising in 1996 (when the US$:Rp exchange rate wasn't nearly so bad). Airlines, travel companies, the auto manufacturers, real-estate agents and telecommunications companies all increased their ad spend in the country, driving it up 33 percent in total over 1995.

Foreign products are often given an Asian angle and advertisers are keen to exploit what they perceive as Asian values. Alcoholic beverage Dom Benedictine apparently helps blood circulation and vitality, according to an ad on Singapore TV accompanied by images of a young mother sipping away. Foreign products are also eager to show that they know what Asian viewers want. Another ad in Singapore attempts to convince viewers that Vidal Sassoon really does 'know' Asian hair.

In China, fast-food giant McDonald's is represented by international ad agency Leo Burnett, which includes other megabrands such as Marlboro, Coca-Cola, Disney and Kellogg's among its clients. It devised an ad for the golden arches featuring Chinese men performing *tai chi* and contorting themselves into the letter *M*. An ad that would have been irredeemably cute and sweet in the west became a way of selling McDonald's as a family restaurant in China to middle- and upper-income families. When it became apparent that many Chinese parents were questioning the value of a McDonald's meal, the company began sponsoring 'Drive Slowly' message boards near Beijing schools.

Sponsorship has become a major business and as the rules regarding who can sponsor what in Europe and the US have become ever tighter, foreign manufacturers have increased their sponsorship involvement in Asia. Ryder Cup Golf is brought to you courtesy of Mild Seven cigarettes, boxing courtesy of Winston and outdoor pursuits thanks to Benson & Hedges. It seems that no keen sportsperson in Asia would be unattached to a brand of cigarette.

Western products that previously were of little concern to Asian audiences are now appearing frequently. For example, as weight gain becomes an issue in Asia thanks to junk food and higher, if not healthier, standards of living, meal replacement product Slimfast has launched an ad campaign on Malaysian TV.

Major advertisers in Asia

China

Advertising is still dominated by product-oriented media. The largest advertisers include Elegbacae anti-freckle cream and Chunlan air conditioners alongside conglomerates such as Motorola. TV ads are overwhelmingly the main outlet. Brands seeking national coverage can find it an expensive business: Elegbacae spends approximately US$7.8 million a quarter on TV ads.

Hong Kong

Banking and finance are major ad spenders, two of the largest being Standard Chartered and Citibank. Consumer conglomerates like McDonald's and Hutchison Telecom also spend heavily. TV is the dominant medium with quarterly ad spend for major brands exceeding US$3 million.

India

Corporate image promotion is the main reason for ad spend at present. The number of car ads has rocketed as have newspaper ads for TV sets. While TV ads are becoming more sophisticated, the main outlet remains print.

Indonesia

The ad industry is product based with the largest advertisers being consumer goods such as Lux bath soap, Indomie instant noodles and Sanaflu cold medicine. Quarterly ad spend exceeds US$3 million for major brands with TV the favored medium.

Malaysia

Ad spend is lower than in many countries in the region and is also dominated by several brands that maintain blanket coverage. Despite this, it still topped US$821 million in 1996. The majority is dedicated to TV but outdoor ads have become increasingly popular, as any visitor to KL's Golden Triangle will testify. Dunhill luxury goods are heavily advertised, with the company paying out just under US$2 million a quarter on TV ads alone.

Philippines

Major advertisers on TV include Philippine Long Distance Telephone (quarterly spend of over US$5 million in 1997), San Miguel beer, Milo (a popular malt/milk drink) and Sunsilk shampoo. The bulk of major advertisers are consumer goods manufacturers. TV is an increasingly important medium, though radio remains heavily used with major advertisers spending between US$700,000 and US$1 million per quarter.

Singapore

Singapore has a sophisticated advertising market with a variety of consumer goods advertised. Major ad spenders such as McDonald's, Courts (homewares) and SingTel Mobile spend in excess of US$1.2 million a quarter to reach a population of 3.1 million. Newspapers remain the main ad medium in Singapore.

South Korea

South Korea is Asia's second largest ad market after Japan. Not surprisingly, advertising is dominated by the *chaebols*, with Samsung, Daewoo, Lucky Goldstar (LG) and Hyundai each spending in excess of US$20 million a quarter across TV, papers, magazines and radio.

Taiwan

The main advertisers are a mixture of international and domestic companies. Major international spenders include Procter &

Gamble and Ford, both spending over US$10 million a quarter in 1997. Local manufacturers such as Kingcar Drinks and Yue Loong Motor are not spending a great deal less. While TV takes the lion's share of ad spend, both papers and magazines remain important. The total market is worth in excess of US$4 billion and is the third largest in Asia after Japan and South Korea.

Thailand

Thailand's ad market is dominated by car and motorbike manufacturers as the country's automobile market rockets and its road system grinds to a halt. Both Honda and Toyota spend in excess of US$4 million per quarter on TV and newspaper ads. Other major ad spenders include the Electricity Generating Authority, Singha beer (the most popular local brew) and the National Energy Policy Office.

Vietnam

Judging by the country's three major ad spenders, booze is big in Vietnam – Tiger Beer, San Miguel and Heineken all spend in excess of US$240,000 a quarter. The country remains a relatively small ad market with spend split between TV and print. Other major spenders include Caltex oil and Chinfon Haiphong Cement.

The effect of the meltdown

Undoubtedly the economic turmoil affecting the region since 1997 has affected the advertising industry. A business whose fortunes are as closely tied to the wider economic health of a market could not have hoped for a continuance of the sustained growth of the last decade. However, as with most things, the fallout has been patchy. Vietnam has seen ad revenues fall somewhat, partly due to reductions in consumer demand but also because new laws mean that only 5 percent of ad spend is tax deductible. Yet the expected decline in revenues has not deterred the many new agencies entering the country.

Thailand has been hit badly, with ad revenues thought to have dipped by as much as 30 percent in 1997 over 1996. This was largely the result of heavy discounting and a drop in real-estate advertising.

The crisis has forced companies to reevaluate their advertising strategies and raised the question of pan-regional advertising. Nobody has searched for Asian hegemony as hard as the advertising industry. To global brands with ad accounts scattered across the globe, finding it would be a major step towards the ultimate prize of global advertising, regional coverage at reduced cost. The turmoil has accelerated this quest.

So far the search for the pan-Asian ad campaign has been fruitless. But eventually campaigns will emerge that can be played across the region, keeping ad agency fees down and clients happy. But they may not be worth the search. Pan-regional ad campaigns in Europe have been almost wholly failures and Europe is less diverse than Asia.

Celebrity endorsements are even more difficult in Asia where local celebrities do not always cross barriers and Hollywood is not yet as pervasive. Korean beer companies use local actresses: goddesses in Seoul, unknown in Bangkok.

In Asia the talk of pan-regional advertising has also been prompted by the need to promote strong regional identities for brands. There has been much talk of the pan-Asian homogeneous aspirational consumer. John Machado, an ad man with a long track record in the Malaysian and Asian ad industry, derides those ad agencies that attempt to sell what he calls 'lifestyle advertising' based around pan-regional aspiration and status seeking. At best, he claims in his book *Creating Desire*, this group represents just 0.5 percent of 1 percent of the total market. Instead he advocates advertising based around consumer values: 'those things people believe in so strongly they place their lives on them'. He cites campaigns such as Nike's 'Just Do It' and Miller beer ads targeted at working women as positive examples.

Of course Asians of all nationalities and social groups are aspirant, of course they seek status, but they pursue these aims on vastly different levels in vastly different ways and with vastly different incomes. The Hunan peasant, the Singapore student and the Bangkok retailer are all aspiring but their short-, medium- and long-term objectives are nowhere near the same.

None of this has stopped the search as ad budgets have been squeezed. Fuji Photo Film in Thailand is thinking on a regional basis as a way to reduce expenses. It believes that it can save more than 50 percent in the production costs of TV commercials by using the same ads across a number of countries in the region instead of producing one for each. There are regional TV commercials for its latest Superia film airing in four languages in the Thai, Singapore, Indonesian and Malaysian markets. Perhaps Fuji has a better reason than many for seeking a pan-regional campaign – as an official sponsor of the Soccer World Cup 1998, it planned to use the opportunity to increase its marketing activity.

And while the market has seen some contraction, new opportunities are also opening. Hong Kong's Chek Lap Kok airport claims to offer an unprecedented opportunity for niche advertisers. Pearl & Dean, the agency responsible for advertising at the new airport, began offering ad space on 1200 baggage trolleys, escalators, light screens and seat backs in March 1998. Panel adverts were priced at US$2300 a week.

Additionally, most of the canceled ad spend seems to be from local companies. Global brands such as Coca-Cola are still spending. It signed up Zenith Media to handle its Chinese account with a budget of US$25 million a year, bringing Zenith's total Hong Kong and Chinese billings to US$3 billion, not bad for a tough market.

The rush continues...

The media rush engulfing Asia is showing no signs of stopping. Despite currency crises and other economic mishaps, advertising expenditure keeps on going up. Newspapers are still locked in circulation battles, as are magazines with publishers convinced that niche publishing will tap the advertising market still further. As the consumer boom continues so titles proliferate on computers, cars, boats, fashion, fitness and anything else people will put their hands in their wallets to find out about. *Newsweek* announced in 1998 that it was launching a Chinese-language edition for sale throughout Asia, with an exclusive ad deal with Johnson & Johnson allowing 23 pages of ad space in an 88-page publication.

As governments release licenses so the plethora of FM and AM radio stations grows. Again broadcasters are looking for the niche: sports radio, news radio, golden oldies, Cantopop, classical, talk radio.

And so too with TV. Cable boxes, satellite dishes, VCD players and pay-TV decoders are all becoming increasingly familiar household items. The number of channels is growing across terrestrial, satellite and cable with increased regional programming to suit all. You want a Bahasa quiz show for the over-sixties, it's there. A Malay teen talk show, it's there. A Chinese car-maintenance program, no problem. Indian music videos, Taiwanese business, Australian home shopping, Filipino serials or Chinese soaps in Mandarin, Cantonese and Hokkien all there alongside *Friends*, *Cybill*, *NYPD Blue* and *Larry King Live*.

Local and international media barons are fighting for viewers and readers across the continent. Despite the turmoil, they will continue to do so as government legislation recedes and advertising expenditure increases. There is room for a lot more expansion.

The twist in the tale for Asia's media is that as consumers cut back on spending after the meltdown, TV viewership has actually risen, sustaining the advertising industry.

11
Retailing

Asian retailing is incredibly competitive: on price, on location, on service and on stock. Increasingly, retailing structures in the region are adapting to resemble its consumers, that is, they are becoming extensive, increasingly sophisticated and competitive. With increasing access to cash and credit, transport, travel and consumer information, Asian shoppers are making active choices about where and how they shop. They have a wide range of choices:

- The region is peppered with large shopping malls providing one-stop shopping facilities in air-conditioned comfort.
- Department stores have proliferated throughout urban areas.
- Supermarkets, convenience stores and minimarts are revolutionizing food shopping and spreading as the suburban sprawl encompasses most cities.
- The number of modern retail outlets across Asia (excluding China) is rapidly approaching 5 million.
- Mail order, home shopping and TV shopping channels have all arrived.
- Discount retailers such as the Dutch group Makro are finding a ready marketplace in the post-meltdown environment.

The retail industry was traditionally dominated by family-run neighborhood stores and market traders. However, with the rapid economic development of the region in the past decade, there has been correspondingly rapid change and modernization in the retail sector. Modern retail-management practices have been introduced, including higher standards of space management, centralized warehousing, inventory control, advanced display and merchandising techniques and the application of technologies such as electronic ordering and point of sale (EPoS) scanning.

The street stalls that traditionally characterized so much of Asia's retailing scene have begun to give way to more concentrated forms of shopping. In South Korea alone the number of markets has shrunk from 686 to 588 in just five years. The large-scale covered shopping center, or mall, is now well established, accounting for up to half of all non-food retail sales in some countries. With shopping increasingly becoming an integral part of the leisure culture, malls offer not only convenience under one air-conditioned roof but also a range of culinary and entertainment attractions that meet some of the traditional Asian reasons for going to the shops in the first place.

The pattern of food retailing is also changing. Although in most countries wet markets and family grocers continue to dominate, supermarkets and convenience stores are increasingly gaining in importance and their numbers have been soaring. Alterations in consumer eating habits such as the move towards frozen, packaged and western foods, along with changes in the mix of households, shifts in population and improvements in food distribution, have led to the growing importance of supermarkets in the processed food trade.

Shopping as a way of life

While the details change, the basic shape remains the same. Asians have always shopped. In countries with large ethnic Chinese populations and those with low ownership rates of refrigerators and freezers, and given subtropical climates, shopping has traditionally been a daily activity. Despite the proliferation of supermarkets, convenience stores such as the 7-Eleven chain and packaged foods, many millions of Asians continue to shop daily.

Invariably shopping is something more than nipping out for a pint of milk and a loaf of bread. Asians have long enjoyed the sociable side of shopping: meeting friends, window shopping and unwinding at the weekend with a family shopping trip. Retailers have not wasted time tapping this trend and have incorporated a vast array of food courts, cinemas, amusement parks, swimming pools and other services into the new 'dream palace' malls that have sprung up from Bangkok to Shenzhen.

The traditions of Asian retailing have been reinterpreted for a new generation. Shops stay open late, new developments stand alongside centuries-old markets which still pull huge crowds, haggling persists and the concept of the bargain and value for money are still prevalent.

Asia isn't the US

Every US city and state has its malls and every UK town its high street. These are replicas of thousands of Main Streets and High Streets dumped out of town, sanitized, enclosed and ringed by acres of parking spaces but essentially composed of the same outlets, the same brands, the same logos – just a little more inaccessible to those without cars.

In Asia, malls and purpose-built shopping centers represent something different. For instance, malls in Bangkok cater to the affluent urban consumer and are designed not simply as one-stop shopping centers but as refuges from the dirt and stress of the city's traditional retailing areas. Across the region clean, air-conditioned malls and plazas offer respite from the humidity and pollution. It is impossible otherwise to imagine the growth of a sophisticated retail infrastructure. Simply put, shopping in KL would be a hectic, dirty, uncomfortable pastime without Lot 10, Sungei Wei and the other plazas of the Golden Triangle.

Out-of-town malls in Asia exclude all but the more affluent by simple distance. With public transport patchy, access is invariably by car. Those without cars don't go, so malls are often hallowed halls of relative privilege.

First it is useful to understand the stages through which Asia's retailing infrastructures are moving and place each nation at its current stage so we can see where they've come from and where they're going.

THE THREE STAGES OF ASIAN RETAILING

***Stage 1*: A gradual move away from a retail infrastructure based primarily on 'wet', or fresh produce, markets and family-run independent general stores towards an emergent system of organized retailing with small supermarkets, minimarts and basic one-stop shopping. Countries at this stage include Vietnam, China and Indonesia.**

***Stage 2*: The development of organized chain retailers such as supermarkets, convenience stores and department stores. Gradually less reliance on markets and neighborhood stores and the emergence of mall/plaza developments. Countries at this second stage of development include Malaysia, Thailand and South Korea.**

***Stage 3*: Further expansion of chain operators followed by a wave of specialty retailers and malls catering to upper income brackets, out-of-town retailing, warehouse and club shopping combined with a growth in the presence of international retailers. Countries that have reached this stage include Singapore, Taiwan and Hong Kong. It is often followed by a slump in mass retailing and a rise in niche markets.**

Countries and stages

Asia is an amalgam of various retailing formats ranging from Vietnam, where wet markets and small general stores dominate and organized retailing is still largely absent, to Singapore, where a recession in retail spending and saturation of the market have led to retrenchment by highly organized retailers.

The level of development of a country's retail facilities is based on a number of factors. There are social factors such as average income which allows purchasing to a certain level, the amount of disposable income left after mortgages, rents, savings, utilities bills and debt repayments. Also in some countries the aggregated costs of health, education and transport don't leave so much for impulse purchasing. In general the new middle-class consumers like to take care of the above categories of expenditure before moving onto life's little luxuries.

Retail infrastructure is affected by secondary factors, not the least of which is local law. Many Asian nations have traditionally banned, or at least restricted, foreign retailers from setting up operations. The Philippines and South Korea, for example, opposed the entry of foreign retailers for many years. However, anti-competitive legislation is being rolled back across the region, including in one-party states such as China and Vietnam, and is destined eventually to be repealed in total following the examples of Hong Kong and Singapore.

The only way is up

Whatever stage a country finds itself at in terms of retailing, the trend is towards greater diversity, competing formats and vendors, as well as the extension of modern retailing forms throughout the country and not just in the big regional retailing centers of the conurbations. The rapid acceptance of new forms is startling:

- In Taiwan it took just three years for supermarkets to move from serving a mere 5 percent of the population to in excess of 50 percent.
- In Thailand the country moved from being largely based on wet markets to having three major supermarket chains and two of the world's five largest indoor shopping malls by 1995.
- From being a region of numerous small, independently owned retail outlets, Asia is developing a growing number of region-

BUY NOW, PAY LATER – ASIA'S FLEXIBLE FRIENDS

Hong Kong residents now invariably carry several store cards while even Vietnamese shoppers can charge it to Amex and Mastercard. Proof of the fact that the stigma of borrowing is dwindling is found in the statistic that spending has shot up to in excess of US$1000 on average per card per annum. The number of outlets accepting charge cards in Asia exceeded a million in 1996, with particularly strong growth in Taiwan where credit has traditionally been avoided. With the credit boom has come a host of financial services providers keen to get in on the act.

Japan's major credit card issuer, JCB, is working with a Thai media firm to bolster its credit card operations in Asia, targeting Thais with high incomes and Japanese living in the country. With an initial fee of 500 baht and an annual fee of 1000 baht, cardholders will be entitled to preferential treatment when they buy goods on credit through a telephone shopping service and at JCB-affiliated stores in Thailand.

However, signs have emerged that not all consumers are able to pay up. The number of unpaid bills in South Korea is growing alarmingly and in Thailand too store card balances are increasingly going unpaid.

wide chain operations introducing the concept of pan-Asian shopping.

- In the last decade there has been a flood of investment by the world's leading international retailers, including Carrefour of France, Marks & Spencer of the UK (which has over 30 stores in the region) and Makro of the Netherlands. The Japanese have been particularly prevalent, with chains such as Isetan and Takashimaya becoming household names across the continent.
- The availability of credit and/or store cards has boosted spending and created a revolution in how shoppers pay for their purchases. Since 1991 it is estimated that over 100 million payment cards have been issued throughout Asia. Between 1991 and 1995 the number of payment cards in circulation grew by 80 percent.

The downside

The emergence of new retailing formats has inevitably meant a downside for some regional retailers. Non-organized retailers are finding themselves squeezed out by mall developments and high rents and maintenance costs. The economies of scale enjoyed by the chains and multiples are placing insurmountable burdens on the small neighborhood retailers, just as they did on US 'mom-and-pop' stores or European corner shops.

However, local retailers are still prominent. Hong Kong companies such as Lane Crawford, Giordano, AS Watson and Dairy Farm have begun to expand throughout the region, as have Robinson of Thailand and CK Tang's of Singapore. Asian retailing may be headed down the road previously traveled by Europe and the US of standardization and formula fascias, but it will have a discernible Asian slant to it. Indeed, several countries have actively promoted buy-local campaigns, most notably Thailand which launched a 'Buy Thai' campaign to help close the trade gap. The London *Daily Telegraph* reported in October 1996 that a former prime minister of Thailand had thrown out his Versace ties and Bally shoes in favor of locally made products – although he kept his £230,000 German-made Mercedes sedan. And enthusiasm among ordinary Thais was muted, the merchandise trade balance not being a topic of everyday concern to most people.

Eventually the 'Buy Thai' campaign took off after the currency crisis when the baht hit an all-time low. It seems that Thais stopped buying foreign and bought local for economic rather than nationalistic reasons. As Piyida Chittangwong, a Bangkok office worker, told the *Straits Times* in September 1997: 'I stopped buying brand name purses, shoes and other accessories some time ago. I also cancelled my plan for a holiday abroad this year. How can one afford an expensive holiday in this economic situation?'

Whatever the downside for local merchants, there is still an upside for manufacturers with products to sell. Retail turnover as a percentage of total consumer expenditure is up everywhere, by 13 percent in Hong Kong since 1991, by 9 percent in Malaysia, by 21 percent in the Philippines and by 7 percent in Thailand. Even more impressive is the growth in per capita retail turnover, which has increased by 206 percent in Vietnam since 1991, 50 percent in Hong Kong, 52 percent in Malaysia, 73 percent in the Philippines, 62 percent in Singapore and 45 percent in Thailand.

No small change

Across the region, excluding China, retail sales are in excess of US$550 billion annually and have doubled every five years since the start of the 1980s. No wonder everyone wants in on a market that contrasts staggeringly well with the developed, some might say overdeveloped, retail regions of western Europe and the US and outstrips growth in the developing regions of eastern Europe and Latin America. Despite the recent slowdown, retailers around the world are increasingly coming to pin their hopes on the Asian shopper.

Western clothing chains such as Benetton, Stefanel and The Gap are moving in. Japanese retailers, such as Mitsukoshi and Isetan, are hoping to escape the domestic slump by expanding throughout the region. Japanese analysts point to the complementary 'push and pull' factors of Asian retailing, the push being the saturated Japanese market and the pull the boom in east Asian retail sales. In addition, niche retailers are finding that the Asian shopper might just be the antidote to sluggish, or even stagnant, sales in the west. Among the hopeful are the Body Shop, Tower Records, Mothercare and Habitat.

It's worth remembering that Asia is not always a cheap option for retailers. Until 1998 Hong Kong remained the most costly retail center in the world with rents twice that of London's Oxford Street and New York's Fifth Avenue and 35 times that of central Manila.

In with the new

Examples of new retailing formats abound. Here are a few:

- The demand for European luxury goods has prompted French retailer Printemps to open 12 stores across Asia.
- Mail-order companies have made major inroads into the Asian market, among them French-based La Redoute and Trois Suisses as well as the UK-based Freeman's operation.
- Door-to-door retailing is booming with companies such as Avon and Amway moving not just sales expertise but manufacturing capacity to Asia to cope with demand from their networks of agents.
- TV shopping companies such as the Australian-based TV Shopping Network (TVSN) operate 24-hour retail channels spanning 100 countries reaching 70 million Asian households.

Hypermarkets are now a staple part of the retail mix across Asia. According to the *New Straits Times* (19.2.97), Malaysia's leading retailing concern, Metrojaya Group, launched a hypermarket called Cosmart Hypermarket in Pandan Indah, Kuala Lumpur. This occupies 85,000 sq. ft in the Pandan Kapitol shopping mall and has a supermarket and general merchandise store under one roof. The group plans to open six such stores in Malaysia by the year 2000. Metrojaya is just one of many retailers, both domestic and foreign, to launch hypermarkets, discount clubs and supermarket chains across the region in the last five years.

Asian retailing concerns tend to operate across formats. Typical of this is one of the region's largest retail operators, Matahari. Established in 1986, Matahari is Indonesia's largest department store chain operating over 90 stores in 29 cities. The company operates four store formats – Matahari Department Store which caters to lower- to middle-income families, upscale retail outlets under the Galleria marquee, Super Economy stores which are established in small regional towns and Mega M, a wholesale retail chain.

International retailers have also entered the Asian market with formats targeting specific consumer groups and aiming to plug current gaps in the retail structure. Loft, a subsidiary of Japan's Seibu Group, sells gifts and games, home furnishings, communications equipment, stationery, design and personal-care products. It already has six branches in Japan. The Loft store covers 1200 square meters on the third floor of the Siam Discovery Center. Many retailers in Bangkok had not previously focused on design products. Loft's merchandise, 70 percent of which is imported, is aimed mainly at shoppers aged between 17 and 35 with incomes of 15,000 baht and up per month.

Franchising has also arrived in Asia. For many years the major fast-food companies such as McDonald's and Kentucky Fried Chicken have been franchising throughout the region and now the concept is spreading across multiple niche sectors. According to Singapore's Trade Development Board, 13 percent of the country's domestic retail sales are now generated by franchised businesses.

Invasion of the malls

Retail malls and plazas have become a little too common for some retailers who have found that the pace of development has occasionally exceeded demand. Often too many malls in too close proximity, too much repetition of retail chains or simply an out-of-town mall finished and staffed before the road to it, or the mass rapid transport system serving it, were completed.

Malls aren't necessarily new in the more developed cities. Kuala Lumpur's Sungai Wang Plaza has retained its popularity after being in business for more than 17 years. In 1992, it underwent a US$8.2 million refurbishment exercise building a new retail floor, bringing in new shops and improved facilities. Since the refit, the plaza has maintained 100 percent occupancy and currently has the highest monthly traffic flow of shoppers in Malaysia, with 2.2 million people visiting it. Just across the road, its competition, the Lot 10 mall, has also undergone refurbishment. In 1996 alone two million square feet of mall space was built in KL. And the number of malls in excess of 3000 square meters in South Korea grew from 1176 in 1991 to in excess of 1600 by 1997.

At first malls were ways for developers to create retailing space outside congested inner-city business districts by utilizing greenfield sites or derelict urban land. They assumed that the new rich and affluent of Asia's capitals would want to be able to shop away from the teeming city centers in palaces of consumption. They were largely right – the first malls were targeted at the rich and the rich came – but the developers' outlay did not always match incomes and retail tenants liked their new customers but didn't always see enough of them.

Developers reacted quickly and began building malls that targeted the middle-income range of consumers, even in some cases the lower-income consumer who needed one-stop shopping. Now a wide variety of malls exist, often in heated competition facing each other across major shopping streets, such as Singapore's Orchard Road or in out-of-town locations. They have become destinations in their own right with food courts, multiplex cinemas and theme parks attached.

Jakarta had more than 45 purpose-built shopping plazas. The recently opened Pasar Festival food and entertainment complex added another 12,000 square meters to the existing 1.15 million square meters of retailing space in the city. Major Indonesian developers such as Lippo were battling for anchor tenants to ensure their sites' success. A mall's anchor tenant is the make-or-break factor determining its success, and tenants have been courted assiduously by developers who had plans for at least another 31 malls by 2000. Lippo entered into a joint venture with US retailing giant Wal-Mart to be the anchor for the company's Jakarta SuperMall, while the capital city's Plaza Indonesia has Japanese department store outfit Sogo as its anchor tenant.

The Indonesian mall developers have been keen to target consumer groups. Melawani Inda Plaza, which controls the Metro chain of stores, created the Metro Pondok Indah plaza in the largely prosperous, largely ethnic Chinese residential area of Pondok Indah. Meanwhile Lippo has big plans with its supermall in Lippo Karawaci, a planned community west of Jakarta. There would be a 976,000 square meter mall, anchored by US-owned JC Penney and featuring a funfair, aimed at a catchment area of four million consumers, while the planned community itself has an international school, offices and apartments and is self-sufficient in services.

MALLS FOR ALL

China	Initial development of upscale malls is giving way to mid-range plazas
Hong Kong	Generally upmarket, though suffering in recession and moving downmarket
Indonesia	Development initially in Jakarta, though moving into the provinces
Malaysia	Established malls in KL with increasing out-of-town and provincial development
Philippines	Upper-income plazas giving way to low-income one-stop malls
Singapore	Upper- and middle-income mall/housing developments boosted by extension of transit systems
South Korea	Large underground shopping centers in Seoul combined with traditional markets and hotel/business developments
Taiwan	Very well developed throughout the country
Thailand	Massive mall developments, particularly around Bangkok
Vietnam	Initial construction of mixed retailing/leisure centers beginning

Initially mall development in the Philippines was driven by the move of the affluent urban middle class to residential communities outside congested Manila. Domestic retailers rapidly became mall developers. Shoemart, oddly enough originally a shoe store, moved into the mall business with the 330,000 sq. ft SM Megamall. Property developer Ayala also went along this route, entering a joint venture with the phenomenally popular Dutch retailer Makro. Ayala has also targeted the affluent new rich with the Ayala Center which contains up-scale retailers including Giorgio Armani, Prada and DKNY. With the booming of Metro Manila and other regions' provincial towns, mall development has become a Philippines-wide trend and the malls are bringing international retailers such as Marks & Spencer, JC Penney and K-Mart to the country.

Other Filipino retailers, most notably Gotesco, have extended the mall concept to low-income consumers with the construction of one-stop, air-conditioned malls in low-wage districts and neighboring university campuses. Typical of this kind of development is Grand Central Mall in Caloocan City, which operates on low margins and high volumes. The format has been so successful that it is spreading throughout the country and creating a whole new group of consumers familiar with one-stop, mall/plaza retailing.

However retailers approach the Philippines consumer market, be it low-income malls or luxury plazas, they are in a market that loves to shop. Sales per square meter in the Megamall average US$1950 (even after the peso devaluation), compared to US$2100 in the US. Given the discrepancy in disposable incomes this is a fantastic retailing environment.

Even Asia's poorest countries are gaining shopping malls. Vietnam is acquiring plazas such as Saigon Superbowl, the country's first air-conditioned mall with 5000 square meters of space and 55 retail units. International retailers, including Swatch, Triumph and Adidas, have taken space so far and Scotts of Singapore is running Vietnam's first food court featuring the Filipino Jollibee fast-food chain.

The great mall of China

In China shopping malls are not out-of-town palaces of consumerism but more downtown retail-cum-office complexes, often with a hotel attached. The simple reason for this pattern of development so far is transport. Chinese citizens, or at least the majority of them, do not have private transport, so acres of parking space in a suburb on the edge of the city would be inaccessible to most. This is why malls tend to be in the main commercial and shopping districts.

In Wangfujing in Beijing is the new Xin Dong'an shopping mall. This ultra-modern mall is built on six floors, with several atria, criss-crossed with escalators and glass elevators. The bottom floors are fully occupied by designer-label stores, modern format bookstores, department stores and so on. It throws into contrast the dilapidation of the surrounding, yet to be rebuilt, parts of Wangfujing and presents a foretaste of Hong Kong magnate Li Kashing's new mega-mall, which is being built on the corner of Wangfujing and Chang'an Avenue – which leads directly to Tian'anmen Square.

This opulence is also seen in the types of stores locating in these malls. Designer-label boutiques, especially of Italian or French origin, are the vogue at the moment, next to mobile-phone shops, computer stores, delicatessens, supermarkets (still a new concept in China) and the flagship department stores, such as the Shanghai Department Store or Beijing Wangfujing Department Store, around which the malls tend to be centered.

In the Beijing Lufthansa Center, such novelties as fast-food outlets and even a pub-cum-restaurant have also been included to create the kind of cosmopolitan, western-style shopping environment so many Asian consumers are now enjoying. Anything, in fact, to move away from the grim realities of traditional Chinese shopping at wet markets and Soviet-style department stores, where service, presentation and a stress-free environment were almost unknown.

The new malls of China appeal to the new rich, who can afford to dispense with the hardships of normal life. You won't see vagrant workers from the countryside in these shopping meccas since there are always security guards on the main doors (often themselves from poor rural villages) to keep out anyone who doesn't fit in.

Redevelopment through retail

Across the region the boom in retailing is propelling the redevelopment of many urban areas as developers change traditional land use patterns to accommodate new desires. Retailing is becoming a major focus of redevelopers from Subic Bay in the Philippines, the Shanghai City Council and Kowloon in Hong Kong, as well as Singapore's Little India and riverside quay redevelopments. In the Philippines the new Mall of Asia will be constructed on 46,500 square meters of reclaimed land in Manila Bay and includes a 10,000 capacity car park, four hotels and a 12-screen multiplex cinema.

The intensifying battle for Asia's retail center – will it be Hong Kong, Kuala Lumpur's Golden Triangle, Singapore's Orchard Road or maybe downtown Shanghai? – is forcing developers to step up their plans. Malaysia has redeveloped Johor on the border with Singapore to take advantage of the boom in cross-border retailing.

Singapore itself has been busily restructuring its retail infrastructure in the wake of several years of recession. Robertson Walk, along the Singapore River, is being redeveloped as a low-rise, up-market mall with a Mediterranean theme modeled on Miami's Coco Walk plaza.

The old face of many Asian cities is being cleared away to accommodate the opulent visions of retail and leisure magnates. As happened in Europe after the Second World War, whole ways of life are being lost as old quarters in major cities are redeveloped and land occupied by cramped, old-style houses is cleared to accommodate new high-rise office/retail/hotel/leisure complexes.

Beijing's infamous Hutongs (a network of back alleys through whole districts of courtyard houses all cramped together) are now in danger of disappearing altogether, so that soon all that will be left of the ancient city will be its more grandiose artefacts.

Reasons to spend

The changes in retailing are not just in the type of stores where Asians are spending their money but also in the reasons they're finding for digging deep. In 1996, most major Shanghai department stores ran Christmas promotions for the first time to cash in on consumers' appetites for western ideas and products. The business reason was to try to extend the prime retailing season in the run up to Chinese New Year in February by starting early in December. Reuters News Service (13.12.96) reported Tong Shenjie, the information officer for Shanghai's seven-story department store Kai Kai Plaza, as saying: 'The idea of Christmas as a time for gifts, cards and celebrations is growing year by year among young people.' Tong went on to say: 'The Christmas factor will boost sales. There is no religious feeling, it is just commercial.'

Bangkok Post (14.2.97) noted that on Valentine's Day many Bangkok retailers, especially those catering to teenage consumers, are full. Though the Thai and Chinese New Years remain the major family celebrations, Valentine's Day has become a significant date for teens on spending sprees. Spending on 14 February has shot up by 25 percent annually with most buying flowers, cards and jewelry. The red rose has become the international symbol of love.

Christmas of the east

The big retail moment in Asia is Chinese New Year, or the Spring Festival as it is known in the communist, non-superstitious mainland. This is the Christmas of the Chinese calendar. Located at the end of January or beginning of February, depending on the lunar calendar, this is the key shopping time for Chinese people, whether they be in China, Taiwan, Malaysia, Hong Kong or London.

This is the festival that welcomes the new spring and marks the time when, traditionally, sowing of crops began. It is also the time to celebrate the lean months of winter and reciprocate the more cheerful weather with more cheerful behavior. This festival sees Chinese, wherever they are, dig deep into their pockets to provide presents for all their close relations, friends and colleagues.

Just as Christmas is celebrated with special foods, the giving and receiving of presents and better than average TV programs, so it is with Chinese New Year. In China, the prices of many luxury goods rise by as much as 10 percent in the run up to and during the festivities. The celebrations can last as long as two to three weeks, despite only two official days of holiday.

Chinese New Year is also a time for families. People on the mainland will make very long and arduous journeys, often from one side of the country to the other, just to spend this festival with their families, despite the fact that every bus, train and plane will be oversubscribed by at least 50 percent.

Empty shops are temporarily taken over by companies which sell the traditional moon cakes, the equivalent of Christmas pudding in the Chinese world, and open markets double in size. Spending on children, already high in mainland China due to the one-child policy, is highest at this time of year, with many families spending almost one month's salary on gifts for their children.

This is why many companies introduce new products to the Chinese market in early January, hoping that demand will boom during the New Year festivities.

The New Year is not the only auspicious time to introduce new products or to open new businesses. Lucky dates, borne out of the often obsessive interest which many Asians have in numerology, are always good times to enter a market. Anything with an 8 in it will be good, such as 8 August. To get a sense of how seriously people take the numbers, one only has to remember the fuss made about any child born on 8 August 1988. According to tradition, these children are supposed to be supremely lucky in life.

Targeting the right groups

Different groups of shoppers want different things – obvious, but the key to successful retailing the world over. Target your customer, provide what they want and get them into your store. It sounds simple, but of course the reality causes major brainache to FMCG company executives, advertisers, small businesspeople and marketing gurus.

Retailers use a wide variety of ideas, promotions, ploys and outright scams to persuade customers to shop with them. The first rule is to know your customer and target them. You need to know their typical age, sex and preferences and a lot more, but primarily you need to know if their wallet is bulging or empty. At the moment it seems that Asia's retailers, both domestic and foreign, are breaking the market down between the new rich, the young affluent, the aspirational and the new consumers who are finding themselves adrift in the world of retail with money to spend for the first time.

Big spenders

It would be a mistake to think that the days of the big spender are over in Asia. Without doubt competition has become fierce for the rich across the region and countries hard hit by economic crisis, such as Indonesia and Thailand, have seen a fall-off in sales of luxury goods. But this isn't the case in China, relatively unaffected so far and with sales of premium cosmetics, clothing and other goods yet far from peaking. Luxury retailers such as Gucci have been adversely affected but haven't gone out of business and as economies recover so will their sales.

Luxury goods are in a world of their own where the rules are different. Varying factors come into play: *cachet*, style, assurance, quality, whim and fancy. The primary question isn't 'how much can they pay?' but still 'will they or won't they buy this item?' – a watch or a bottle of wine, the influencing factors are the same.

Of course at the very top the big spenders of Asia are proving their wealth by moving into the traditional sectors of the super-rich: art, private jets, yachts, antiques, fast and very luxurious automobiles.

Vietnam Investment Review reported that Siber Hegner & Co had opened a liaison office in Ho Chi Minh City in November 1996. Siber Hegner represents brands including Cartier watches, Montblanc pens, Yves Saint Laurent, Baume & Mercier and Wonderbra. Not exactly a typical shopping list in a country with an average per capita income of US$260.

In Singapore a rash of specialist retail parks has sprung up to target the most affluent groups in society. Holland Village is just a 10-minute walk from Orchard Road and largely caters to the country's sizeable and generally wealthy US and British expatriate professional communities. Another exclusive development is the Millennia Walk in the high-cost Marina Center which features upmarket outlets including Valentino, Liz Claiborne, Burberry's and Trussardi.

Even China has its big spenders. They may represent just 2 percent of the country's total population, but then 2 percent of a billion is a good starting point.

The affluent young

Across the region boutiques have sprung up to cater to the affluent, brand-conscious young. The spate of new boutiques appearing in Hong Kong have been designed to appeal to the young rich with a taste for international fashion and the *avant garde*, along with the dollars to pay for it.

More traditional, larger-scale retailers have also hopped on the bandwagon. Lane Crawford has a 60,000 sq. ft outlet in Hong Kong's Times Square mall aimed exclusively at the younger, more contemporary consumer, stocking fashion, accessories and homewares. Traditionally Lane Crawford had been a little more sedate and conservative, an Asian version of New York's Lord & Taylor or London's Dickens & Jones. A number of other Hong Kong retailers, including Sincere with its Signature store in Causeway Bay, have followed suit, stocking Italian shoes alongside the most fashionable European and US designer names. This 'fine tuning', as the *South China Morning Post* dubbed the phenomenon, is bringing the young with cash to spend back into stores they had forsaken as places their parents, and only their parents, would ever go.

Among young, affluent and brand-conscious consumers trends change fast. Companies with brand success have often found that to tap the market they need to set up shop outside of the usual department store concessions. A prime example was the Levi's brand which was becoming unfashionable largely because it was sold through concessions in stores that had lost the younger, more affluent consumers. It set up dedicated boutiques for its products featuring advertising centered on the younger consumer. A year later its Asian sales had doubled.

Now that we have money ... what?

Behind the aspirants are those who are finding that for the first time they have money – maybe not a lot, but enough to provide a disposable income to go shopping with. For them the world of retail is opening up as never before. Their shopping list is long and encompasses everything from food to clothing, beer to books and medicines to cosmetics.

Across the region shoppers are browsing for things they've never had before. If they buy they will become first-generation purchasers. But in each country the first-generation markets are different. Once they buy their current dream they reach a little further: now a TV, next a VCR; now a generic makeup product, next a branded lipstick. Catching the now/next wave is crucial for FMCG manufacturers and retailers. Too slow and people will have gone somewhere else, bought something else. Too fast and you'll be paying out while you wait for the wave to reach the shoreline.

Retailers are finding that simply targeting the rich is not necessarily profitable. Japanese retailing group Yaohan had begun establishing supermarkets in Beijing and Shanghai with joint-venture partner Pacific Concord Holdings. It already had seven stores in China but was repositioning itself to draw in the new consumers, those entering the middle-income group, in order to break free of reliance on the still small group of affluent consumers. Ultimately it was the fall of the Japanese economy and Yaohan's credit limit problems that ended the company's expansion across Asia.

In very rapidly emerging retail markets such as Vietnam, where retail spending has grown by 250 percent since 1992, the race is on to supply the new consumers with what they want as a growing number of people move beyond the stage of merely requiring food and shelter. So far few international, or regional, retailers have committed to Vietnam and the market is in danger of being consumed by pirated and second-rate goods. However, the signs for the country's retail future are good: 35 percent of the population currently aged under 15, a growth in urbanization, 2 percent per annum population growth, low housing, utilities, health and education costs, and a growth in per capita GDP of 210 percent since

1992. All this is combined with an ever-opening marketplace as reforms continue.

Vietnam suffers from a number of problems typical of a country on the cusp of a retail revolution: a chaotic distribution system, lack of warehousing, an underdeveloped credit system and a lack of outlets. But the Vietnamese are getting ready to buy. In 1996 a magazine was launched targeted at new consumers and aiming to explain new products, with tips about spotting counterfeits and dangerous goods. A recent survey of baby clothing purchasers in Hanoi found that those buying clothing with the Disney trademark did so largely because they believed it to be superior to Vietnamese-made items since it was American. Indeed, Vietnam is rapidly acquiring a taste for all things foreign-made: Heineken beer, Marlboro cigarettes, Stimorol chewing gum. As the market moves beyond beer and fags to PCs and CD players, this should translate into a ready market for foreign brands, even if they are not necessarily manufactured in the countries that gave birth to them.

The fact that an increasing number of people have money means that retail structures have to adapt. Retailers who don't get left behind and squeezed out. There's a great deal of revamping going on across the region. Take the Wangfujing Department Store in Beijing. Wangfujing was founded just six years after the revolution, but as retailing has taken off international department stores in the city like Galéries Lafayette have stolen its market share. So Wangfujing is being revamped. The store has a new target audience: families with an income of between 1500 and 2500 yuan (US$180–300) a month who want one-stop shopping. Wangfujing may be the oldest and best-known brand name in Beijing, but that isn't helping it. What the store has had to do is bring in consultants, team up with successful international retailers like The Gap and float on the Shanghai Stock Exchange.

The Wangfujing empire is three stores with a combined turnover of US$190 million. At the moment, a stroll through the store is a bewildering experience. Ladies' underwear is alongside stereos and jewelry is next to sports equipment. But it seems that plenty of people want to aid Wangfujing in its makeover. In June 1997, 2000 executives crowded into a room (the store was expecting no more than 100 people) to buy space in the store. Clothes retailers and fast-food brands all mixed in together to consider getting a slice of the new Wangfujing cake. And the old lady of Beijing retailing couldn't have left it much later to take action – on the opposite side of the street Hong Kong property developer Sun Hung Kai is building 120,000 square meters of retailing space.

The wise consumer

While discount outlets have found a ready home in countries with large numbers of aspirant consumers who want to spend, they are also finding potential in more developed countries where consumers have become accustomed to shopping around and are becoming increasingly concerned with value and bargains than simply acquiring what they didn't have before. This is the new generation of 'wise consumers' and in post-turmoil Asia this is the most crucial group of consumers to capture.

In South Korea the major discount stores have moved in to target this group, offering everything from food to appliances to clothing. The discounters have certainly worried the department stores, which have retreated without a fight and concentrated on capturing the high end of the market. Many, including leading retailer Shinsegae, have also started up discount stores of their own, deciding if you can't beat them join them.

Another example of the new power of the wise consumer is the success of the international category killers. IKEA, Mothercare, Office Depot and Toys 'R' Us are spreading throughout the region, attracting consumers who want wide choice and high-value pricing.

Value retailing is springing up across the region, its growth fueled by careful consumers watching their pennies. In Hong Kong, US retailer Wal-Mart and Thai-based Ek Chor Distribution Systems have established a chain of Value Club membership stores similar to Wal-Mart's Sam's Club outlets in the US. In Indonesia, Makro has six stores with in excess of 40,000 members; and in Thailand Siam Makro has been accused of single-handedly

PRIVATE LABEL

Private label has long been important in the western retailing canon, both in food and non-food retailing. Leading private-label manufacturers have also found success in Asia, not least British retailer Marks & Spencer and more latterly US giant Wal-Mart.

Asian retailers have begun to realize the potential of own brands. Major regionally-based retailers such as Singapore's NTUC Fairprice, Cold Storage and Guardian Pharmacies are introducing new private-label products on a regular basis, targeting the wise consumer with slogans such as 'No Frills'.

So far, private-label products have proved most successful in South Korea, Hong Kong and Thailand. However, east Asia is yet to see penetration levels of private label equivalent to Japan, which accounts for 11 percent of all own-brand sales in the region. However, with leading Japanese private-label retailers such as Jusco and Daiei active across the region, it looks likely that private label will be a growing business.

revolutionizing the retail scene since its introduction in 1991 of low-margin retailing and warehouse clubs. One of Singapore's leading retail operations, Metro Holdings, has begun opening US-style factory outlets to attract the value-conscious consumer. South Korea now has a growing number of value store chains including Bargain Price Clubs and E-Mart. In Taiwan leading retailer Far Eastern Department Store has entered a joint venture with France's Promodes retail group for a chain of out-of-town hypermarkets in Taipei's suburbs.

Shifting sands

Of course, a look back at Asia's recent history would tell you that the income categories discussed above are not rigid, fixed phenomena. Twenty years ago a Nike superstore in Beijing would have been unthinkable and a Porsche dealership in Hanoi a risky undertaking to say the least. But every year more and more people enter the realm of basic purchasing power and live in regions with retailing infrastructures to help them part with their new cash and push their credit limits to breaking point.

One thing is certain, however. The number of first-generation purchasers will fall, although there will be more people who grew up with washing machines, fridges and VCRs. They will see these appliances, along with cars, bottled beer and credit cards, as everyday items, things you have to have if you are to maintain a decent standard of living. People whose mothers had washing machines tend not to revert to hand washing.

We do need to strike a cautionary note here. Without doubt over the last 20 years Asians have been buying more, consuming more, expecting more. In the new economic climate they may have become more cautious and wiser, but they retain their Asian values. Just as in the first part of this book we explained how social phenomena such as teenage rebellion and women's emancipation are occurring within the remit of established Asian values, so these values also affect retailing.

Despite the increasing ease with which credit is available and growing per capita incomes, the retail market may not boom in direct proportion. Financial security is still crucial and savings are rising faster than consumer spending. The old favorites of stock, land and property remain major repositories of the growing wealth. Asians like their money to make money and instant gratification comes a poor second to long-term family stability and wealth. The vast majority will forgo consumer durables and extras like holidays if that expenditure jeopardizes their children's education, or indeed their own further/higher education in an increasingly competitive job market.

Brand love

For several years now western newspapers and magazines have been full of stories detailing the Asian love affair with brands. Certainly some of these tales reveal the fact that Asian consumers have been able to afford previously inaccessible brands. When Italian fashion house Prada opened its Hong Kong store it sold out even before the official launch party. It's also true that Asian magazines are full of adverts for luxury brands. A recent issue of Malaysia's English-language *Her World* magazine contained ads for Salvatore Ferragamo, Tommy Hilfiger, Estée Lauder, Lancôme, Clinique, Louis Vuitton, Anne Klein, Calvin Klein, L'Oréal, Christian Dior and Chanel in the first 20 pages alone. Impressive, but not necessarily any more than in an equivalent US or European publication.

Brands in Asia are really large mixed metaphors. Certainly wearing a branded suit conveys status and affluence, but Asians are not the brand-blind suckers many in the west have portrayed. Brands are a sign not of labels but of quality, applied craftsmanship and good materials and ingredients, attributes that have long been appreciated in the region. This mindset is revealed in the success of brands that definitely represent quality, such as Gucci and Louis Vuitton, and the decline of a brands-for-brands-sake mentality that has meant many hip names in the west having short lives in Asia.

Brands can also be means for a younger, more outwardly thrusting generation to reflect their international perspective. The retailer Club 21 in Singapore has opened a fashion outlet called Black Jack which specializes in modern streetwear. It stocks labels from Europe and the US alongside the Australian Mambo brand. Most of Black Jack's clients have been young, brand-conscious Singaporeans who are very obviously in touch with minute shifts in world tastes and are keen to be seen as just as cool as any western fashion victim.

In general, the vogue for branded goods is strongest in countries which have not traditionally had access to them. Hong Kong and Singapore have latterly taken a more blasé attitude towards brands, most international labels having been available for a long time now. However, nations such as Vietnam, Indonesia and China are more brand obsessed. In part this is because brands allow those with money to move up from often poorer-quality local produce and in part a sign of interest in the new.

A survey by Indonesia's Central Bureau of Statistics confirms this trend. Imports of luxury and mid-range brands are a relatively new phenomenon and middle- to upper-income consumers are reported to be increasingly opting for foreign-made goods. The big initial gainers in this market have been the international retailers such as Japanese-owned Sogo department stores which has 90 percent imported stock. However, even the main retailers of imported goods are bracing themselves for the shift in consumer attitudes as foreign goods become more everyday and Indonesians begin concentrating on quality and value for money. Gauging just when the fad for foreign goods will die down is the tricky part of the equation and often this can occur sooner rather than later.

Despite the adverse effects on incomes caused by the turmoil in some Asian countries, there has not been a rejection of brand worship. Fewer are being purchased and not so many brands will succeed, but branded generally remains best.

The China brand syndrome

China has seen interesting shifts in brand loyalty which have surprised overconfident foreign invaders. When in 1979 the government finally lifted restrictions (rationing) on all cigarettes, including famous local brands and foreign imports, novelty-hungry Chinese consumers – which in the case of cigarettes is some 80 percent of adult men – were keen to show off their cosmopolitanism by smoking premium foreign brands, the more expensive and famous the brand the better.

However, foreign brands were not the only ones that had been unavailable for decades. The top brands made in China, Hong Zhonghua and Panda, were the sole privilege of the ruling classes and were unavailable to the man on the street. Access to foreign cigarettes was almost bound to win customers, as anything foreign was the vogue for much of the late 1980s and early 1990s. But what the Marlboros and Dunhills of the world did not reckon on was that, despite their products having great brand appeal and being of high quality, the leading Chinese brands would ultimately win top place.

Why? The first reason is that Hong Zonghua and Panda brand cigarettes were the high-profile brands smoked by the 'great leaders'. Only Mao Zedong himself was known for smoking a foreign brand (555 State Express), which is why that particular brand is now so popular in China and demands such high prices. Panda, made in Shanghai, was the favored puff of Deng Xiaoping, the hero of China's economic miracle.

Another reason is linked to the sharp rise in the popularity of foreign cigarettes when the forbidden fruit became freely available. When the laws were relaxed, there were not enough to go round because for so long they had only been made in quantities sufficient to supply top officials. So these brands remained at a premium and retained their luster as luxury brands, which conferred status to anyone who was able to flash a packet in their local bar.

The final blow to foreign competition was that the local brands are good and compete on a par with Marlboro and others. And they taste like Chinese cigarettes. Being brought up on Chinese tobacco, smokers in the country are used to and prefer the local flavor.

The result has been a resurgence in the popularity of high-quality local brands at the expense of imports, even though Marlboro (among others) is now made under license in Shanghai using local tobacco. This example serves to illustrate that local tastes and preferences, and even associations with prominent historical figures, can all serve to boost local products over imported goods, and that foreign goods don't always win instant kudos just because they are foreign.

Further proof of the attraction to quality rather than just labels is found in the fact that Asians are very keen on branded appliances and electronic goods and that brands certainly do not have to be foreign to have *cachet*. The success of Lexus as a car brand to rival Mercedes shows that Asians can also take a pride in domestically designed and produced quality products.

The great 'sorting out'

In 1994 a curious thing occurred in Hong Kong and Singapore – a retail slump. Nobody had been expecting it but suddenly the combination of rising rents and overheads in the two leading retail centers met a slight slowdown among consumers, compounded by the rise of alternative retailing centers throughout the region. The result was what some analysts have described as the great 'sorting out'.

Both Hong Kong and Singapore were at an advanced level of retail development with mature retail infrastructures, broad-based consumer markets and heavy investment by local and overseas retail operations. The falls in store operating profits left scars on local retailers. Singapore's Orchard Road was forced to have its first sale. Hong Kong department stores such as Wing On (which has 13 stores in Hong Kong and a further two in mainland China) and Sincere had to cut costs for the first time. It struck a deal with Japanese retailer Seiyu to reduce costs further. Many retailers were left feeling bruised and battered and wondering what happened to the Asian consumer miracle. Some newspapers and magazines even went so far as to announce the end of the consumer as a power.

In fact, the process was a replica of movements in retailing in the US. The big, department store retailers – Macy's in New York, Wanamaker's in Philadelphia, Filene's in Boston and the Sears Group across the US – have been weakened if not bankrupted over the last 15 years. The US has seen the rise of the specialized store – Crate & Barrel, Pottery Barn, Banana Republic – catering to the high end of the market while large volume discounters – Wal-Mart, TrakAuto – have captured the low end.

The same thing is happening in Hong Kong and Singapore. Their central shopping districts had grown up on middle-class money and aspirations. Department store companies have now been weakened and several major names have exited the market, including French-owned Galéries Lafayette. In their place specialist malls and stores such as the Body Shop and Episode have risen to prominence. Additionally, it appears that the 'sorting out' is not deterring foreign investment. More and more international retailers are entering the market. In 1997 Boots, the leading pharmacy chain in the UK, announced its intention to create a joint venture in Thailand. Regional retailers are keen to expand too. Watson's of Hong Kong is planning 60 stores before the year 2000 outside its home base.

The economic turmoil of 1997/8 accelerated the pace still further, with older, less organized malls suffering and niche retailers finding themselves able to cope better in a contracting marketplace.

Niche filling in China is still ongoing and at a furious pace. Gift giving being such an important part of the culture, and consumer spending being on the up, a rather large number of people own perfectly good, yet unwanted presents. This can be as a result of getting married and being given two of the same kind of electric toaster, or receiving an expensive watch when you already have a gold Rolex.

Seeing the need for so many people to offload their unwanted, unused and perfectly resaleable gifts, shops have opened specifically to sell them. These gift shops sell goods brought to them on a sale-or-return basis and take a commission on the sale. Prices will be determined by perceived demand and the original retail price. Customers of these shops are bargain hunters who are out to find top-of-the-range products at a reduced price in comparison to the main retail outlets.

Value for money is therefore one of the key issues concerning the Asian consumer and thus also the Asian retailer. Just as consumers have been learning to spend, they have also been learning to flex their muscle in terms of demanding proper protection from poor goods and poor service.

In China in the late 1980s, you could walk into a shop, see what you wanted to buy (in one personal experience, a can of tomatoes), ask the bored shop assistant (dressed in what might be mistaken for a surgical gown and cap) for that item, indicating its position on the shelf, only to be told that it was 'not in stock'. Getting hot under the collar, pointing frantically, cursing the assistant for their lack of efficiency (tantamount to utter laziness if said correctly in Chinese), all failed to gain me the can of tomatoes which was only three feet away.

Now you don't even need to confront a clinical shop assistant in order to shop. Gone are the counters, now it is self-service and you can make sure your tin of tomatoes does not have a rusted dent in it. You can even check the sell-by date, the holographic certificate of hygiene, the ingredients etc., etc. And when it comes to paying – well, it's just like any supermarket chain in the west.

As soon as retailing was commercialized, consumers rejected the old ways and became very demanding about service and quality. Consumer protection agencies have sprung up, publishing their own magazines which expose poorly made products and their manufacturers, along with retail ruffians, direct mail sharks and all the other scams which have flourished during the naïve beginnings of consumerism.

Consumer News, a leading magazine which runs a very similar format to *Which?* in the UK, illustrates many of the problems facing retailers and consumers in these developing markets. Take the woman who received a TV as a wedding gift which, when delivered, did not work. She lived in rural Hunan, the company was based in Nanjing, mountains, lakes, rivers and poor roads away. Persistence got this consumer a new, working TV, after sending back several faulty units over a two-year period.

In order to deal with the increasing complexity of every transaction, including guarantees, warranties, returns, exchanges and so on, the retail industry has had to become better equipped. Stores now need trained employees, who can understand and deal with complex consumer and product issues, advanced retail technology and sophisticated sales and promotional skills.

Many of the old-style department stores are having to become specialists in everything they sell in order to compete with specialist retailers in terms of quality of service. Such staff are expensive, as is the administration of consumer protection issues. Which begs the question, how long can the predominant department store format continue to remain on top?

Some Chinese stores have ended up in drastic price-cutting wars to keep customers passing through their doors at the same time that new stores continue to open, especially in the commercial hub of Shanghai. The fallout has been weeding out of the less commercially viable stores, leaving openings not just for better equipped department stores and the leading local store chains (Shanghai Number One being one of the most notable), but also for specialist retailers.

FAKE GOODS IN CHINA

In a state circular, authorities said that the findings of product-quality inspections would be published weekly in the official media. More than 900 Chinese were killed or injured by faulty household products in 1996, by official estimate.

Exploding beer bottles injured and disabled 255 consumers in the same year, prompting Xinhua (the New China News Agency) to describe bottles produced by state-owned breweries as 'hidden bombs'. Food poisoning put another 688 people in hospital, while authorities blamed faulty gas heaters, electrical appliances and other shoddy products for hundreds more injuries and deaths.

In January 1998 the China Consumers' Association (CCA) pledged to help all townships establish consumer protection groups following a nationwide poll that revealed that rural consumers were more at risk of fake and dangerous goods than were urbanites. Already 26,000 townships have set up such groups. Meanwhile in Beijing, a consumer protection hotline established in March 1998 received 150 calls on its first day.

A study in 1996 found that nearly a quarter of all China-made consumer products surveyed failed to meet federal standards, while 35 percent of safety products – including gas-leak alarms and safety belts – were unacceptable.

In the past, public disclosure of faulty products by the official press has met with swift retribution from Communist Party censors. The president of the *Beijing Youth Daily* was sacked after the paper revealed that yoghurt drinks produced by state-owned Hangzhou Wahaha Group had resulted in the fatal poisoning of several children.

The winners and the losers

While there were many reasons for the fall in retailers' profits linked to operating procedures (outdated distribution and management practices, rising labor costs etc.), in the main it was the rise of niche markets that adversely affected the stores.

Luxury retailers such as Dickson Concepts and the Joyce Boutiques chain in Hong Kong were winners. Their high-income target market did not feel the economic woes and in Hong Kong were less susceptible to pressures connected with the handback to China that are said to have discouraged many middle- and lower-income shoppers from spending. Indeed, both operations expanded their outlet numbers and the range of exclusive labels they stocked. It is better in this environment to target one income group specifically rather than attempting to hit everyone with everything.

The losers were those stores that attempted to be all things to all types of consumers. The Japanese-run Daimaru stores group was one such operation and found itself scaling back its outlets and range in Hong Kong in 1996.

In Singapore the main evil was apparently the strong Singapore dollar which rose by more than 10 percent against the US dollar between 1994 and 1996. The ensuing mismatch between supply and demand led to 'sorting out' Singapore style. There were further substantially important underlying reasons. Singapore had become weak while neighboring Malaysia and Thailand had significantly upgraded their retail infrastructures, and Singapore had also had to contend with the reduction of its vital role as a hub airport and duty-free location for Asia.

Additionally, Singapore was becoming sophisticated, with specialist retailing malls targeting high income earners, expatriates and families taking business at the margins and leaving the traditional Oxford-Street-of-the-East, Orchard Road, trying to be all things to all shoppers. Consequently the big Orchard Road retailers, who were anyhow reeling under horrendously large rents, took the hit. Lane Crawford reduced its operation from five floors to two, French-owned department store Galéries Lafayette withdrew from Singapore completely and the leading Singapore department store retailer CK Tang suffered major losses (though its Malaysian store in Kuala Lumpur grew in value, showing the success of other regional retailing centers). A property specialist and retail analyst in Singapore commented in 1996 that 'speciality retailers with strong concepts, niche marketing and suburban retailers are doing well.'

Direct selling

In Asia's increasingly competitive retailing market, companies have sprung up to provide direct marketing and selling to the millions of new consumers. It's no small business, with revenues from direct selling in Singapore alone at upwards of US$26.8 million a year. In part the rise of direct selling reflects the retailers' need to respond to an ever more crowded marketplace, though in part the explosion of companies such as Avon and others reflects the growth in consumer sophistication and technological advances. TV shopping networks only work when a certain percentage of consumers have cable access. But when cable becomes commonplace, as in Singapore, direct sellers are quick to go into action. The magazine *Asian Advertising & Marketing* reported that television infomercials on late-night TV had become an 'epidemic' in Singapore.

Direct selling now comes in a variety of methods, from the basic door-to-door salespeople and colorful mail-order catalogs targeting specific niche groups to sophisticated programs on cable television. In Malaysia, Mail Order Gallery (MOG) has 14 shops, 19 concessions and 38 dealers with a turnover in excess of US$10.7 million and 20 percent a year growth in sales. However, seeing, touching, smelling and experiencing the product are still important, as MOG's regional operations manager, Nigel McKenzie, told *Business Times* (Malaysia) (26.2.97): 'Research has indicated that about 70 percent of consumers will never buy what is merely advertised on the television. To this group of consumers, shopping is actually a social experience.'

Avon calling Asia

Direct sellers don't come much bigger than Avon: 34,000 employees worldwide, operating in 130 countries and utilizing 2.3 million representatives, all adding up to annual revenues around the US$5 billion mark. Avon has been in China since the late 1980s, setting up and expanding its network of door-to-door, direct salespeople, beginning in the southern consumer catalyst of Guangdong province.

This was the first example of direct-sales marketing in China and remains one of the most successful. Others have followed, such as US giant Amway, but none has the spread of territory or expertise in the market that Avon has accumulated. In fact, the government ceased all direct-sales trading in 1996 for several months, while it tried to separate the bona fide from the bogus companies, due to consumer complaints about many.

Avon's formula – an attractive young girl visiting potential customers at home, saving them the trouble of wading through busy shopping streets and making available to them reasonably priced cosmetic goods – won almost instant appeal. Whereas in the west such concepts are seen as rather *passé*, in China they are all the rage.

The fact is that after years of impersonality, the Chinese are very open to such intimate selling situations. Avon representatives are seen as welcome guests, rather than pushy nuisances. The Avon identity, and the chance for Chinese women to join in by themselves becoming Avon reps, has only added to the appeal. The women not only feel that they are getting good products at a good price, but that they are part of some kind of corporate family, which wasn't prescribed to them, which pays them well and also offers them a new social arena, outside the extended family or work unit.

Avon's main competitor internationally is Amway. The company has built up a salesforce of 2.5 million in more than 75 countries. In the Philippines it has found particular success. Its core distributor base is approximately 25,000, with distributors required to purchase a business kit which contains sample products and literature. The kit costs US$68 – pay up and you are in business for Amway.

As this type of selling has increased, so have the applications. Everything from small plastic goods to large and expensive home electrical appliances is now being sold by direct means, in one city or another, and this is all developing alongside the development of the more traditional retail outlet. What this is likely to mean, in the long run, is a much more open mind towards differing types of retailing method, without the cynicism of the west.

Direct selling and marketing have perhaps been more successful in Thailand than anywhere else in Asia so far. A survey by Ogilvy & Mather found that 75 percent of Bangkok residents had purchased goods through direct marketing, with a 90 percent satisfaction rate. Most of these sales were traditional door to door but catalogs, newspaper ads and direct mail were encroaching on the traditional methods. Most sales were of cosmetics, periodicals, clothing and books. Perhaps most surprising of all, the survey found that 57 percent of respondents read all their junk mailshots.

Shopping sprees on the screen

Shopping traditionally means going to the shops in person to look, touch, hold and try out before making a purchase. There is nothing like trying on shoes, pants, a shirt or a dress before deciding to buy any of them. However, a host of high-tech retailers are going regional instantly by establishing TV and Internet home-shopping services.

- In Hong Kong, SmarTone has launched a new Internet Web site enabling customers to choose their preferred service plan from home and allowing them to tailor their services to their own needs.
- The Mall of Malaysia has also gone on to the Net in an attempt to boost sales by tempting its stores to go online and reach the Net surfers.
- Teleshopping was first introduced into Malaysia by TV3 in October 1994. It was followed by Regal Shop a month later and Kayla Beverly Hills through the Metrovision station. Analysts estimate the home-shopping industry to be worth US$3.6 billion with some nine million television viewers as potential customers.
- In Thailand, the Direct Media Group has put a shopping home page on the Internet, targeted at 10 million potential buyers worldwide. Home delivery is provided and credit cards are accepted as a form of payment. The home page offers 15 types

of goods and services ranging from gifts, handicrafts, toys, high technology, audiovisual equipment, sports and leisure goods and decorations to fruit and flowers.

Perhaps the most interesting home-shopping TV service is the Television Shopping Network (TVSN), based in Sydney and owned by Hong Kong interests. TVSN, which has rapidly been dubbed Buywatch, broadcasts 24 hours a day, seven days a week to Japan, Korea, Taiwan, Hong Kong and the Philippines. The thought of tens of thousands of newly affluent Asian consumers calling in and using their credit cards meant that TVSN was not short of backers. But there are others. Hong Kong's Wharf Cable operates a 24-hour shopping channel reaching 200,000 subscribers and sells five-minute segments for US$28,000. The competition for TV home shopping is also hotting up as international players such as Interwood and K-Tel get in on the act.

The future

As a general rule, the poorer a country the greater its expenditure on food as opposed to non-food products. Every country in Asia is witnessing a growth in non-food sales. Of course, everyone is still buying food. And food sales are growing as consumers turn to more packaged foods, expensive imported foods and snack foods. The markets for meat and dairy are expanding and premium foods and beverages such as wine and pet food have emerged. However, it is non-food sales, household items, clothing, medicines and so on, that are driving the market the hardest.

With the Asian retail scene becoming ever more crowded, local retailers are having to take a good look at just where the new consumers will be handing over their cash and plastic in the future. A recent Singapore Retail Industry Conference made a point that is pertinent to all the region's retailers: 'With shoppers of the nineties becoming increasingly knowledgeable, sophisticated and well-traveled, product differentiation and good customer service have become key ingredients of success.'

The conference went on to describe the difficulties in Singapore's retail industry. While Singapore had for many years been the region's shopping paradise, its neighbors have now caught up. The modern shopping complexes that have become common in capital cities such as Jakarta, Kuala Lumpur and Bangkok have become threats that are all too real. For example, Bangkok already has SEACON, arguably the largest shopping mall in Asia, which contains a small theme park. Kuala Lumpur boasts a 10-story Japanese-owned Sogo department store. And the new megamall at the Petronas Twin Towers occupies a total of 162,000 square meters. Mega Mall, a 130,000 square meter five-story shopping complex, has been completed in Jakarta. More are being built to make Singapore's beleaguered retailers even more nervous.

The conference also rightly noted that such complexes were not confined to the capitals: they have sprung up in the region's cities and large towns. ASEAN tourists, who make up more than 30 percent of Singapore's tourists, have less need to shop in Singapore, since Orchard Road does not have the pull it had barely five years ago.

But the conference also noted the domestic factors, the demand side. Most Singapore homes are now very well equipped with refrigerators, televisions, videocassette recorders and washing machines. The sales potential of the more common household goods declines as the ownership level of these items gets closer to saturation point and manufacturers and retailers rely on second- and third-generation purchasing or, more simply, replacements only.

Singapore retailers have also been partly a victim of their own success. On the supply side, retail space has increased sharply in the last few years compared to growth in retail sales. In 1993, retail space grew by 12 percent while sales rose only 2.8 percent. The gap was smaller in 1997 – retail space grew by 4.3 percent and sales by 3.7 percent. The inevitable result is that even more retailers are sharing a retail pie that has grown only marginally: a smaller slice for most retailers, crumbs for the uncompetitive.

The changes underway in the Asian retail sector as a whole appear to be unstoppable. The drive towards more modern forms of retailing is spreading into even the most remote areas. Retailers are having to cope with changing structures, technology, design and marketing. In the next 10 years who knows what will happen?

The attitude of many retailers was summed up by Viroj Phutrakul, executive chairman of the Central Patana retailing group, in the *Nation* in March 1996:

'Traditional retail outlets will be replaced by modern retail outlets within the next ten years. These modern retail outlets include department stores, supermarkets, hypermarkets, cash & carry outlets, convenience stores, minimarts, drug stores and discount stores. To remain in the competitive retail market in Thailand, Mr Viroj advised traditional wholesalers and retailers to adapt to the changing retail environments. These include implementing information technology and undertaking marketing and promotional activities. These are necessary due to the changing lifestyle of consumers.'

Many Asian retailers have suffered in the economic turmoil and certainly some have gone out of business. However, in many countries such as Taiwan, China and the Philippines growth has carried on regardless. International retailers such as Marks & Spencer, Carrefour and IKEA remain committed to the region and at the height of the turmoil announced new investments. Maybe we would all do better to stop thinking of Asian retailing as a declining industry but rather to view it as a sector where competition has become as acute as many of the international retailers are used to in their home markets.

12

Asia's Free Time

Across Asia people's incomes are increasing, they are living longer, they are healthier and the five-day working week is catching on. People have more time – more time for entertainment, leisure and travel. More time to spend their wages and enjoy themselves.

As with so many things, the Japanese have been a major influence on the region's leisure. In 1994 Japan declared its intention to become a 'lifestyle superpower' and learn to enjoy itself more. Many other countries have decided to follow suit.

Sonic the Hedgehog meets Ho Chi Minh

Perhaps nothing reveals the extent to which leisure has changed in Asia than the news in late 1997 that giant Japanese electronic games company Sega was planning to launch a series of high-tech amusement parks in Vietnam. The announcement that the first theme park would be situated in Hanoi's Lenin Park was justified by the Vietnamese government as an answer to how to develop computer skills rapidly in a country with minimal PC ownership.

The 1000 square meter arcade featuring virtual reality games and the latest Sega products will arrive in a country which in the summer of 1997 had just 10 secondhand commercial games machines to go round. Now an estimated 300,000 Vietnamese will find themselves becoming acquainted with Sonic the Hedgehog and the world of computers.

In China, in an attempt to get its citizens to spend more of their increasing incomes, the government reduced the working week, first to five and a half days (every other Saturday being worked) and then to five days in 1995. The Communist Party wanted its citizens to go out, spend money and enjoy themselves!

Now, across Asia, people are buying computer games, videos, widescreen TVs, karaoke machines and video compact discs. Japan is supplying most of the impetus, flooding the market with Manga comics and cartoon series, tamagotchi (electronic virtual pets) and even virtual pop stars like Kikyo, with 700,000 avid fans in Japan buying this electronic ghost (who bears a striking resemblance to Audrey Hepburn) in the form of CD singles, radio shows, magazine articles and fashion shoots. Kikyo even has 'her' own biography.

Asians have a thirst for both Hollywood and locally created 'culture'. Japanese Manga is still more popular than US cartoons, Hello Kitty still draws more interest from children in Taiwan and Japan than does Mickey Mouse, badminton is still the top spectator sport in Malaysia despite Manchester United opening a store in KL. The gap in popularity between more traditional forms of leisure and what is now being imported from the west is closing, but western culture is not predominant and local tastes have to be entertained, not ignored. Maybe Disney should adapt classical Chinese tales, such as the Water Margin, into feature-length cartoons, just as one Chinese studio is planning an animated version of the classic tale of the Monkey King's journey to the west?

The announcement that DreamWorks (Steven Spielberg's production company) had sold an 11 percent stake in its business to Cheil Food and Chemicals, a Korean *chaebol*, surprised many. Cheil has the right to distribute DreamWorks' products throughout Asia, a seat on the board and the opportunity to use DreamWorks' expertise to aid Cheil's own film studio J-Com. Hopefully, this sort of partnership will fare better than the ill-fated Hollywood film studio acquisitions of Japanese companies that ended in losses and management infighting.

And what is it about karaoke? In the west it's something embarrassing one does when really drunk in a bar – in Asia it's serious stuff. Housewives in Asia don't vegetate in front of banal daytime chatshows and cookery programs. For them it's more a case of practicing their karaoke repertoire in between getting the kids to school, doing the ironing and preparing the evening meal. Many take this further and enter amateur karaoke competitions. Visit any bar with karaoke equipment in Taipei on a Wednesday afternoon and they'll be there, not to drink but to chat with friends and practice their favorite songs.

New middle-class families will often be in the market for a karaoke machine before a hi-fi system. Asians like to entertain in company, not just because they live in such cramped cities that being a loner is impossible, but more because they like to belong to their society. Their entertaining is inclusive, rather than exclusive – except where serious money is concerned, and places at the local golf club are strictly by invitation only. Karaoke is just an electronic focus for entertaining, whereas before there was Mah Jong, going out to eat, a visit to the park and so on.

Socializing is part of the social fabric of Asia, which partly explains why the Chinese are so into soccer, enjoy dancing the foxtrot in the municipal park and getting up ridiculously early to practice *tai chi* by the lake. Being members of clubs and associations is still cool in Asia because being part of society is part of the whole culture. This is why in business it is as important whom you know, and in which circles you mix, as what you know and where you work.

This is perhaps why so many Asian women enjoy selling for Avon and Tupperware, as this not only gives them a lucrative job but also makes them a part of a big club. It is also why corporate life seeps into social life. Loyalty to the company comes from all the social benefits of being in the club, rather than from any robotic subservience to the employer. Being part of a group, out for a night down at the bowling alley, on holiday abroad or just sitting down for a game of chess at the local teahouse, is the way Asians entertain each other.

This is changing, of course, and television will have a major role to play. However, social cultures have been long in the making and are strongly rooted, so entertainment needs will continue to have a social edge to them. This explains why so much advertising uses the image of a family (including grandma) enjoying a product together, or a group of young people all enjoying a night out on the town, personal pleasure always in the context of a social group. It's fine to advertise a product with the idea that it will make you an individual who stands out in the crowd, just so long as you are still part of that crowd.

Asia on the move

Higher levels of consumer spending have meant that Asia has moved from a destination for western businesspeople and backpackers to a region that generates tourists of its own, both within the continent and further afield. Londoners, Parisians and New Yorkers are used to the gaggle of Burberry-clad Japanese huddling behind their minicams, but people from across the region are now hopping on jet planes to see the world. Increasingly the tourist destinations of Europe and the US are finding themselves welcoming Singaporean, Taiwanese and Korean tourists.

Likewise, Asians are finding out more about their own region. The reasons for the growth in domestic tourism are the following:

- Better living standards have meant that more Asians have the cash to shell out on a holiday abroad.
- The general easing of tension between nations has meant that freedom of movement is more possible within the region than at any time previously. Both Taiwan and South Korea have eased exit regulations and China has eased access regulations.
- Every Asian country has at least one national airline and several secondary carriers. Airlines like Cathay Pacific, Malaysian Airways and Singapore Airlines are now among the biggest players

ASIAN TRAVEL AND TOURISM

Growth in tourist receipts earned between 1992 and 1996	63.2% to US$49 billion
Growth in the number of hotel rooms between 1992 and 1996	42% to 821,000
Average room occupancy rates across Asia in 1996	between 55 and 90%
Growth in tourist arrivals to Asia between 1992 and 1996	40% to 50 million
Growth in Asians traveling abroad between 1992 and 1996	40% to 78 million

Source: National statistics

in the airline industry. By the year 2005 Asians will comprise over 50 percent of global airline travelers – nearly half a billion people.

- The relaxation of travel regulations regarding entry to China has caused a boom in visitor numbers as the millions of ethnic Chinese around the region visit the country for many reasons, from tending ancestors' grave sites to cruising down the Yellow River.

Tourism is becoming something on which the Asian economies are coming to rely as exports decline and the home market becomes more important. Hong Kong derives over 5 percent of its GDP from tourism and Singapore fully 8 percent. The tourism industry also accounts for over 2 percent of the labor force in these two countries. However, with the economic turmoil tourism has taken a downswing and this has hurt many local economies. This is in fact another example of the interdependency of Asian nations. The real pain that Hong Kong felt through falling tourist numbers was not because of the number of Europeans or Americans but the mass cancellations by Taiwanese and Japanese. For westerners travel to Asia has never been cheaper, but it was always the other Asian visitors that spent the most.

In Indonesia, the number of tourists visiting the country had tripled since 1991 and this earned the country in excess of US$15 billion annually. Bali alone received nearly 1.5 million tourists a year – their loss will be keenly felt.

Travel is a growth industry to rival any other in Asia. The Chinese airline industry reported that growth was running in excess of 30 percent a year and the demand for trained pilots is in excess of 600 a year. Boeing in Seattle estimates that Chinese carriers alone will buy 800 new aircraft over the next 15 years to expand fleets that already carry 50 million passengers.

A decade ago every Asian country rushed to set up its own national airline in the same way that in the 1990s they rushed to set up their own car manufacturers. However, there is a new tranche of carriers in the light of the subsequent wave of air privatization and liberalization.

Typical of this direction is the Philippines, where the Manila government sold its 67 percent holding in Philippines Air to a private consortium in 1992. Since then, the government has granted a wave of new licenses and new companies have appeared such as Grand International Air, which competes with Philippines Air on routes to Hong Kong and elsewhere. Air Philippines (AP) is another secondary carrier. It was established by William Gatchalian, a plastics producer based at the Subic Bay airport, formerly a US army base. AP has started a service between Manila and Cebu with 12 leased Boeing 737s. Demand has been exceptional.

The tourist industry has also been seen by national governments as a way to bring investment into the country as well as tourist cash. Vietnam, a destination still largely for the entrepid traveler, has attracted US$6.6 billion in tourism infrastructure investment.

Hotels

A tour around the building sites of Asia reveals the large number of new hotels popping up in both the big cities and the resorts. The growth in the hotel industry reflects the growth in travel between

Asian countries and also the influx of western tourists. But perhaps most of all the market has been stimulated by the region's newly affluent consumers.

Rohan Dalziel, an investment analyst with Barings Securities, recently commented: 'People in Asia are riding the back of rising disposable incomes and, with the transition from some of the older Asian values to more relaxed western work ethics, they're beginning to travel further afield.'

Hotels are often social centers for the middle class – the sumptuous buffet lunches available in KL's luxury hotels attract as many diners from the Malaysian business community as tourists. In provincial towns and cities hotels are becoming the central entertainment. When two hotels opened in Surabaya, Indonesia's second largest city, traffic came to a standstill as the street outside the new Majapahit Hotel filled with imported luxury cars. The *Singapore Business Times* described the opening night as Surabaya's 'coming out' party.

Asia needs the additional hotels

Vietnam estimates that it needs to build another 25,000 hotel rooms by 2000 to keep pace with tourist arrivals. The country currently has 42,000 rooms but less than half are up to international standards. Vietnam had in excess of a million tourists in 1996, earning it US$4 billion in receipts and creating 15,000 jobs.

Asian hotels are large-scale projects

Philippines property developer Megaworld Properties is working with international hotel giant ITT Sheraton to manage its Marina Hotel and Residential Suites site near Manila Bay. The project includes a 26-floor, 250-room hotel and 32-floor apartment building.

Foreign investment is pouring in

Examples of foreign hotel chains entering the Asian market are numerous. The US Days Hotel chain is one such foreign company. It is planning to spend US$192 million to build 25 hotels throughout the Philippines catering mainly to locals holidaying at home.

But the locals are building fast, too

Asian hotel chains have become major conglomerates with the growth in both overseas and domestic tourism. Shangri-La hotels, a local player, has seen 40 percent growth in profits and 65 percent growth in turnover as the market has boomed. The company has expanded successfully throughout the region with a 77 percent occupancy rate at its new hotel in Shanghai and 84 percent at its resort on Mactan Island in the Philippines.

And laying the groundwork for the growth of tourism

In Taiwan there has been a dash to build additional hotel rooms. The country has opened its first hotel school to provide staff to the industry where previously those looking for a career had to go to Switzerland or elsewhere in Europe.

Not forgetting the niches

The 400-room Taipei Hilton is not the first and won't be the last Asian hotel to start addressing niche markets. Like others in the region, it has created an executive floor to build a 'hotel within a hotel' catering to the high end of the market with more room space, fax and phone lines along with Internet connections. Other hotels have created women's rooms with additional bathroom space and a more feminine color scheme along with additional security.

Theme parks

Asia's tradition of family seems ideal for the theme park industry. While corporations like Disney bemoan the fact that European parents want to bring their children to Disneyland Paris, drop them off and then find a bar (a trend which forced Disney to relax its no-alcohol rule at its French theme park), Asian families apparently enjoy the world of theme parks. Such establishments as Lotte-World Adventure in South Korea, Leofoo Village in Taiwan and a whole island that is essentially a theme park, Sentosa in Singapore, are major money spinners.

South Korea's Yong-in Farmland theme park located in Kyonggi-Do is Asia's most popular theme park outside of Japan's Disneyland. In excess of 7 million visitors arrive at the gates annually. Asia's theme parks are usually water based with a penchant for aquaria. Increasingly the trend has been towards technology, with a growing number of Namco Stations and Segaworlds across the region.

Brunei, which is in the process of trying to sell itself as a cool tourist destination for families, has Jeudong Park built by the Sultan for his people. Many believe it to be the best in Asia and certainly the Sultan's money has raised the level of attractions, including Michael Jackson and Whitney Houston. The Michael Jackson concert is remembered nightly at Jerudong Park with a laser show in the great performer's honor.

Theme parks are big business and it seems that just about every leading property company is jumping on the bandwagon and finding little trouble locating investors for a slew of new fun-packed family-oriented parks:

- Hong Kong is planning Film City, to cover 25 hectares on Ma Wan, a small island between Lantau and Tsing Yi that serves as a landing point for the new suspension bridge. The theme will be domestic and international films along with a 1000-room hotel.
- Thailand's largest theme park, Siam Park, is getting a US$128 million facelift to compete with the plethora of regional attractions. Funding is coming from German, Swiss and British banks. Siam Park attracts a million visitors a year to its water-themed rides.
- Sega Enterprises has captured a large slice of the leisure industry across Asia and beyond. Now the company is opening amusement arcades across India in Chennai (Madras), Mumbai, New Delhi, Calcutta and other Indian cities.
- A group of Australian entrepreneurs has been contracted to build Hualien Ocean Park on Taiwan's east coast, yet another water-themed amusement center.
- Johor Baru, Malaysia, is the location for Southern Magic, which is forecast to attract 3.5 million visitors within five years of

opening. A US$1.4 billion project, this is aimed at attracting the well-heeled Singaporean funlover living across the Causeway.

The entertainment business

As economies become more advanced, the supply of more sophisticated goods increases, as does the way these are marketed. Consumers begin to learn a new language and become more varied in their tastes. This phenomenon spills over into how people spend their leisure time and as leisure pursuits change so do consumer aspirations.

In countries where economic development has happened over a period of a few years, rather than a century or so, the changes in leisure activities have been dramatic, with people demanding more diverse forms of entertainment backed up by their increased expendable income. The suppliers of entertainment have been quick to see the potential for new entertainment businesses, such as the inevitable influx of the Disney empire into just about every corner of Asia.

A sign of the significance of Asian consumers as *the* new potential market for entertainment corporations is the fact that Michael Eisner, head of the Disney Corporation, visited China 24 times in 1995, shuttling between top leaders in China in an attempt to corner rights to set up Disney theme parks and franchises.

Sitting in the back row

More people in China have seen the film *Jurassic Park* than in the US and western Europe combined, most of them below the age of 40. But equally, the Chinese film industry is hitting back with its own product, such as the 52-part computer-animated film version of the classic Journey to the West titled *Uproar in Heaven*, the local answer to *The Lion King*. In Hong Kong and China, the *kung fu* movie genre has received a new lease of life, modeled on Hollywood action blockbusters.

Cinema is a longstanding leisure activity in China. After the Cultural Revolution (1966–76) it became the main leisure activity, attracting ten billion viewers in 1982. *Popular Cinema* magazine had a circulation of over ten million in the 1980s, the largest of any monthly Chinese magazine at the time. Cinema admissions now exceed six billion annually, with box office takings in excess of US$500 million (remember that admission is cheap).

Singapore Technologies Industrial Corporation (STIC), a Singaporean government-owned company, is moving into China following moves by the Beijing government to allow foreign ownership of cinemas. In April 1997, STIC established a US$2 million joint venture with Hong Kong's Golden Harvest to build cinemas in Shanghai that would form the start of a nationwide chain. Multiplexes are planned in Wuhan.

South Korea still produces around 65–70 domestic movies annually despite local cinemas thriving on a diet of Hong Kong and Hollywood fodder. Traditionally, Korea's cinemas were family-owned businesses. Now in the highly competitive leisure market of the new Korea, the *chaebols* have moved in on the act – Daewoo, Hyundai and Samsung are all developing multiplex cinema chains across the country.

The media rush and the growth of TV have begun to eat into cinema's potential as a leisure activity. But there is one country where the cinema is still king – India. It remains the world's leading film producer and is now a top producer of 'made-for-TV' movies. The market has box office receipts in excess of US$550 million (remembering again that average ticket costs are far lower than in Europe or the US). Hollywood films while on show account for only 2 percent of total receipts. What the continued success of Indian films shows is that local output can be popular and good and varied – it ranges from the internationally acclaimed *Bandit Queen* with very high production values to mass entertainment Hindi musicals that are produced on what seems to be a daily basis.

Every Asian country has seen the invasion of Hollywood to an extent, but each has also produced strong local content. Vietnam has a film industry that continues to attract international interest. The industry that was initially built on propaganda, with films such as *Steel Ramparts* made on location in the underground tunnels used during the war with the US, is now producing films that look in closer detail at modern Vietnamese life, such as *Cyclo* and *Scent of the Green Papaya*, and are winning international awards.

Soccer

The national soccer league has made football one of the most popular spectator sports in China, backed up by sponsorship from Marlboro. This has circumvented the total ban on tobacco advertising in the country, thanks to the league's lobbying the government to be allowed to keep Marlboro's support because it would not have been able to continue otherwise and the league is now so popular.

The fact that Manchester United Football Club has an official fan club in Malaysia, with an accompanying franchise retail outlet, is another significant indicator of how important sport is as a leisure pursuit for Asians. Malaysia's subscription satellite TV station Astro has built its subscriber base largely on the back of screening 10 English Premier and Division One games a month live along with an average of three international games. English football is big business across the region and sponsors such as Dunhill are keen to get involved.

In Japan the most popular spectator sport, after the indigenous Sumo wrestling, is baseball, imported from the US after the Second World War. This influence has also spread to Taiwan, thanks to its close links with both countries.

Sports traditionally popular in Asia, such as many of the racket sports (badminton, squash, table tennis and so on), have retained their significance, despite the large amounts of sponsorship money being put behind newly imported sports. Malaysia is more likely to come to a standstill for the badminton World Cup, which it has won several times, than the soccer World Cup.

All these spectator sports rely on TV coverage and the advertising slots around the televising of major sporting events, such as big volleyball matches in China, can draw the most expensive advertising fees. Governments are also happy to allow their citizens to become hooked on sports, seeing the benefits of better health gained through sports participation and the sense of patriotism kindled in supporting national teams.

It's not just the masses who are being catered for, as country clubs begin to appear all over Asia and the passion which is golf continues to claim new addicts all the time. The golf phenomenon, most fanatical in Japan but spreading ever outward, is attracting big money. New courses are springing up all over Malaysia, Singapore and the Philippines. In China, the central government tried to curb the 'waste of productive farming land on the building of golf courses', especially in the south, but local interests have had their own way. One such development near Shenzhen, called the Mission Hills Golf Club, boasts courses designed by such golfing luminaries as Jack Nicklaus, Nick Faldo and Jumbo Ozaki. These places are as exclusive in China as they are in southern California.

Sport also tends to be non-political and a 'safe' form of entertainment for citizens who might otherwise be led astray by 'immoral' or 'subversive' pastimes. So governments are happy for sport to become the new opiate of the masses, even in China where soccer violence has reared its ugly head.

Sex and violence

Pornography is another, much more sinister and, in many countries, frowned-on opiate of the masses. The fact that erotic art and eroticism have existed for centuries in Asian cultures has not helped the official purge of such material, which has enabled peddlers of hardcore pornography to find a ready and willing market.

Japan and China form an interesting dichotomy in this respect. Japan is openly flooded with erotic/pornographic images (we will not debate the definitions here), but in China even the most innocent form of eroticism (such as a passionate kiss) is strictly forbidden to be displayed in any context or art form, whether in the performing arts, cinema/TV or in fine art. Hong Kong's street newspaper stands had been used to displaying a large selection of erotic titles, but since reunification with China they have had to play much more carefully.

Both countries share a wealth of erotic art in their cultural backgrounds, in China dating back to the Tang dynasty and in Japan almost throughout its history. The fact that the two countries now have opposing situations is thanks to modern history and the point at which western involvement had most influence.

This is no time for a history lesson, but we can look at the effects the difference has had on consumerism. In Japan the media is awash with images of eroticism and violence, even in children's Manga comics. In China, death sentences are handed out to those caught infringing its morality laws, in an attempt to control the trade in pornographic material.

At the same time, however, 'sex shops' have begun to appear on the streets of China's cities. The government, mindful that it must bring its population problem under control and aware that levels of awareness and understanding about sex among its population are low, decided to bring sex out into the open, though within moral limits. Shops selling condoms and other 'marital aids' have therefore started to receive government licenses to sell safe-sex products and 'informative literature'. Needless to say, some have appeared which are unlicensed and sell literature that is rather too informative, but China has officially admitted that sex exists.

Other parts of Asia see sex quite differently. Majority Muslim countries obviously have strong views and censorship in Malaysia and Indonesia is strict. It is the same in secular Singapore – local court judges, dealing with a case where a woman claimed that a man forced her to have sex with him, more or less banned oral sex as an indecent act unless it led to full intercourse!

Thailand and the Philippines are two countries where sex has been freely available and openly displayed. Abuse of minors by visiting tourists and businessmen has forced their governments to try to curb their libertine sex industries.

In China, along with eroticism, 'excessive' violence in films is seen as a potential pollutant of the moral integrity of the masses and is treated with the vehemence any enemy of the state might expect to receive. But violence is a part of Chinese life and history, as it is of Asia in general. There has always been a strong current of violence in films and will continue to be so, as long as demand is still there. Asian movies have always been generally more violent than their western counterparts. For example, in the 1960s when people were being shot in westerns in the US (but without showing blood), in Japan decapitation was not an uncommon effect. In the 1970s, a glut of violent *kung fu* movies were made, continuing a tradition which first appeared in the middle of the century.

The future of fun

Lim Kim Hong, CEO of the Sumurwang Group, thinks he knows the future of fun in Asia. In fact, he's so sure he knows that he's getting on with the job of building it. It has a name and a location – it's called the Sumurcity Spaceport and it's in Malaysia's Klang Valley. Apart from fun, Lim Kim Hong has some thoughts on the future of housing, manufacturing, retailing and finance – that's why he's building a whole city. Sumurcity is projected to be 72 acres and represents a US$925 million investment by the *taipan*. The city center is described as an 'encapsulated hub, called the entertainment-driven retail complex (ERC), covering 25 acres'. It's fun, it's new and it's covered.

Of course it doesn't exist yet, even though Lim describes it as a low-risk investment. Only someone with a big vision would describe building the world's first covered city as a low risk. He wants to redesign the theme park that has become the standard in Asia – water based and historical – and go for something rooted in technology and science. Rides planned include Cosmos which allows you to experience genuine G-forces and Max Q which launches you upwards at amazing speed, similar to taking off in a rocket. There's also Flash Landing which simulates reentry to earth's atmosphere and splashdown while those on the ride are spun at fantastic speeds. The whole park is based around exhibits explaining science in the more traditional sense for those who think that G-forces and reentry are best left to astronauts.

It seems that the future of fun in Asia is a mixture of tradition and technology.

Part Three

The Future

13

Bouncing Back

Asia hasn't gone away – it's bouncing back. Life goes on and Asians are applying their traditional or, in the case of the Chinese and Vietnamese, recently found business sense to the new times. And the multinationals are staying. Simple mathematics dictates that they should. According to *The Economist*, the average Chinese household shoots half a roll of film each year. If it could be encouraged to finish the roll and persuaded to use Kodak film, the company would double its global sales. Obviously Kodak has realized this and announced in May 1998 an investment of US$1 billion in China. George Fisher, the company's CEO, stated: 'I think that in 10 years you will find this is the most important thing Kodak has ever done.' Times may have got harder in Asia, but the prize is still worth fighting for.

Value for money

Competitive pricing and stores renowned for value for money are leading the bounce back. While retailers are finding the going tough in Hong Kong shopping malls that feature almost exclusively luxury goods, Malaysia has found a different route. Despite the collapse of the ringgit and the country's continuing economic woes, its largest shopping mall (1 million sq. ft), Kuala Lumpur City Centre next to the Petronas Twin Towers, opened for business in May 1998 with 80 percent of available space let. This Malaysian–Dutch–Australian joint venture features notoriously strong value-for-money retailers such as Isetan and Britain's Marks & Spencer, as well as local retailer Parkson Grand. Several retailers have reduced the price of their goods to their local franchisees, believing in the location as fundamental to their long-term strategy of strong positioning in Malaysia.

Isetan's store is twice the size of its other KL store in the Lot 10 mall and aims for the middle and upper income brackets. Its managing director Toshiyuki Asano told the *New Straits Times* at the opening: 'We believe that the economic situation is temporary and we're confident about Malaysia's economy and its ability to recover.'

The everyday example of food also illustrates the importance of value for money. Prices have increased in most Asian countries and this has led to widespread looting and rioting in Indonesia and contributed to Soeharto's downfall. However, most Asians are still able to exercise a choice about where they purchase their food.

Competition continues to grow in the Chinese supermarket business. Shanghai is rapidly moving away from traditional grocery stores and markets as the number of super- and hypermarkets expands.

French-owned Carrefour unveiled plans in April 1998 to open three more supermarkets in Shanghai, building on the success of the two stores it already operates in this booming coastal city. Another foreign entrant is the German retailing giant Metro with three hypermarkets in the city.

In retailing in general, A&A Mall is perhaps the most interesting example of inward investment in China's retailing infrastructure. This is a joint venture between a local Shanghai real-estate firm and a Taiwanese investor. The store is located in the city's northwestern suburbs, has attracted crowds since it opened and now the company has also announced that it will construct six or seven similar malls along the Shanghai–Nanjing and Shanghai–Hangzhou highways.

These examples all have certain elements in common that also characterize many of the 'bounce-back' businesses thriving in the new Asian environment: they are big, they target the mass market and they offer extremely competitive pricing as well as an introduction to new products and retailing methods. A&A, Carrefour and Metro often have what seem at first to be poor locations for the Chinese market – on the fringes of the city, at best half an hour by car and one hour by bus from the city center. But still they are attracting business. Without doubt the magnet is price.

All these stores are run as what in the west would be seen as wholesale operations. They are combining this with the successful western formula of out-of-town or edge-of-town locations that are less expensive than high streets and take into account growing car ownership, improved public transport and the move away from daily shopping. When all these factors are combined these companies are bouncing back even as the first wave of in-town supermarkets, such as Shanghai's Lianhua China, are losing ground. Now China's problem is that the smaller, first-generation supermarkets that put the grocery stores out of business are themselves threatened with extinction by the next-generation hypermarkets.

But the supermarkets themselves are fighting back. Lianhua plans an additional 145 outlets in 1998 and rival Hulian anticipates 90 more outlets. Shanghai's market is further boosted by Dutch company Royal Ahold, which bought now defunct Yaohan's Shanghai stores in 1997 and is converting the city's 22 Yaohan supermarkets to Ahold's Tops format. Shanghai may be the main center of investment at present, but Beijing is also attracting new waves of retailing money, as the numerous building sites along the city's premier retailing street Wangfujing testify.

In addition, retailers have begun to move from their locations in the city center out into the suburbs. Across Asia, smaller retailers are reacting to the growth in the larger out-of-town stores by becoming more local and therefore filling the niche between the corner store and the hypermarket. The Chinese–Japanese joint-venture supermarket chain Huatang is opening stores in Beijing's suburbs, typically 15,000 square meters in size, and is backing up the expansion with an investment of US$130 million.

The strategy of being bigger than the competition is working for retailers across Asia, not just China. Much troubled Thailand is seeing a similar bounce back. Its largest cash-and-carry operation Siam Makro is investing in new information technology and two new stores. Despite the economic meltdown's adverse effect on sales of expensive goods, Thailand's discount stores, convenience stores, cash-and-carry outlets and supermarkets are finding that they are growing the volume of their business by lowering prices. And in South Korea, despite a downturn in fortunes, Carrefour (which opened its first Korean hypermarket in 1996) has announced plans to open 20 more stores by the year 2000.

Attracting shoppers in new ways

Festival Supermall, a 20-hectare integrated shopping mall and leisure complex, opened in Manila in May 1998. It is a four-story complex with two department stores, two supermarkets, a 27-outlet food court and 450 specialty shops as well as an indoor family entertainment center with rides, a ferris wheel and puppet shows. The investors behind Festival Supermall knew that in the current economic climate a purely retailing venture would not succeed. Therefore they have built a family entertainment destination where you can also shop, located within the heart of Manila's southern area as a community focus point.

Developers and retailers are looking for new ways to attract shoppers. From August 1998 Beijing's Henderson Center will give Chinese consumers the opportunity to pay US$10 to thrill themselves at a mini Universal Studios. The center is the result of a strategic alliance between Hong Kong property group Henderson Land and Universal Studios. The US movie company is establishing an interactive entertainment complex to anchor an 80,000 square meter shopping and housing development on Chang'an. The complex will be known as Hollywood Location.

Customer service is becoming a watchword across the region, not least in China, where one store manager told *China Daily* that good service now had to be understood as 'much more than a Colgate smile'.

And of course there's always the store that will still find a market whatever the consumer's mood because some things are more important than economic recessions. Manchester United Football Club is planning to open a chain of stores across Asia, perhaps as many as 50 in countries as diverse as Thailand, Singapore, China and Hong Kong. Another example is the recently discovered penchant for platinum jewelry among China's S generation. Young consumers consider it to be elegant and sophisticated compared to their parent's taste for gaudy gold jewelry and sales doubled in 1997.

Still expanding

Without doubt retailers took a pounding in the meltdown. Many went out of business, mostly operations that were in a weak financial position prior to the crisis or were outdated – Yaohan was the prime example, Maria's Bakeries in Hong Kong another.

But retail expansion actually looks set to continue. Rents have fallen as businesses have gone bust, increasing the volume of available property. Landlords have also learnt that lower rents help tenants stay in business and keep paying. Retail rents in Hong Kong's main tourist shopping district Tsim Sha Tsui fell by 50 percent between November 1997 and March 1998. Empty retail property benefits no one and intense renegotiations have been ongoing since the New Year in 1998.

In Chapter 1, we offered some examples of how retailers were taking the opportunity of the post-meltdown period to expand their operations in other Asian countries: Marks & Spencer across the region and Hong Kong's Giordano chain into mainland China. Stagnant markets at home – there are few high streets in Britain without an M&S and not many shopping areas in Hong Kong, Singapore or Malaysia that don't have a Giordano or three – have meant that expansion overseas is essential for growth and profit spread. Others are following suit:

- Dominant British pharmacy chain Boots is expanding in Thailand with 40 new stores and an investment of US$14.6 million. The company claims that the Thai recession has bottomed out and finds the low retail rents and flexible lease terms attractive, combined with the country's growing middle class. Martyn Bell, MD of Boots in Thailand, says that the company plans to train Cantonese-speaking Thais as managers who can be sent to China as that market opens up.

- Hong Kong-based New World Development Co opened its sixth general store in China at Ningbo (Zhejiang) in May 1998. After success in Wuhan, Shenyang, Wuxi, Harbin and Tianjin, New World is now targeting Beijing, Qingdao and Dalian.
- Costco is ramping up plans to extend its chain of discount stores in South Korea.
- The UK's leading supermarket chain Tesco has announced plans to invest US$239 million in the recently acquired Thai hypermarket chain Lotus. Another 12 outlets are planned along with redevelopment of the existing 13 branches.

Financial services

For many companies the need for fixed premises that incur overheads is being dispensed with altogether. Financial services are a growing sector of the Asian economy and one that will become increasingly important as the region bounces back. For providers of financial services, from pensions to insurance, healthcare to mortgages, Asia is now a booming market. Indeed, Eagle Star Asia has recruited 200 people as the company bids to be one of the top three insurance agencies in new business income in the Hong Kong market (and ultimately China) by the year 2001. The 200 newcomers will make a total of over 1000 for the SAR alone. Britain's Royal & Sun Alliance has identified Asia as a growth market to compensate for the slowdown in European business.

Even pretty well covered Hong Kong is way behind coverage levels in the US, Europe and Japan, however. Of all the Asian countries, only Singapore has insurance coverage of over 70 percent of the population. But in the last few years the number, range and promotion of financial products in Asia have rocketed. All of a sudden, several factors have become more important:

- A growing number of unemployed professionals are looking for jobs – direct selling of financial products is one route out of joblessness.
- With unemployment and financial hardship looming, medical insurance, life assurance and income protection insurance all suddenly look like something one should have.
- With government spending under strain, many Asians are questioning whether or not the support networks and financial safety nets they have taken for granted will still be there when they need them.
- And in China, the housing market is poised to be thrown open and bank mortgage-lending ceilings have been tripled. An urban public housing population of 370 million Chinese are all about to receive the 'right to buy'.

Local banks in China now seek to attract new accounts from stalls arrayed in such places as along the junction between Beijing's Chang'an and Xidan streets. In addition to qualifying for a bank account, successful applicants can also use the growing number of ATMs sprinkled around the city.

The Chinese government has earmarked Shanghai as the testing ground for the country's insurance market. Previously the People's Insurance Company of China (PICC) was the sole provider of policies, but currently over a dozen competitors are in the Shanghai market, including joint ventures and foreign companies from the UK, Japan, Switzerland, Canada, Germany and France. International names are commonplace on Shanghai policies, including AIG, Commercial Union and Allianz. All of this activity of course backs up Shanghai's bid to be a financial center for Asia, with the new Shanghai Stock Exchange Building completed at a cost of US$3.7 million.

Direct sales

Direct selling is also booming as the bounce back provides new opportunities. We have already talked about the rise of catalog and home shopping and these relatively low-cost, low-overhead operations are expanding in the new consumer environment. The only exception is China where in April 1998 the government banned direct selling following concerns about pyramid selling and investment schemes such as those that caused riots in eastern Europe several years ago. However, it seems likely that this restriction will be lifted for reputable operators such as Amway and Avon. Avon already has 'beauty boutiques' in Malaysia and Taiwan allowing for a mixture of direct and traditional shopfront sales. Companies such as Yves Rocher have followed a similar path. With US direct-selling operations in China having already invested over US$130 million and employing perhaps as many as two million Chinese, there is a great deal at stake.

And all the time companies are seeking to expand home-shopping opportunities using new media. One consequence of the recession in Asia is that more people are watching television (something that just might save the region's advertising industry from plunging profits). Home-shopping networks and the additional channels on cable, satellite and digital TV, as well as the Internet, are being seen as low-cost post-meltdown shopfronts.

In March 1998 Hong Kong's long-awaited interactive television system, ITV, was finally launched. It is not yet clear whether it will be a success, but Hong Kong is better cabled than Japan or the US and over a third of its homes have immediate access. The SAR's massive tower-block apartments also mean that connection costs are half those in Europe or the US, where connections require more cable and a greater number of manhours. According to Hong Kong Telecom's research, 87 percent of SAR residents are prepared to sign up for interactive. ITV may have to incur losses for some time to come but a combination of Hong Kong's appetite for shopping, leisure, TV, movies and technology should ensure that it wins in the end. The consortium behind this experiment is already planning its assault on Singapore and SingTel.

Fast food

Other sectors of the Asian economy have also found the economic downturn a strangely profitable time and are building on previous success to emerge stronger than before. One such sector is fast food.

Local Filipino franchiser PhilKing Restaurants announced in April 1998 that it would be opening at least 64 Burger King restaurants over the following five years. At present BK has only a handful of stores in the country. With additional competition it is highly likely that the two main competitors, McDonald's and local key player Jollibee, will have to cut prices to boost volume sales. But it would appear that the burger giants are willing to play the price-slashing game in Asia.

In early 1998 James Cantalupo, president and chief executive of the international division of McDonald's, announced investments of US$1.5 billion over three years for further expansion in the Asian market. Another 2000 outlets are to be added to the existing 4500 in the region's 17 countries (including Japan and Australia). Cantalupo does not see the Asian financial crisis as a significant threat to the plan – and anyway McDonald's has reached virtual market saturation in the US and Europe and is left with only minor markets to exploit such as Moldova (which got its first Big Mac in 1998).

KFC, Malaysia's leading fast-food operator, is planning to open an additional 25 outlets across the country in 1998 to add to the 265 outlets that already provide it with nearly 70 percent of the fast-food market. In April 1998 a KFC representative told Bernama, the Malaysia News Agency: 'So far, we have not seen much change in our customers' spending pattern and we are projecting a growth in sales.'

As we explained earlier in the book, the multinational fast-food chains have not had Asia all their own way. And the meltdown will not change this. Hong Kong's Café de Coral has announced plans to invest in 12 new branches to add to the company's existing 110 outlets in a bid to stay on top of the SAR's fast-food market.

The magic moment

There is no scientific definition of a consumer market. It is impossible to say when one starts and when it becomes the norm. Does a country have a consumer market when 5 percent of the population can afford items over and above the basic necessities of life? Or is it 10 percent, 20 percent, 50 percent?

One Billion Shoppers tries to show that defining this 'magic moment' when consumerism arrives is almost as much a feeling, an emotion, as a reflection of a nation's bank balance. GDP per head calculations and the formulations of comparative spending have a place; economists have grappled with such calculations for years. More important is how Asia feels – the buzz, the rush of the region, quite unquantifiable but also undeniable. Is there a consumer market in Asia? Yes, the figures tell us that. But is there a consumer culture, are there consuming passions? Yes, but it was our visits to the region over the years that told us that, putting faces to the figures.

Deng Xiaoping came up with the theory of Xiao Kang. This was his definition of the 'magic moment' for the Chinese economy and it was an average yearly income of US$1000 per head by the year 2000. Without doubt if this was achieved then consumerism would leap forward in China – but US$1000 a head in rural China by the century's end is unlikely.

Identifying this 'magic moment' anywhere in the region is extremely difficult. Take India as an example. Many foreign companies have started entering the market in the same way that western companies rushed to establish joint ventures in China in the 1980s. In China few companies found the great riches they were expecting. Invariably they faced bureaucracy, corruption, shifting politics, a weak local market and a culture they rarely understood. For many India has been a similar story. Sony, Matsushita and Whirlpool all announced in early 1998 that they were scaling back their initial levels of involvement in the Indian market and all claimed to have overestimated the size of the country's middle class.

In a country of nearly a billion people, the consuming middle class can be both spread out and hard to find. Early estimates of 250 million active consumers were wrong. More realistically, under 3 percent of Indians are currently active consumers. By 2010 that percentage could be above 10 percent, but India's magic moment remains elusive.

Future developments

In this book we have attempted to look at what is really happening in Asia rather than being swayed by the advocates of doom or those who overhype the region. What is needed is a sober assessment of what has changed at ground level and how that is affecting Asian society and will determine its future development.

Examples of the changes are found throughout this book, but when we group them together we can see various patterns emerging.

Global vs local

Asia can appear to be the best proof yet of the much overused (and abused) term 'globalization'. The existence of McDonald's restaurants, department stores, Audis and consumer goods across the region can give the impression of a homogeneous, mutually understanding Asian culture. It is as if the ability to eat a Big Mac and ride in a Mercedes in Beijing, KL and Manila means that the countries are the same. To add to this false impression, the visitor spending time in similar-looking hotel rooms all over Asia will probably agree that the media is furthering this process as he or she watches the same channels in each country. But this is just a casual glance. The real key to Asia is localization.

The Audis and washing machines and cosmetic halls are about aspirations more than globalization. In truth, at ground level, what Asia is about is modification. Take these examples:

- At McDonald's in Beijing, Chinese spend a sixth of an average month's salary on a meal that is a chance to sample a taste of the west. And it is far from being fast food – customers linger over their milkshakes enjoying the experience of something different.

- Sales of cosmetics and haircare products are growing. Initially this growth was fueled by the arrival of western products and brands simultaneously with a rise in image consciousness and income. As the region's consumers have become more sophisticated, there has been a growing demand for quality color cosmetics that suit Asian complexions. Haircare products offer the quality and packaging of western imports but incorporate Asian ingredients such as ginseng.
- Western-style clothes shops have appeared all over the region, but a new breed of store blends in Asian characteristics. David Tang's Shanghai Tang store in Hong Kong is laid out like a western boutique but features good-quality Chinese-made and designed clothing such as padded suits and silk *cheongsams*, along with a *feng shui* master for customer consultations. Other examples include Joyce Ma's chain of Hong Kong boutiques.
- Asia's Channel V has attracted a massive audience among young Asians with its MTV-style graphics and format. But along with the western videos are the stars of Cantopop and Mandopop. In each country local programming reflects local taste. In the Philippines Channel V broadcasts in Tagalog and in India Hindi videos feature prominently.

Asian consumers have reacted warmly to many western concepts – fast food, video music channels – but have absorbed those concepts and made them local, made them Asian. This applies not just to western concepts but often to Japanese as well.

Marketers have to be aware when entering the Asian market that although they might have a product that works in the west, they must adapt their packaging, branding and marketing to suit multiple Asian tastes. Yet again, this requires an understanding of Asia at a local level rather than treating it as a homogeneous whole.

Modern vs traditional

Increasingly, modern technologies, products and services are being adopted by Asian consumers to support traditional values. For example:

- As discussed in Chapter 9, computing and computer ownership in Asia are growing rapidly. Education remains a traditional value which is being enhanced and maintained by parents purchasing computers for their offspring along with educational CD-Roms. Companies such as Dorling Kindersley have found a ready market by providing modern products to suit traditional aims.
- As discussed in Chapter 11, shopping malls have arrived in Asia and represent a complete shift from traditional environments. Shopping mall outlets tend to be glitzier versions of traditional stores. The international chains are present but, for example, the Xin Dong'an mall on Beijing's Wangfujing features slicker traditional-style tea houses, Chinese pharmacies and branded Chinese restaurants.
- As demand for housing has grown, so new developments have mimicked US suburban architectural styles on the outside but, more often than not, the decor inside reflects Asian tastes. New homeowners are buying traditional Asian furniture and wall hangings but because the setting is new, the approach to Asian design has been modernized.

Asians have not been afraid to adopt concepts and products that have improved their lives, been of better quality or just plain new. However, they have used these products to create a modern version of the traditional, invariably supporting long-held values and practices.

As Asians create their own version of modernity so it has become a creative force in itself. Local companies have been quick to pick up on this trend and foreign companies need to be aware of these forces.

The new Asian generation

For the younger generations in Asia, the past appears distant and old values are lost in the maze of the 'tiger' years. In Malaysia everyone under 40, in other words the majority of the population, was born in an independent country, as was every Indian under 50.

Perhaps this is obvious, but today's young Asians, and in most cases the middle aged too, were born into countries of their own: independent nations with ties and squabbles with their neighbors and their region rather than the old colonial powers. The youth and younger professionals who form the backbone of Asia's consuming classes know not just independence but economic self-sufficiency and global influence. A young person embarking on a career in banking in Singapore is aware that they are beginning a career in an important global location for their chosen profession. Likewise, someone entering the lower rungs of management in an Indian software company or an Indonesian footwear manufacturer knows that they are competing globally with factories in the US, Europe and Africa.

The next generation of consumers in Asia has grown up in nations where living standards improved annually, where new options and choices presented themselves monthly, where they have access to global media and where new 'toys' – from a new pager to a new car – arrived almost daily. And they have now experienced their first economic dip.

But the flame of consuming passion has been lit and expectations remain high, so the desire to advance will not go away. Asians have still not all attained the lifestyle enjoyed by many in western Europe and the US. Some have reached high levels of prosperity, but will this wealth continue to grow and trickle down to the large mass of people who are on the lower rungs of the ladder? The answer must be yes, as the aspirations of those on the lower rungs continue to drive economic growth.

No matter what happens as a result of the economic slump in 1997/8 Asia remains dynamic, even if at present much of this dynamism is directed towards correcting mistakes. Once recovery is reached – something that is in everyone's interests, both in Asia and the west – dynamism will be refocused on the business of consuming. Even if the process of recovery takes several years in some countries, the seeds of consuming have been sown. Once smitten, Asian consumers are not likely to forget their new aspirations and desires; they will merely find new ways to create the fundamentals which will allow them to attain what they want.

Asia will continue to be a market for the future and cannot be ignored or written off. However, to succeed in Asia requires both commitment and understanding at a much more significant level than before. A potential market of one billion shoppers, in all their diversity, must be worth the effort.

Further Reading

The literature concerning Asia is growing daily. As the region attracts attention so it needs interpreting, both to the other four continents of the world and to itself. While there are a large number of books available, we have mostly omitted the more academic texts in favor of titles that provide flavor and insight through examples and experiences.

John Naisbitt's *Megatrends Asia* (Nicholas Brealey, 1995) first raised many of the points that we have dwelt on in greater detail and Jim Rohwer's *Asia Rising* (Nicholas Brealey 1996) was also a consummate roundup of the region with particularly interesting thoughts on India and China. Also worth noting is *The Changing Business Environment in the Asia-Pacific Region*, edited by Henri-Claude de Bettignies (Thomson Business Press, 1997) and, although a little older, John Andrews' book *The Asian Challenge* (Longman, 1991) still raises some useful ideas and arguments about how Asia will develop.

Many people have dealt with the new rich and the wealthy business class in Asia and their role as catalysts of growth and trends. Geoff Hiscock's *Asia's Wealth Club* (Nicholas Brealey, 1997) provides a useful picture of the region's business leaders and their multifaceted, diversified and interlinked interests. In addition, Claudia Cragg's *The New Taipans* (Arrow, 1995) offers a useful series of 'mindmaps' to the new Asian business leaders.

Most countries of the region have begun to start examining themselves in closer detail, often from dissenting points of view and often with a degree of humor. The rise of the middle classes and the growth of consumption have frequently been topics for discussion. Particularly revealing in this vein have been Karim

Raslan's collected columns for various Malaysian magazines and newspapers called *Ceritalah: Malaysia in Transition* (Times Books International, 1996). Malaysian consumer society is also discussed with wit and insight in Lee Su Kim's *Malaysian Flavours* (Pelanduk Publications, 1996), a collection of her columns for *The Star* newspaper. John Machado's *Creating Desire* (Sym Press, 1996) gives an insight into Asian consumerism from a leading Malaysian ad man. Another book of particular interest for those attempting to understand the different habits and tastes of Asian consumers is *Golden Arches East: McDonald's in East Asia* (Stanford University Press, 1997), edited by James L. Watson.

China has been the subject of many books, though most have dealt with its political and diplomatic history rather than the social changes afoot in the region. Nicholas Kristof and Sheryl WuDunn's *China Wakes* (Nicholas Brealey, 2nd edn 1998) is a book from two *New York Times* journalists that manages to combine both the social and political shifts in China's recent history. *China Pop* by Jianying Zha (The New Press, 1995) provides an insight into the effects of popular culture on the Chinese from a *Village Voice* journalist. Jim Mann's case study of western business in China, *Beijing Jeep* (Westview Press, 1997), also outlines the pitfalls and potential rewards of doing business in China from the point of view of carmakers. Conghua Li's *China: The Consumer Revolution* (Wiley, 1998) is a good starting point for an understanding of China's burgeoning consumer market. Somewhat older but also still interesting on changing China is Orville Schell's *Discos and Democracy* (Pantheon, 1988), as well as *China Rising: Nationalism and Interdependence* (Routledge, 1997), edited by David S.G. Goodman and Gerald Segal.

India remains the country with the least written about it. Despite the outpouring of words on the country around the fiftieth anniversary of independence in 1997, the new India and the thoughts and tastes of its citizens were little talked about. However, the magazine *Business India* has begun to cover the marketing industry in greater depth recently. Two interesting introductions to the country, its people and markets are Claudia Cragg's *The New Maharajahs* (Arrow Books, 1997) and Mukesh Eswaran and Ashok

Kotwal's *Why Poverty Persists in India* (Oxford University Press, 1994).

It is difficult to fully understand Asia, its development and likely future trends without at least a passing knowledge of Japan. The literature on Japan and the Japanese is voluminous and not always helpful. However, there are some useful books that look at the habits and actions of Japanese consumers. Among these are John Clammer's *Contemporary Urban Japan: A Sociology of Consumption* (Blackwell, 1997) and the Australian journalist Richard McGregor's *Japan Swings* (Butterworth-Heinemann Asia, 1997), which reveals just how far Japan's leisure and entertainment culture has permeated Asia. The *Asian Wall Street Journal* also published a collection of vignettes on Japanese culture, consumption and consumer markets called *Let's Talk Turkey (About Japanese Turkeys)* (Charles E. Tuttle, 1996) that revealed a little more about consumers than cold statistics can.

The number of publications dealing with Asia as a whole is increasing monthly. Particularly useful are *Far Eastern Economic Review*, *Asia Inc.*, the *Asian Wall Street Journal Weekly* and the *Vietnam Investment Review*. Naturally, the *Economist* continues to cover the Asian scene comprehensively, as does *Asia Business Week* and *Asiaweek*. For those particularly interested in the advertising industry in Asia, the weekly *Asian Advertising and Marketing* is a useful roundup, as is *Asian Retail* for those concerned with developments in retailing. The number of English-language magazines around the region has grown in the last five years, with titles such as *Malaysian Business* and *Directions* being useful sources. Additionally, the global business magazine *South* contains much of interest on Asia.

For those wanting deeper research on consumer markets in Asia, a number of companies produce useful reports on the region. Euromonitor's series of reports on the consumer markets of southeast Asia and China are a useful starting point, as is its annual publication *Consumer Asia*. Other research publishers covering the region include International Business Strategies which provides a series of reports on various Asian consumer markets. Several online services have multiple Asian sources, among them Dialog

Corporation's Profound service which includes news from the very good Asia Pulse news agency and the Financial Times China Business Intelligence Service.

The Internet has become another way to gain direct access to Asia. Perhaps its most useful function is the ability to keep up with news. The following Web sites all contain daily news from Asia:

Hong Kong and China

South China Morning Post – http://www.scmp.com
Hong Kong Standard – http://www.hkstandard.com
China Daily – http://www.chinadaily.com.cn
China News Digest – http://www.cnd.org

India

Times of India – http://www.timesofindia.com
Indian Express – http://www.expressindia.com

Malaysia

Malaysian Star – http://www.jaring.my

Philippines

Philippine Star – http://www.philstar.com
Philippines BusinessWorld – http://www.bworld.com.ph

Singapore

Straits Times – http://www.straitstimes.asia1.com

South Korea

Chosun Ilbo – http://www.chosun.com
The Korea Herald – http://www.koreaherald.co.kr

Taiwan

China Times – http://www.chinatimes.com.tw

Thailand

Bangkok Post – http://www.bangkokpost.net

Index